Voice of the Voiceless

Conceptualizing the Marginalized Psyche

Gulshan Das

G. A. Ghanshyam

AUTHORSPRESS

Publishers of Scholarly Books

Worldwide Circulation through Authorspress Global Network

First Published 2012

by

Authorspress

Editorial

Q-2A Hauz Khas Enclave

New Delhi-110 016

e-mail: authorspress@rediffmail.com

Marketing

E-35/103, Jawahar Park

Laxmi Nagar, Delhi-110 092

e-mail: authorspress@rediffmail.com

Voice of the Voiceless: Conceptualizing the Marginalized Psyche

ISBN 978-81-7273-625-5

Printed in India at Tarun Offset, Delhi.

Dedicated to

Late. Prof. Nirmaljeet Oberoi

Head, School of Studies in English
Vikram University, Ujjain (M. P)

who has been a perennial source of
our inspiration

Preface

In the beginning there was no centre.
In the beginning there was no margin.
In the beginning there was no margin, for there was no centre.
If there was no margin, how did centre come into existence?
Then what existed before margin and centre?
There must have been something, for there can never be nothing.

(*Rig Veda*)

The debates pertaining to the margin and the centre attained significance with the individual's frustrations, sense of failure, keen awareness of the futility of their existence and threat to their identity. The individuals and some segments of society were marginalized and discriminated on the basis of religion, race, region, community, caste, gender, nationality and ideology. Such a relationship between the centre and the margin could not last long. The centre could only suppress the marginalized voice but could not silence them forever. The whole equation changed when the marginalized registered their resistance upholding the banner of self assertion. Once they were eloquent, they ceased to be marginalized.

We wonder often whether the marginalized can speak. The culture of silence with regard to the marginalized section of the society has found an outlet of their fears and tears, anguish and despair, apprehensions and aspirations through literature. When silence becomes eloquent, it often makes history. The question of their identity has assumed different dimensions amongst creative writers. Dennis Wrong points out that the term "identity" and "identity crisis", have become the "Semantic beacons of our time" for these "verbal emblems express our discontent with modern life and modern society".

While conceptualizing the marginalized psyche in the pluralistic social setup we have incorporated a broad interpretation of the texts that are marginalized by the academy or marginal to the academy, and mediums that are considered marginal, such as those that result in oral literature or popular cultural artifacts.

The twenty-six papers in this volume have made a sincere attempt to trace the journey of the marginalized from the shadows of anonymity and obscurity to the centre of focus in the society. With the dawn of awareness the victims, marginalized section, group or individual those were in the periphery, reacted against it and thought of de-centrering the centre at least by voicing their marginalization through literature. Due to the creative and critical works by the member of the marginalized community and on the marginalized groups of our society, margin and centre were radically redefined. This humble academic endeavour will perhaps provide a fresh approach to the issue of marginalization and may lead to the conviction that:

> In the end there will be no margin,
> In the end there will be no centre,
> In the end there will be no play,
> In the end there will be a free play of playlessness
> Without margin.........
> Without centre..........

Voice of the Voiceless: Conceptualizing the Marginalized Psyche includes twenty-six insightful papers focusing on the issue of marginalization. This volume encompasses comprehensive and detailed approach to most of the issues related to marginalization encouraging innovative thinking and pragmatism. The book has been a dream project for us, which could not have seen the light of the day without the helping hands that have encouraged and supported us throughout the venture. We are beholden to *Prof. Kapil Kapoor*, an academician par excellence and a noble human being for his unconditional support, guidance and timely help.

We extend our heartfelt gratitude and acknowledge the encouragement and support of all our learned contributors. We place on record our gratitude to *Prof. C.B.S. Chauhan, Mr. Pradeep Das, Dr. Prashant Mishra, Dr. Shabnam Das Manna, Rajat Dave, Dr. Tanjeen A. Khan, Dr. Ajay Sharma, Dr. Devasree Chakravarti, Rakhi Nara, Swetanjali Pradhan, Mrs. Usha Iyengar and Mahendra Gupta* for their unceasing support and faith in us.

We extend deepest gratitude to Shri. *Sudarshan Kcherry* of Authorspress, New Delhi for showing this volume the much-needed light and reposing confidence in us. His encouragement is immense and noteworthy. We are deeply moved by his kind gesture. We compliment the staff at Authors Press for giving this volume an excellent shape.

We are hopeful that this volume will be patronized by the academicians, scholars and students. Constructive suggestions are requested from well-wishers to improve the quality of the content and presentation in our future endeavours.

Vijayadashami
6th October 2011

Dr. Gulshan Das
Dr. G. A. Ghanshyam

A Tribute

In the passing away of Dr. Nirmaljeet Oberoi ji, a lady of much grace and dignity, her family, her friends and her students have suffered a grievous loss. For me it is a personal loss as I shared a very affectionate relationship with Nirmal ji, as I used to call her.

As one proceeds in life, one experiences both joys and sorrows and as one grows older there are more sorrows than joys because human life is by nature transient. Death of a loved one has been accepted as among the deepest *duhkhas*.

One of the Yaksha *prashnas* in *Mahabharata* is—"What is the greatest wonder/surprise in life?" Yudhishthira says "We see people born and die every day—yet we expect immortality." But such is the grief that afflicts us when a loved one separates from us that no wisdom; no sage advice assuages our suffering. In *Hitopadesha*, it is said:

> *We are clasped to the bosom by mortality—first as a nurse, then as a mother.*
>
> *Why should there be all this grief?*
>
> *Where are the great rulers of the earth, with their guards, their armies, their chariots? To this day the earth bears witness to their departure.*
>
> *Each day the outward form wastes away imperceptibly, like an unbaked jar standing in water. Until the jar has disappeared, it is not known that it is vanishing.*
>
> *As a victim approaches the altar, step by step, so death comes nearer day by day to every living being.*

Youth, beauty, life, riches, power, friends, all passes away. A wise man fixes not his hopes on these

As a plank of timber may meet another plank in a mountain stream and then part asunder again, even so is the meeting of men in this world...

Separation no doubt is the law of life and yet, equally, grief is a fact of life. I knew Nirmaljitji since 1990 when I met her in her university, a very charming, caring and thoughtful person. In the evening, she took me to her home to meet her noble father and loving mother and that evening my long relationship began with the whole family—Bauji and Biji, her brother, her Bhabhi Renu, her nephew whom she particularly loved, her sister Gulshanji and her *jijaji* Das Sahib. Every visit to Ujjain meant every evening eating at home as a member of the family. Nirmalji, every time I met her, would unfailingly inquire about Mrs. Kapoor, whom she called Bhabhiji, about our daughter Saumya, about Saumya's small daughter—her generous heart never forgot anyone. And once she learnt that Saumya's husband liked Ujjain *namkeen*, every time she used to quietly put five packets for Hitesh in my bag and towards me, she was always unfailingly polite, obedient and affectionate.

I have seen in her a great devotion towards her parents, Bauji and Biji, and her endless service to them till her last day at home. I also know of her care for those beautiful courtyard trees and plants which she tended with great attention and gentleness.

Everything in that house marked her presence. Last time I had food with the family, she was unwell and withdrawing from life. But her courtesy her desire to serve was intact.

Now she is gone and the home has fallen silent and her people and her friends deserted. But wherever she is and wherever she takes re-birth she will be the same loved person that she was in Ujjain.

02. 04. 2011

Kapil Kapoor

New Delhi

Our Contributors

Ali Ahmed Khan, Assistant Professor of English, Shobhasari, Sikar, Rajasthan.

Anurag Chauhan, Lecturer, Department of English, Guru Ghasidas Vishwavidyalaya, Bilaspur, Chhattisgarh.

Behzad Pourgharib, Assistant Professor, Department of English, Golestan University, Golestan, Iran.

Binod Mishra, Assistant Professor of English, Department of Humanities, IIT, Roorkee, Uttarakhand.

Chetna Tiwari, Assistant Professor of English, University School of Humanities and Social Sciences, GGSIP University, Delhi.

Devasree Chakravarti, Assistant Professor of English (Adhoc), Guru Ghasidas Vishwavidyalaya, Bilaspur, Chhattisgarh.

G. A. Ghanshyam, Professor of English, Government M. L. Shukla College, Seepat, Bilaspur, Chhattisgarh.

Gulshan Das, Professor & Head (Retd.), Government Bilasa Girls' P.G. College, Bilaspur, Chhattisgarh.

Indrani Singh Rai, Department of English, Durga Mahavidyalaya, Raipur, Chhattisgarh.

James R. Aubrey, Professor of English, Metropolitan State College of Denver, Denver, United States.

Meeta Ajay Khanna, Assistant Professor of English (Adhoc), Guru Ghasidas Vishwavidyalaya, Bilaspur, Chhattisgarh.

Oorja Rajan Sinha, Assistant Professor of English, D.P. Vipra College, Bilaspur, Chhattisgarh.

Prashant Mishra, Professor & Head, Department of English, Govt. P. G. College, Neemuch, Madhya Pradesh.

Prerna Hiradhar, Head, Department of English, Delhi Public School, Bilaspur, Chhattisgarh.

Protibha Mukherjee Sahukar, Department of English, Durga Mahavidayalaya, Raipur, Chhattisgarh.

Shabnam Das Manna., Trainer in Soft Skills, Hyderabad, Andhra Pradesh.

S. K. Tripathi, Professor of English, Government E.R.R. Sc. P.G. College (Autonomous), Bilaspur, Chhattisgarh.

Shrabani Chakravorty, Dept. of English, Government Mata Shabari Girls' College, Bilaspur, Chhattisgarh.

Shubhra Paikra, Department of English, Durga Mahavidyala, Raipur, Chhattisgarh.

Somali Gupta, Department of English, Government V.Y.T.P.G. Autonomous College, Durg, Chhattisgarh.

Sucheta Mukherjee, C/o Dr. Mukherjee's Dental Clinic, Badi Omti Chowk, Jabalpur, Madhya Pradesh.

Swetanjali Pradhan, SK (Gr. I), Government High School, Kodapuri, Dist. Bilaspur, Chhattisgarh.

Tanjeen Ara Khan, Asst. Professor & Head, Department of English, BIT, Raipur, Chhattisgarh.

T. K. Sandhu, Assistant Professor of English, Government College, Navagarh, Durg, Chhattisgarh.

Uma Ram, Professor & Head, Department of English, Government P. G. College, Jagdalpur, Chhattisgarh.

Usha Masram, Assistant Professor of English, Office of Additional Director of Higher Education, Jabalpur, Madhya Pradesh.

Contents

1

Identity Crisis in Dalit Short Stories from Maharashtra

— Ali Ahmed Khan

Literature by the dalits has today become a potent tool for projecting their identity by providing critical insights on the question of their identity, their literature projects, their victimization and social subordination, which no other writing could do as subtly and as pointedly. The writing of the dalits is directly or indirectly linked up with the social, political and cultural ethos of the dalits, however this literature does not constitute a homogeneous or unified entity. There are divergent currents and tendencies, which these writers use to voice their anger and protest. This literature seems to emphasize the economic structure as primary and consequential, and it seems that their identity issue is located within a larger matrix of the market economy. This literature exemplifies how relations of inequality and dominance are primarily governed by structures of economic and political power and not merely or significantly by the cultural forces.

The literature that we are going to analyze subsumes the writings of various sections within the dalit fold including Muslims and Christians, and Buddhists whose changed religious status has not insulated them from social inequities and humiliations arising out of their earlier low-caste origin. This literature taken from the dalits of Maharashtra demonstrates very visibly that their social location is strategic and it enables them to capture the depth of their social reality. This literature is insistent on using a very different imagery and is rooted in experiences and perceptions that make this imagery set of the callousness of the others and the marginalization of the self.

In a story by Waman Hoval, *The Storeyed House* (1992) we come across a very typical dalit household full of children living on the fringes of exclusion. A Mahar by caste, Bayaji, has been fortunate to have got a job in the city as a lifter of heavy loads and towards the end of his career retires as a supervisor. Making his way home with Rs. 2,5000 in his pocket he becomes the butt of envy of the higher castes. The unacceptability of him is evident in the first conversation that he has with Bhujaba, the high caste rascal of the village. He would have greeted Bhujaba with:

> 'My humble salutation to you, Sir, who are my father and mother'. So, when Bayaji merely said, 'Greetings' Bhujaba became furious and said, 'Do you think you can become a Brahmin by merely saying 'Greetings? Can you forget your position simply because you have turned Buddhist?' (156).

Two things emerge from this brief encounter: first that no amount of persevered attempt by a dalit can upgrade their status, the hostility from the other castes is subversive for an identity renewal; once a dalit always a dalit. Even though Bayaji had converted to Buddhism there was no inversion to his identity. Another thing that surfaces is that though the Mahars amongst the dalits emerged as distinctly assertive due to several reasons including, social movement within that caste, education and availability of new economic opportunities in urban areas, yet within the closed community of their rural environment they cannot think of scaling another step upward in the social ladder. We know that among the literate Mahars there is an urge to closely observe the deteriorating conditions among the rural untouchables and express their feelings towards them.

Bayaji also gives expression of his assertiveness by trying to build a two-storeyed house. It is with his all efforts that his family is doing well, that his two daughters have been married and his elder sons look after the fields, the next two sons are in government service, the one after them is a school teacher and the sixth is still studying. All this projects a kind of a well-to-do-ness which is unusual for a dalit. Bayaji now opens up his secret wish to his family—he wishes to build a house out of his earnings, a storeyed house for the usual three portioned house won't be adequate for the likes of him. He wants to get out of a typical dalit syndrome whereas Zelliot describes the men and women in a deplorable condition surviving merely at a subsistence level: distanced from mainstream life, in unhygienic conditions and lacking the most basic necessities.

But as the news of the Bayaji's storied house spread, the upper castes became more caustic. Kondiba Patil remarked:

> Baiju, you shouldn't lose your head simply because you have set aside some money. Do you aspire to an equal status with us by building this house? The poor should remain content with their cottage, understand? (158)

Bayaji was non-plussed and Kondiba uttered a threat that he may go in for a storeyed house only if he didn't wish to stay in the village. Kondiba shot out the warning and walked away. Other ruffians in the village threatened Bayaji in a similar manner.

However, the house was completed and a huge house-warming ceremony planned. There was a lot of fuss by the family, and devotional singers with their troupes were also invited. Some of the elders of the town grew very uneasy at the sight of the brand new house, the impressive pandal and the cleverly conceived second storey, which had been carved out from a loft. As the sound of the bhajans rose to a crescendo Bayaji's new house caught fire from all sides. Panic struck as the house went down in ashes and with it Bayaji too. The entire family was shattered by this calamity and their spirits dampened. Since it was Bayaji, a low-caste dalit evidence was mutilated and records put 'right' according to the wishes of the higher-ups, "Bayaji's death was the result of an accident due to petromax flare-up," (161) was their conclusion.

Such a fate does not surprise anyone who knows the social mores of a caste-ridden Indian society. The life of a dalit here is a grim struggle and if demeaning situations like poverty and immiseration, hunger and starvation, homelessness and economic exploitation are not there, they are bound to be subjects of insidious and nefarious violence. But in the wake of all this dalits have been known to suffer their atrocities with unusual grit. It seems that despite these adversities and powerful adverseries the dalits have become brave, have shed their diffidence and their complexes. Bayaji's sons show this kind of an unconsumed spirit and an urge to overcome obstacles. At the end of the story they amaze the gathered guests by declaring that their father's soul cannot rest in peace unless they rebuild the house, not one with a concealed first floor but a regular two-storeyed house. And the six brothers resume with determination the work of digging the foundation of a two-storeyed house.

It is as if they want the hollowness and the cunningness of the hegemonic classes to be realized and simultaneously to assert their identity which will not be cowed down by any distressing attempt. As Punalekar (2001) has pointed out "the Mahars among the dalits have been the foremost, with the agenda for upliftment' and 'crusade against untouchability."

In a story by Arjun Dangle, 'Promotion', it seems that Bayaji and his likes, that is, Waghmare in the present story, have succeeded in getting jobs as clerks in a government department. The dream of both economic and personal upgradation have come through. But now there is another dialectics that has to be gone through. The higher-up community clerks despite being under him, do not listen to him and are even derogatory in their behaviour towards him. Waghmare wants to preserve this identity, a distinct, different identity that his sustained hard work and education have created. In his efforts to isolate himself he steels himself when others from his community greet him with, "Jai Bheem"; when he encounters the word "reserved" anywhere. The fetish becomes so pronounced that when his wife's aunt from a slum 'chawl' comes to visit them, he lashes out at his wife, "learn to maintain your status. After all, you are an officer's wife" (172). But the tragedy is that this kind of an immunization does not last for long and even though he might cocoon himself, the society has ways of puncturing into his self-created identity—his son is pushed for drinking water from Ganpati's pot, his wife finds fruit expensive and of course the haunting image of Godbole from the office who turns a deaf ear because he is an SC. His tragedy is the tragedy of dalit identity formation, "His newly-sprung wings of promotion fall off and a mere mortal named Pandurang Satwa Waghmare crashes helplessly into the abyss below" (172).

Despite social mobility and the acquisition of literacy skills to secure employment, a dalit cannot ward off the evil of caste divisiveness for long. The upper castes have a way of asserting an overwhelming presence. For whatever efforts being made by the British in the earlier regime, yet the struggle against the evil forces was never diminished. Gavaskar points out that brahmins in new incarnations of Kulkarni and Bhatkamagar are maintaining day-and-night vigil over their interests in villages and urban centres and poisoning the minds of the British against the shudras. In *Brahmanache Kasab* (Priest Craft Exposed), Phule, by depicting the omnipresence of brahmins in the roles of a priest, a schoolteacher, a Kulkarni, a Mamlatdar, a reformer, a clerk in the public works, a reporter in the vernacular press, builds a demonology of gram-rakshasas (village demons) and kalamkasais (wielders of pen) out to gobble up the ignorant shudras. Behind this demonology lies Phule's sharp grasp of power relations that make him boldly state, ". . . that the Brahmin will not descend from his self-raised high pedestal and meet his Coonbee (*sic*) and low caste brethren on an equal footing without a struggle" (Phule 125). And it is this acumen that drives him to search for an anchorage in an alternative centre of power that would overthrow the inegalitarian social set-up of his times.

Integration within the dominant structure is an impossibility, and no amount of personal upgradation can bring about even a bare minimal of equality that the dalits strive for. The chains of the horizontal structure of society are so tightly knit that any dream of breaking these and ascending onto a vertical ladder is impossible. Within this grooved nexus of brutal defining, the dalits do not find sufficient access to either natural or human resources. Despite the decentralization and democratization of power the dalits are no better-off and as Runciman (1966) points out, "this questions the validity of the concept of relative deprivation which primarily presupposes the perception of contrasting one's situation, even at the most primal level" (Runciman 9). Studies understanding the dalit movement in terms of relative deprivation and social mobility help to reveal the role of castes and inherited status that have for long influenced the monopolizing of the available jobs by the upper castes which viewed caste mobility as dangerous and disruptive of the social fabric. It is in this context that studies establishing a connection between the dalit movement and the above concepts bring out the latent contradictions of a socioeconomic and political nature. Moreover, such studies also reveal that relative deprivation leading to socioeconomic mobility has after all a democratising impact on the socioeconomic, political and bureaucratic structure of India.

According to Gopal Guru, given the happenings in the rural areas where the upper castes or class forces are committing brutal atrocities on the dalits, and when the state's response is either callous or repressive, the dalits do not feel a sense of relative deprivation so much as a total alienation and exclusion and the threat of physical liquidation.

Such then is the plight of the low caste that even the most demeaning work is not a sustained materiality for them; they are destined to live from hand to mouth, to be shooed away from better vicinities and if the worst comes to worst to live a dead-like existence. They have no right to live, and when they assert this right to live they are beaten up by adverse logic.

The attempts by Arjun Dangle, Baburao Bagul and others have been to undermine the cultural hierarchies constructed by the upper castes. They have tried to present the existential reality of the dalits with remarkable ability and courage. Their writings have offered an opportunity and promise to raise awareness about the subjugation of the dalits. They have concentrated their literary energies to explore the cultural gaps and the brahminical social order in order to win support for the downtrodden. Very objectively they have worked out the vulnerability of their low caste protagonist and made their writing political. The portrayal of the absolutely adverse material conditions is done purposely to beg support for such of them that are scavengers if not worse living on the dregs of the upper class and on the edge of survival. Such representations of the dalit identity that we get are enough to set the mind's thinking—are we still living in an age of inequality? How are we a democratic nation? How has the millennial change ushered in a more global order? S.P. Punalekar remarks that dalit literature upholds the view that this vast majority which is vulnerable and poor, untouchable and isolated, must be brought together. And to bring them tighter, they must be made conscious of their capacity as creative and worthy members of humanity. It is not a matter of shame or indignity to be a Mahar or Mang, Dhor or Chamar, Berad or Kaikadi, Christian or Muslim. Caste or community does not pollute or criminalize the society. It is rather the other way around; it is society, meaning its social (economic) institutions and the underlying cultural system, which upgrades some members at the cost of others, i.e., by degrading them, by dehumanizing and marginalizing them.

Baburao Bagul, a leading dalit intellectual, asserts that dalit sahitya (literature) is not a literature of vengeance. It is not a literature which spreads hatred. It first promotes man's greatness and man's freedom and for that reason it is an historic necessity. He had further explained this point at the Dalit Literature Conference held in Nagpur in 1976. He said that anguish, waiting, pronouncements of sorrow alone do not define dalit literature. We want literature heroically full of life for the creation of a (new) society.

Thus, there is clear evidence that dalit literature is deeply concerned with identity formation and its assertion to regain the self-confidence and self-worth of the marginalized sections in our society. Most of their creative imagination is structured around these premises. Theirs is an agenda of rebuilding society on values which promote honour and dignity, justice and equity. Tryambak Sapkale's poem 'Mother India' expresses this sentiment poignantly.

Don't despair.
This day will depart too.
Now, this day is pregnant with day.
Our day is not far away.
Look, from the day is born the day.

(*Sapkale*)

Dalit literature began with an agenda for upliftment and a crusade against untouchability. Today its frontiers are expanding and more and more of the group are questioning the complex set of social, economic and cultural ways, dwelling largely on the question of identity.

Works Cited

Dangle, Arjun. *Poisoned Bread: Translations from Modern Marathi Dalit Literature*. Delhi: Orient Longman, 1992. All page numbers of short stories are from this collection.

Phule, Jyotiba. *Mahatama Phule Samagra Vangmaya* (MPSV). ed. Yeshwant Dinakar Phadke. Mumbai: Maharashtra Rajya Sahitya ani Sanskriti Mandal, 1991.

Runciman, W. *Relative Deprivation*. London: Routledge and Kegan Paul, 1966.

Sapkale, Tryambak. *Times Weekly Supplement*. 25 November 1973.

2

Overt and Covert Dominances in Toni Morrison's *The Bluest Eye* and Gabrielle Roy's *Windflower*

— Anurag Chauhan

Toni Morrison's *The Bluest Eye* and Gabrielle Roy's *Windflower (La Riviere sans repos)* are both two fictional works that explore many dimensions of marginality. Although the two works show two protagonists of different ethnicities, African and Eskimo, their fates are subjected to and shaped by circumstances similar in many respects. *The Bluest Eye* shows the African-American community in Ohio, America, inundated by external conditions and ideology constructed by the "central", American culture there. *Windflower* is the story of an Eskimo mother, who becomes alienated both from her own culture of the Canadian North and that of the white South because of her love for her child. The protagonists of both, Pecola and Elsa, are victims of circumstances, especially as produced by an overwhelmingly dominant alien culture and its values. Both the works show a protest against the threats of cultural assimilation and dissemination in their own ways.

The issue of marginalization needs an insight into the social, economic and political ideologies and practices of the majority groups. The white community frames its rules and implements them in both *The Bluest Eye* and *Windflower;* it also conveniently winks over or dismisses as unimportant those things which it feels to be so. Why does Elsa have to come back to the white ways? Why is the sexuality of black women a hush-hush issue? Every action or inaction, overt or covert, is a political statement. Innocent as it seems, this dominance of the English and 'white' cultures percolates to the marginalized Eskimo and black communities in such a way that it is not seen, except in its more obvious ways as alien or subversive. The 'central' and powerful culture has just to seed its values and ideology and prove itself as superior to the 'other' culture, the marginalized one. It does not need to be actively involved then. Even if there is no such design or intention, yet the fact remains that the minority culture gets inspired and often, corrupted by such an influence. This can be seen clearly in *The Bluest Eye* and *Windflower*. Elsa does flee but before that she too has adapted the white ways in upbringing Jimmy. This is an unconscious conditioning or brainwash which makes its victims of Elsa, Pecola, Pauline and Sammy. In fact, words like 'centre' and 'periphery' often become misnomers when applied to the Canadian Eskimos and the Afro-Americans and can be convenient and usable only in a broad, vague sense because these communities and races are self-sufficient in cultural terms, even if they are more prone to disease, poverty and death. This is an issue for a Marxist study, surely. Yet, the cultures of these marginalized communities have the potential to sustain themselves, if not to face the onslaught of foreign cultures.

Nor is this contained in a watertight compartment of economics but affects every aspect of culture. When this onslaught takes place, the communities in *The Bluest Eye* and *Windflower* find themselves alienated and uprooted in a land which is as much theirs as of anyone. Here, in the clash of traditions and the intangible ways of living with the more concrete and productive system of the white, English community, it is the latter who assumes the central position. It adds to the female predicament and the growing realization or the growing incomprehensibility that has a benumbing effect which is the start of alienation. Both Elsa and Pecola become alienated, and gradually, deranged.

In her book *Playing in the Dark: Whiteness and the Literary Imagination* Toni Morrison questions the cannons of literary reading and understanding of Africanism and says:

> As a disabling virus within literary discourse, Africanism has become, in the Eurocentric tradition favored by American education, both a way of talking about and a way of policing matters of class, sexual license and repression, the formation and exercise of power, ethics, and accountability. (Morrison 1792)

This misreading can is true even for the French-Canadian identity represented by Gabrielle Roy and for the Eskimo culture depicted by her in *Windflower*. This way, these cultures and their discourses are considered as peripheral or insignificant.

In case of both Elsa nd Pecola, they are doubly marginalized, both as women and as members of marginalized communities. Pecola is of the black American community, with many privileges denied to her. Elsa's condition becomes clear with this comment by Allison Mitcham:

> Several outstanding contemporary Canadian novelists seem obsessed with the plight of characters doubly isolated, characters who are isolated, first, from the two main streams of Canadian culture—the French and the English—because they have been born Indian, Eskimo or Jewish, and second, isolated from their own tribe, group or race because, for various reasons, they reject their own racial or tribal patterns, or for some reason, cannot conform to them. (Mitcham 43)

As such, subversion is inevitable to them.

A precipitating point in this subversion is the sexual exploitation of both. Before this point, the dominance of a system, an ordered social hierarchy is already accepted by our protagonists. In this, the two works show not the out of ordinary, rebellious characters but an indictment of this order by showing it as it is. The dominance of the system is such that the identities of the two female protagonists are already erased and when the sexual violence occurs it leaves many ripples in its wake. Rape is not an extraordinary happening in case of both the communities. We know already in *The Bluest Eye* how Frieda and other girls are sexually harassed; in *Windflower* too, rape is taken passively, philosophically, by the community. Of course in Pecola's case it is an incest-rape, by her own father but the response of the community is quite callous about Pecola, "Ought to be a law: two ugly people doubling up like that to make more ugly" (Morrison 149). Overtly, the society allows them to exist, does not exorcise them, but covertly, has little means or desire to blame the culprits, let alone punish them.

In both *Windflower* and *The Bluest Eye* we find the pull of opposite forces in the search for identities by the protagonists from the Eskimo and the African communities. This results only when a land becomes a battleground of two contending ideologies or of tradition with a strong capitalistic culture. We find this capitalistic angle in both the novels. Dorothea Drummond Mbalia has very clearly done a Marxist interpretation of Morrison's novels and contended that in her initial novels Morrison shows a growing consciousness of capitalism as the most powerful and destructive of Western forces that oppress the people of African heritage.

Elsa's love for her son is unconditional in spite of her rape by an American soldier and the divided result: her son is half Caucasian, half 'south'. She wants to give him the benefits of the white, Western culture and yet she wants to preserve in him the North, Eskimo culture. But this happy compromise does not work. It is not simply something innate or genetic in her son that makes him part away from her and her Eskimo culture. The dominance of the 'central' white culture with its attractions, cultural and economic artifacts and paraphernalia is such that Jimmy's adoption of the white culture and rejection of the Eskimo ways is not surprising.

In Pecola's case, the patterns of dominance, not only of the society, but also through family, with a drunk for a father and an unloving mother, are so overwhelming that she can not afford to choose or to reject. Pecola might have been less unfortunate were she self-dependent in economic terms. She is in a worse condition than Elsa, as her conscious and subconscious have not become strong enough to discriminate or to judge. Unable to decide, choose or flee, she takes recourse in a fetish, which provides but a temporary solace and erodes her active cognitive faculty. The support of sympathetic but young and powerless friends like her does not work as a strong physical or mental support system against the oppressive realities at home and in society.

Rejection, shame, escapism—incompatibility with an overtowering, unsurmountable, and unaccommodating system and values, and a half-objectification of her unrealizable fantasy—blue eyes—drive Pecola to madness. But for Elsa, it is less of escapist tendency because hers is not a scarred psyche like that of Pecola but an element of hurt added to anger and shame, the causing element being her own blood. The fairy tale story created by her to tell her son about his birth does not deceive him; but neither does it elicit sympathy, which she deserved most from him. The dominance of the white culture is not accidental; it is simply covert. It is ironical though that Elsa had to forsake the Eskimo ways of living because of Jimmy and it is he who deserts her primarily because he considers her a representative of what he considers an inferior culture. In Pecola's case, she is a child and is not calcified enough into adulthood to differentiate between the rights and wrongs of the adult world so the element of hurt is absent but there is a subdued hurt or fear of rejection and a desire for acceptance in her.

A means for acceptance is beauty. John Leonard says, "*The Bluest Eye* us an enquiry into the reasons why beauty gets wasted in this country. The beauty in this case is black; the wasting is done by a cultural engine that seems to have been designed to murder possibilities..." (Leonard).

Greta Garbo and Shirley Temple become symbolic statements as well as cultural icons. Thus, the sustaining elements of the mental and emotional landscape are eroded. Yet, the reality is different and the result is incompatibility. In case of Cholly, Pauline and others, this incompatibility or lacuna, results in either taking it out on others in a sadistic way or in passive alienation. Rafael Perez-Torres remarks rightly about *The Bluest Eye*:

> In addition to race, the novel takes as a primary issue the position of women within marginalized cultures. The "double marginalization" experienced by the characters is

> due to the emphasis on standards of beauty and the exploitation of their budding sexuality. This marginalization has its source in a community's internalization of oppressive systems of value, which fragments both individual psyches and the community as a whole." (Perez-Torres 21)

It is this conditioning done by Soaphead Church and others and internalization of the standards of beauty that bring about Pecola's doom.

In contrast, in *Windflower* the begotten child is a reality, not absent like the bluest eyes that Pecola desires or like the stillborn child she gets. Not only that, he is beautiful too. "His eyes were the blue of those glimpses of sky between the snowy April clouds. His hair, as silky as the down on baby ducks, was already long. Elsa could give herself up for hours to the pleasure of rolling it on her fingers..." (Roy 17). One can conjecture well the degree and form of this love if the child had been black. But the beauty and goodness of the child, Jimmy, is in sharp contrast to his cruel behaviour when he grows up. But it also shows how the indirect influence of a system, a powerful "central" culture can make inroads into the personality of a person.

The individual harassers and victimizers in both the novels are males. It attests to the generally held view about the male dominance. Here, the male dominance is lower in the hierarchical pattern of power but whereas the ideological or cultural level of dominance is higher and affects the whole community; the male dominance also is an ideology governing the society and has more of an individual thrust. It must also be said that the victimizers in both the novels are victims themselves and that is how Morrison and Roy have tried to show them, sympathetically. They carry scars with them and are product of a system where a system dominates with all its overwhelming power. The cycle of abuse, maltreatment, shock, alienation, perversity, sadism which they go through culminates when they start hurting others. But the society has no remedy only legal recourse, sometimes. In *The Bluest Eye* Cholly has faced rejection and hurt and so has his wife, Pauline.

It passes on to the children Pecola and Sammy, in varying degrees. The cycle of victimizer-victim-victimizer has its roots in the social reality, which is harsh and inhuman. On the one hand Cholly and Jimmy can be seen as players/victimizers having power and a male identity in a society that does not thwart them and on the other hand they can be seen as pawns/victims in a set up where they are caught up in an existential condition and are played upon. In *Windflower* Jimmy shows a callous and cruel behaviour towards the Eskimo culture and towards his mother, Elsa. But he himself has had the devastating shock of knowing about his begetting. After his boasting in the sky in his fighter plane, father Eugene considers him "cynical and twisted" (Roy 149) which, it can be said is a punishment or retribution, as it is for Cholly, in his condition.

What both the novelists want is a greater understanding of cultures and of the need of retaining identities. The authorial voice is subdued in both *The Bluest Eye* and *Windflower* but the authorial tone in *Windflower as* far as the questions of dominance and race are considered is one of compromise. Jimmy's misdoings are pointed out at individual level; there is no blaming of a race or culture. Roy is non-commital about making a verdict. In *The Bluest Eye* Morrison is equally non-commital about making a verdict; in fact, some may read it as blaming the black community for their downfall. But in fact, Morrison, through the hetroglossia in the novel, including the Dick and Jane narrative, the symbolism of Claudia and Friedas's unproductive marigolds and other symbols makes a quiet but strong statement about marginalization of the Afro-American females in particular, and about a whole system that sustains this marginalization, although this statement is very much encoded and covert.

Works Cited

Leonard, John. qtd. Backcover. in Toni Morrison's, *The Bluest Eye*. London: Picador.

Mitcham, Allison. "The Isolation of Protesting Individuals who Belong to Minority Groups", U. of Regina: *Wascan Review* 7:1, 1972.

Morrison, Toni. *The Bluest Eye* (*BE*). London: Picador, 1994.

_______. qtd. in *The Critical Tradition*, Ed. David H. Richter. Boston: Bedford/St. Martin's, 2007.

Mbalia, Dorothea Drummond *Toni Morrison's Developing Class Consciousness.* Selinsgrove: Susquehanna UP, 1991.

Perez-Torres, Rafael. "Tracing and Erasing: Race and Pedagogy in *The Bluest Eye*" in *Approache s to Teaching the the Novels of Toni Morrison*. Ed. Nellie Y. McKay and Kathryn Earle. New York: MLA, 1997.

Roy, Gabrielle *Windflower,* Trans. Joyce Marshall, Toronto: McClelland and Stewart, 1970.

3

Position of Women and Women Writers in Society in Virginia Woolf's *The Common Reader I and II*

— Behzad Pourgharib

Virginia Woolf has left behind her life five volumes of essays, but her fame as an essayist and literary critic rests entirely on the two volumes entitled *The Common Reader I and II*. Indeed, most readers are not even aware of the fact that she has three other collections of essays to her credit. The popularity of *The Common Reader I and II* was immediate, and it has also been enduring. *The Common Reader I and II* was organized and edited by the essayist herself. In these essays, she was intensely aware of the intrinsic frustrations and the increasing exasperations of the women of her generation which made the problems confronting her sex not only of academic interest but of vital concern to her. With her unflinching honesty and singleness of purpose Virginia Woolf succeeded in revealing the deplorable position of women in society.

Virginia Woolf pursued her search well into the seventeenth century before she discovered in the *Duchess of Newcastle*, ('Duchess of Newcastle', *The Common Reader I*) an instance of a woman capable of intellectual communication. Margaret Cavendish, the Duchess of Newcastle, was certainly not a writer of any great standing or merit. Though "her poems, her plays, her philosophies, her orations, her discourses- all those folios and quartos in which she protected, her real life was enshrined—moulder in the gloom of public libraries," (98), her chief merit lay in variously overcoming the belief that writing was an act unbefitting her sex. While the impressive range of the Duchess of Newcastle's writings is well brought out, Mrs. Woolf at no time is concerned with their literary or critical merit. She was more taken up by the somewhat incongruous literary style that the Duchess adopted to give vent to her many sided nature.

> She similized, energetically, incongruously, eternally; the sea became a meadow, the sailors shepherds, the mast a maypole. The fly was the bird of summer, trees were senators, houses ships, and even the fairies, which she loved better than any earthly thing, except the Duke, are changed to blunt atoms and sharp atoms, and take part in some of those horrible maneuvers in which she delighted to Marshals the universe. (98)

Virginia Woolf's interest in the Duchess arose not only because of the latter's gifted mind, but because of her unorthodox upbringing which gave her the liberty to gratify her taste for reading and writing. This enabled the Duchess to formulate her "philosophies" no matter how illogical, diffused and wild they were. It is the "erratic and lovable personality" of the woman who flew from "subject to subject", never bothering to pause, or to correct, or to feel diffident about her ignorance, or conscious of her sex, that Virginia Woolf celebrates, as volume after volume is finished by the remarkable Duchess, in spite of censorious objections leveled at her, not only by the men, but also by those of her own sex.

"Sure the poor women is little distracted, she could never be so ridiculous else to venture writing books and in verse too" ('Dorothy Osborne's Letters', *The Common Reader II* 98), Dorothy Osborne remarked at the publication of one of the Duchess's books. She admitted her own reluctance to be ever reduced to this distraction, "If I could not sleep this fortnight I should not come to that". (60)

But Virginia Woolf points out that woman, though still wary of the art for writing, had advanced to the stage of writing letters. With great ingenuity and intrepidity they hit upon a medium of expression which need not be denied them as it could be "carried on at odd moments... among a thousand interruptions, without exciting comment...." (61). The writer of letters, besides, needed neither privacy not economic independence, both of which, Virginia Woolf reminds us, the women of the period were denied. So, in their letters, at last, "the silence is broken... for the first time in English literature we hear men and women talking together over the fire". (60)

In spite of its many drawbacks, the art of letter writing gave women a chance to express themselves without fear of "unsexing" themselves. Thus an almost new form of literature came into existence and women could contribute to its development without undue exposure or display of vulgar pride. Dorothy Osborne's letters, writes Virginia Woolf, "make us feel that we have our seat in the depths of Dorothy's mind, at the heart of the pageant which unfolds itself page by page as we read" (62) although, here again, we feel that Mrs. Woolf takes more cognizance of Dorothy Osborne as a woman than as a gifted literary writer. Her temperament, her humour, her intense love for Sir William Temple, the womanly virtues of her time—these are all conveyed with subtle but compassionate irony till the complete portrait is arrived at. Virginia Woolf primarily viewed the letters, the diaries and journals, all that was jotted down and scribbled by women, as the first faint stirrings of the feminine sensibility. She was trying to discover, as it were, not only why women had not written earlier, but at exactly at what moment in history they underwent the process of transformation and emerged as writers of account in their own right. So she studies the letters of Dorothy Osborne "as she filled her great sheets by her father's bed or by the chimney-corners" recording the events of the time "gravely yet playfully, formally yet with intimacy, to a public of one...".(61)

It is not that Mrs. Woolf intended to write a history of women writers and yet she is almost the only writer of the twentieth century from whose critical writing accrues a vast fund of material which is absolutely indispensable in determining the social position of women during the last three hundred years. She searched through their obscure lives and brought out the subtler lights of their intelligence throwing into relief their fortuitous sufferings and reluctant rebellions. With great ingenuity and intrepidity she digs out characters like Laetitia Pilkington (1712-1759) whose only attraction could be her femininity and whose memoirs are "so imbedded with the old tradition of her sex that she wrote, as ladies talked to give pleasure" ('Laetitia Pilkington', *The Common Reader I* 161). Yet Laetitia Pilkington, according to Mrs. Woolf, is almost a landmark in the feminine fight for academic independence. She is deserted by her husband, this great-granddaughter of the Earl of Killmallock, in order to earn her living, "set up, as her advertisement had it, to write letters upon any subject, except the law, for twelve pence ready money, and not trust given" (164). This Mrs. Pilkington makes history and becomes the first instance of a woman writer utilizing the craft of letter writing for making a living.

The fact is that Mrs. Pilkington steadily descended in social scale "till she ended in prison for her debts, does not much bother Virginia Woolf. Nor is she much concerned about the shifts and shades of an adventurous career." What impresses the writer of *The Common Reader* is Laetitia Pildington's inordinate passion for scribbling verses and an incredible hunger for reading books" (164) and the fact that her language was corrected by no less a person than the "great Dr. Swift" which even if it is a "trifle coarse" still places her "in the great tradition of English women writers...". (164)

Mrs. Thrale (1741-1821) appealed to Mrs. Woolf, not because of her "impressionable, generous, intellectual qualities," or because of her association with Dr. Johnson, but because she was "by nature an innovator". She was almost the first woman who was concerned with the style of her writing and the form of her sentences. "Why, she wondered, should there be one set of words for writing and another for speaking?" ('Mrs. Thrale': *The Moment and Other Essays*). Her colourful prose "crowed with familiar phrases and vulgar idioms," which "roused the disgust of the conventional," only proved Mrs. Thrale's preoccupation with the usage of words which had hitherto remained an exceedingly male concern. Moreover, Mrs. Thrale broke another convention which made her "a subject for her enemies to exults over, and for her friends, if she [had] any left, to forget or pity" (47). By marrying Mr. Piozzi, an Italian music master, she had shown the same rebellious unconventionality that she had displayed in her style of writing. This determination to find her happiness and her keen desire to employ fresh words made her an intriguing character even though she showed "coarseness in her fiber and commonness in her vision" (48) which made her observations vastly inferior to others of her own times.

In spite of their various letters, memoirs, and diaries, women did not yet feel encouraged to make writing their full time occupation. The odds were heavily against any woman who wanted to take to her writing seriously. "Writing was held to be slightly ridiculous in a girl; rather unseemly in a woman," ('Dr. Burney's Evening Party', *The Common Reader II* 108) observed Virginia Woolf, as she reviewed Fanny Burney's life and novels. Fanny Burney (1752-1840) with her keen power of observation and a "most retentive memory" which equipped her to be a naturally gifted writer was yet compelled to do her writing in secret. "It was only in the afternoon that she allowed herself to scribble—letters, diaries, stories, verses, in the look-out place which overhung the river, till the oaths of the sailors drove her in" (108-109). The mornings had to be devoted to the more serious task of household work, sewing and in learning the accomplishments proper to a lady. Whenever she could no longer resist the temptation of writing down her thoughts, Miss Burney had to steal away to a private hidden place, "to write at full till exactly as the words came into her head" (113). Out of the pages of her diary and the letters that survive, Virginia Woolf reconstructed not only the influences at work on Fanny Burney, but drew a most vivid and striking picture of a married woman ('Fanny Burney's Half-Sister', *Granite and Rainbow*) of the last quarter of the eighteenth century.

With characteristic firmness, Virginia Woolf searched for the reason why women could not yet, late in the eighteenth century make writing a career or a profession. So that even Jane Austen, whom the writer of *The Common Reader* characterizes as "the most perfect artist among women, the writer whose books are immortal" ('Jane Austen', *The Common*

Reader I) wrote in almost complete obscurity. Almost all her novels were "written stealthily under the cover of a creaking doer" (172). They were published gradually and mostly because of the persuasion and intercession of her brother. Jane Austen, herself, was too ready to admit her limitations and ignorance. Small wonder that, when the Reverend James Stanier Clarke, Librarian to the Prince Regent, suggested to her the possibilities of introducing more accomplished heroes, Miss Austen replied, not without any admixture of irony:

> Such a man's conversation must at times be on subjects of science and philosophy, of which I know nothing: or at least occasionally abundant in quotations and allusions which a woman, who, like me knows only her mother tongue, and has read little in that, would be totally without the power of giving. A classical education, or at any rate a very extensive acquaintance of English Literature, ancient and modern, appears to be quite indispensable for the person who would do justice to your clergymen... and I think I may boast myself to be... the most unlearned and uninformed female who ever dared to be an authoress. (*Jane Austen*: *Her life and Letters* 443)

Virginia Woolf drew attention to this lack of education in women, their inherent poverty (*A Room of One's Own* 30) and its effect on the feminine mind, without in any way passing any judgments or over-rating their literary talents. She merely placed them where they could be viewed from a proper perspective. Mrs. Woolf had concluded from her study of women and their position in society that the "extraordinary woman depends on the ordinary woman." She maintained further that as this was the case the "extraordinary woman" would reveal the extent of her struggle before she could rid herself of her inhibitions and create an environment propitious for creative work. It was from this point that Virginia Woolf explored through the ages, discovering in each milieu some of these "extraordinary women," who, each in her own way, had endeavored to emancipate her sex from various handicaps and repressions. She achieved her objective by sifting the biographical elements an depicting the shifting points of view, arranging memoirs, letters, diaries, novels as kaleidoscopic lenses or as multiple perspectives, till the characters achieved a rounder, deeper and living complexity, revealing the various knots of their struggle.

Virginia Woolf had set out to find at what stage women had begun to emerge as full-fledged and independent writers and what social transformation had provided them the gift of right education and economic freedom so that they could use their literary talent without any social restraint or inhibition. The eighteenth and early nineteenth centuries abounded in obscure memories and not so obscure diaries and letters that women produced in such abundance, but they hardly record many outstanding writers of merit. This obscure mass of writing, however, revealed the feminist state of mind, their skepticism and cultivated rationalism, their ministrations to the poor and their pet charity works conveying above all the converging need of some useful vocation. One reason for the generally low standard of feminine writing was their inadequate experience and conventional mode of living, whereas the novelist in order to write well had to be "terribly exposed to life" (*Granite and Rainbow* 41).

The 'life' to which women writers were 'exposed' was essentially narrow, paltry in experience, limited by certain fundamental taboos, in spite of the "innumerable slight changes in law and custom and manners," that gave women of the nineteenth century a better education and more leisure than earlier. Though women lived almost solely in their homes, and their observations and conclusions were consequently immature due to their inexperience and seclusion, some women writers did utilize with a discriminating mind whatever observations they could form, in spite of their immense handicaps. Instead of filling their works with passivity or cloying sentimentality all the time, they began to write with vigour hitherto unsuspected. Charlotte and Emily Bronte had arrived on the literary scene. Virginia Woolf groups these two writers together not because of their blood relationship, but for the 'commonness' of their genius, which was vehement and strong, though highly personal in Charlotte Bronte and determinedly impersonal in Emily Bronte. Their writings are charged with a dynamic affirmation of life.

Their writings are charged with dynamic affirmation of life. Though Charlotte Bronte was obviously conscious of her sex, as her writings teem with please on behalf of women, (Charlotte Bronte 392) and though she "never learnt the smoothness of the professional writer or acquired his ability to stuff and sway her language as he chooses", ('Jane Eyre', *The Common Reader I* 200) nevertheless she had latent powers and talent, almost gigantic, well out of proportion to her restricted education and cloistered mode of living. If Emily Bronte transcended all the limitations for her sex and "could free life from its dependence on facts" (204) it was due to her specific emotional vitality which gave a spiritual poise and fluid continuity to *Wuthering Heights*. But the conventions of their times hedged the Bronte sisters and they could neither break the rigidities of the social pattern nor escape its consequences.

Allen Tate has specified the commitment of the literary critic "to a particular stance". The stance (Allen Tate 1955) which Virginia Woolf adopts in her study of the women writers enables her to highlight not only the awakening of women to their social environment and the consequent urge for its improvement, but bring to the foreground the numerous disadvantages that they had to overcome before writing became possible for them. Though Mrs. Woolf denied the dichotomy between the so-called objectivity and subjectivity in literary criticism, her presentation of these writers enhances her won subjective approach. This is based primarily on her gradual unfolding of this slow but growing awareness of women and their struggle for emancipation. The specific contributions that these writers made to these struggles, their awareness of their own limitations, were more vital to her than the literary merit of their writings. The essay on Christina Rossetti is not the only instance where the emphasis is laid not so much on critical appreciation or evaluation of her poems, as on highlighting the figure of a frail but determined woman who, like the Bronte sisters, was 'self-centred and self-limited'. She had earlier made up her mind that writing poems was her true vocation. Her education was in no way different from that of other women in the conventional middle class families of England, nor was she professionally trained to earn her living. The reader is reminded that Christina Rossetti's writings never brought her more than ten pounds a year nor did she write poetry with a view to reform the world. As an "instinctive poet" possessing a "keen sense of visual beauty," (Christina Rossetti, *The Common Reader I* 243), Christina Rossetti detested the limitations imposed upon her by conventions. Yet her sensitivity allowed her to be restrained by them. She cheerfully put up with the limitations of her sex, retaining its brave dignity in the consciousness of her feminine superiority.

Virginia Woolf did not select Aurora Leigh as the representative poem of Mrs. Elizabeth Barrett Browing, because Mrs. Browning singled it out as "the most mature" of her works conveying her "highest convictions upon life and Art," ('Aurora Leigh', *The Common Reader II*) but because it dealt primarily with the problems of women and represented Victorian life in all its complexities. Aurora Leigh, the heroine with her "passionate interest in social questions, her conflict as artist and woman, her longing for knowledge and freedom, is the true daughter of her age" (212). The feminist in Virginia Woolf was more interested in the poem as a social document focusing attention on the restraints and restrictions that disabled the women of the period than in the poetical faculties of Mrs. Browning. The character of Aurora's maiden aunt had a special moral appeal for Mrs. Woolf because it was drawn with an ingenious deftness and compelling plausibility. Further, such a woman posed the problem confronting many single women of Victorian times. Similarly Virginia Woolf was fascinated by Mrs. Browning's pungent description of women's education of the period.

Another nineteenth century writer that Virginia Woolf found of interest was the lesser-known novelist Geraldine Jewsberry. She did not attempt to formulate any elaborate theory of minor Victorian women writers or stress their personal point of view. Her attempt was more to sift the biographical material till there emerged the pattern of living which governed these women writers from middle class household. Miss Jewsberry was not only a writer but an intimate friend of Jane Carlyle, and the letters that flowed into

Cheyne Row, revealed serious preoccupations of particular interest to the feminine mind. They echoed and reflected the growing feminist awareness of their social limitations, "It may be that we women are made as we are in order that they [the men] may in some sort fertilize the world..." ('Geradine and Jane', *The Common Reader II*).

The autobiography of Eilen Terry is reviewed from the same point of view that Virginia Woolf had brought to the character sketches of women (important to the extent of their furthering the cause of women and their struggle for emancipation). Ellen Terry, the housewife or mother, has little fascination or charm for Mrs. Woolf. But she celebrates the writer in the actress: "It never struck her, (Ellen Terry) humble as she was, and obsessed by her lack of book learning, that she was among other things, a writer." Virginia Woolf goes a little further and emphasizes that "... this mutable woman, all instinct, sympathy and sensation, is as painstaking a student and as careful of the dignity of her art as Flaubert himself" (*The Moment and Other Essays* 169). It was as if Virginia Woolf wanted to bring sharply into focus the amount of incessant toil and ruthless hard work women were capable of, once their genius had a chance of developing along the right lines.

Virginia Woolf might not have been what Dr. Daiches calls a "systematic critic" (Daiches 132), but she was "systematic" in her search for any material available which would throw light on the reasons for the paucity of women writers and the generally backward position of women in society. She had reviewed almost the entire social and literary history of England in these critical essays and had arrived at certain conclusions. Poverty and ignorance, she surmised, were closely connected, whereas education and economic independence were largely responsible for intellectual maturity of any kind. The history of women writers, she discovered, was the history of feminine emancipation.

Works Cited

Austen, R.A. and Austen-Leigh, W. *Jane Austen, Her life and Letters.* London: 1913.

Bronte, Charlotte. "Shirley": *World's Classics*. London, 1907.

Daiches, David. *Virginia Woolf.* New York, 1942

Tate, Allen. "Preface" *to The Man of Letters in the Modern World.* New York: New York Press, 1955.

Woolf, Virginia. "The Duchess of Newcastle", *The Common Reader I.* London: Hogarth, 1948. 98-109.

———, "Dorothy Osborne's Letters", *The Common Reader II.* London: Hogarth Press, 1953.

———, "Laetitia Pilkington", *The Common Reader I.* London: Hogarth Press 1948.

———, "Mrs. Thrale": *The Moment and Other Essays.* London: Hogarth Press 1952. 45-49.

———, "Dr. Burney's Evening Party", *The Common Reader II.* London: Hogarth Press, 1953.

———, "Fanny Burney's Half- Sister": *Granite and Rainbow.* London: Hogarth Press, 1958. 192-204.

———, "Jane Austen", *The Common Reader I.* London: Hogarth Press 1948. 168-183.

———, A *Room of One's Own.* London: Hogarth Press, 1959.

———, "Jane Eyre", *The Common Reader I.* London: Hogarth Press 1948.

———, "Christina Rossetti", *The Common Reader I.* London: Hogarth Press 1948.

———, "Aurora Leigh", *The Common Reader II.* London: Hogarth Press, 1953. 202-203.

———, "Geraldine and Jane", *The Common Reader II.* London: Hogarth Press, 1953. 186-201.

———, "Two Women", *The Moment and Other Essays.* London : Hogarth Press, 1952.

4

Voicing the Voiceless through Literature: A Study of Major Works of Hindi and English Stalwarts

— Binod Mishra

The aim of literature lies not only in the unfolding of human beings' life and their ambience but also in creating awareness about certain shortcomings and incongruities, which require rethinking and reconsideration. A sentinel of society looking towards change and like an integral link between man and society, literature records the longing and regrets of all sections of society. It is also responsible for representing the voices of individuals through various tenets viz. poetry, drama, short stories and novels.

Many of the characters, which we find around ourselves neglected suddenly, become vociferous because of their delineation through texts. What we as readers realize through texts often tend to ignore in mundane affair of our life. The deluge of characters, which once seemed marginalized, came to limelight through different literatures of the world.

The question of their marginalization being manifold, the texts portraying them have an indelible imprint on our psyche. These characters are marginalized not because of their inability but because of their innocence and their utter neglect most often by the centre, the ruling class. In literature, we have plethora of such cases. The present paper attempts to unravel the circumstances of these marginalized characters whose plight enabled writers such as Munshi Premchand,

Phaneeshwarnath Renu in Hindi and Mulk Raj Anand and Arundhati Roy in English to present the panorama of their times. The delineation of these characters often takes us back to William Butler Yeats, an English poet of protest. What he says can be an eye-opener not only for the centre but also for the people living on the margins:

> the centre cannot hold;
> Mere anarchy is loosed upon the world,
> The blood-dimmed tide is loosed, and everywhere
> The ceremony of innocence is drowned;
> The best lack all conviction, while the worst
> Are full of passionate intensity.
> Surely some revelation is at hand;
> Surely the Second Coming is at hand.
>
> (W.B.Yeats 'The Second Coming')

Surely, there have been revelations and revolutions as well. The veterans of literature have provided voice to the voiceless and the world today appears to be coming out of the notions of marginalization. The voice of the voiceless is being realized and we are nearing a consensus where the narrow divides are to stop and we are likely to accept that these gaps exist neither in letter nor in spirit.

The first novel to be discussed in this paper is Premchand's *Godan* (1936). *Godan* can be read as a social documentary which unfolds the milieu of an age when the more powerful ruled the less privileged class. The novel clearly has two plots and the writer shows the gaps existing between the two more overtly on the basis of their financial capabilities. But we cannot ignore the presence of subdivisions even in these two classes. The village atmosphere is clearly segregated into various factions—one of the farmers, the other of patwaris, sahukars, moneylenders and yet other of the younger generation.

Hori Mahto is a middle class self-reliant farmer. As a typical Indian farmer, he depends solely on his land and considers land as his first and last resort. Conscious of his stature as a prosperous farmer, he wants to have his own oxen and a cow. He brings a cow on loan though on high interest rates. The jealousy of his own brother results in the killing of the cow and this changes the course of his life. Faced with guilt, grief and the further fear of police harassment, his brother flees. Hori's faith in his own individuality is not shaken. The great-hearted Hori considers it his responsibility to help Heera's wife and children in tilling, sowing and harvesting. Hori represents the ilk of people who have been sent on this earth to head the family despite the fluid making way to separation. Troubled, torn and dejected even by his son's attitude of fleeing secretly because of his association with Jhunia does not deter him. Hori lends a voice to others though his own voice gets stifled in the mad race of sahukars, patwaris and other moneylenders.

Hori's suffering arises because of his love for land and also because of his being morally alive. Conscious of his prestige in society he beats his wife Dhania when she opposes to comply with the atrocities of moneylenders. His inability to protest against the exploitation of patwaris and his fealty to these power centres makes him a scapegoat. Land, though his first love, he borrows money on it and towards the end of the novel marries his daughter Roopa to man older than her. He considers it his moral duty to get his son and daughters settled though he has to suffer humiliation. His belief that his daughters should have a better-married and prosperous life leads him ultimately to his grave. Cheated tough by his son, Hori reassesses himself and gets ready to face the music considering this as the go of the world. He feels baffled though he does not refuse to accept Jhunia as his daughter in law. His act of giving shelter to Shiliya, a kept of Matadin shows Hori's fearlessness and his helpful attitude devoid of all biases. He also realizes the truth of Dhania's strong and straightforward views but rejects it because of his established stature as a loyal farmer and a follower of feudal system. Premchand tries to give voice to voiceless through Gobar, who represents a new generation. Having suffered much the atrocities of the exploited class, Gobar inherits the strong views from his mother who does not fear to call spade a spade. He has strong views and he hates to love the orthodox ideas of his parents. Mentally weak and physically strong, Gobar is infatuated by the charms of a widow, Jhunia and flees her to his house. Unable to face the parents, he flees to the town to earn a livelihood. He reappears after a year and is drunk with the little pleasantries of urban life. His urban exposure adds some voice and he seems to bring a change in the conditions of his parents. He soon becomes the hero of the village boys who are highly impressed by the opportunities of better life available in Lucknow. They consider urban life as a Pandora's Box and soon see their imagination fructified in Gobar. Gobar is also highly surcharged with the villager's change of attitude for him. He wants to bring a charisma and wants to turn the table on the moneylenders and sahukars. He wants his father to protest against the privileged classes and also goads him to ask for the receipt of land revenues. He is unable to resist the new fangled ideas and seems to be in a hurry to bring an overnight change in the village. What he tells his father is full of a new voice, a voice of awareness and a mantra of protest:

> Why do you go to flatter your masters? If the dues are not paid, the messenger comes and abuses. We work at a less payment and also give gifts. Then why should one respect them? (16)

Gobar is shocked to see that some other hawker has occupied the place of his shop at Lucknow. The fast changing conditions of town life put him into oblivion. He becomes jobless and finds Jhunia and their son Lallu weeping. Jhunia feels dislocated in the congested confines of the rented house and her son gets no one to swing him in arms. The expectation of another baby and the lack of adequate facilities fall heavy on her health. Emaciated and bereft of milk, Jhunia is unable to satisfy either her husband or her son. Lallu dies and leaves her mother in despair. Jhunia's troubles do not end here. Bearing the brunt of Gobar's frustration and his unemployment, she cries for help. Chuhia, the tongaman's wife comes to her rescue and a son is born to Jhunia. She seems to have more knowledge of the world and always cautions Gobar from joining the strikers. But the divisive forces of money and the yearning for a better life with wife and children make him blunt and blind. He forgets the voice of his conscience and joins the strikers in factory and pays a heavy price. His physical prowess blinds his mind and he eats a humble pie. And as ill luck has it, Gobar is beaten badly by the new group of workers. Jhunia not only bandages his bruises but also makes him understand his fault. he is ashamed and full of repentance. He takes a vow never to hurt Jhunia who has awakened him. The novelist draws Gobar's condition in the following lines:

> When we do an injustice to our dear and near ones and when we realize the acute sting of adversity, we feel awareness in our souls. We become ready to regret for our misdeeds. Gobar was getting impatient for such repentance. (238)

Premchand not only portrays the picture of society ridden with poverty and exploitation but also tries to hint at the possible solution. He shows Gobar's life taking new turns at every step. But aware of father-son relationship, he makes Gobar realize his faults. When he receives his father's letter informing about Sona's marriage, Gobar persuades Jhunia in the following way:

> It is not good to be at attrition with one's parents. They have given us birth, we can quarrel and be cross with them but they have tended us. We should be patient even if they say something. These days I remember them too much. I don't know why I became angry with them. I had to leave him because of you. (293)

Gobar's stay in Lucknow and his encounter with the new world gives him a new voice. The pulls and pressures of industrialization disillusion him. The masters and the factory owners in the towns appeared to him the extended version of village sahukars and patwaris. Gobar becomes numb, mellowed and experienced because of his frequent change of his jobs. In his second visit to his village, he becomes more cordial and finds no fault in his father's decision to marry Roopa to Ramsevak. Rather he sympathizes with his father's predicament and lends a voice to him.

> When a man has no control over circumstances he leaves it to his fate. How long shall this muddle go on? All pelf and prestige is a pomp and show for those who cannot meet two ends. You too could have been a prosperous person had you but throttled others neck and embezzled other's deposits You never left your ideal and that is why are paying for. Had I been in your place, I could have either been executed or been in a jail. (16)

This acute realization of Gobar not only lessens Hori's anxieties but also soothes his guilt like a balm. Gobar's approval of his father's action voices both the father as well as the son. Both feel inspired and awakened. Gobar's words also reveal the ostentatious and hollow life style of the so-called big people both in village as well as in towns.

Raisaheb feels his voice challenged when his son wants to marry Saroj, the girl of his choice. Having spent a lot in election and licking dust to his rival Suryapratap, he had earned an immense respect in society. He had an edge over Suryapratap by winning the case and the election. Becoming a minister was another laurel but all that seemed stunted when he got Suryaparatap's proposal to marry his daughter with Raisaheb's son. But he felt a jolt at his son's defiance of fleeing to England with his fiancée. Raisaheb's trouble took a tragic turn to know about her daughter's separation with her husband. Thus we find that the younger generation felt more comfortable in listening to their own voices and this is what the novelist has endeavored to outline.

Premchand has tried to portray Gobar as the new voice who can earn, who can burn and who can also make others learn that there can be many other alternatives in life. His escapade to Lucknow is a device to show Gobar's determination, his waywardness and his rebel ideas. But he fails because of his bluntness and lack of reasoning. What makes Premchand memorable as a writer of social fiction is to introduce the device of creating awareness in the new generation, which could bring an end to the persecutions of the old. The rise of capitalistic forces encourages the suppressed class to think of an alternative. Cheated, defeated and despite several struggles to maintain his home and hearth, Hori tumbles at last. His death can be seen as a surrender before man, God and social structure.

Dhania, Gobar and Shiliya represent the rising forces whose voice cannot be curbed for long. The sympathies of Dr. Mehta and Malati for the downtrodden people, their voluntary services in Bellari village strengthen the causes of the voiceless. Their endeavours put stumbling blocks in the elite class' exploitation represented by Raisaheb, Khanna Saheb and Tankha. The novel also lends a voice to the dormant society of downtrodden represented by Hori who considers poverty and class divisions as ordained by Fate and God.

A serious reader of Premchand discovers that as a writer, he has come above minor issues usually becoming the plot of imaginative writing. He as a conscious writer has been able to unfold the stigmas and propose a solution to these problems. In this connection, the writer himself becomes the voice of the suffering class and tries to solve the crisis enveloping the psyche of the masses. Women characters in *Godan* also seem to be dissatisfied with the prevailing conditions and are in search of a new alternative. They seem to console, support and fight each other's cause by whatever means possible. Dhania's acceptance of Jhunia, her approval of giving shelter to Shiliya, her goodwill with her sisters-in-law are clear indications of sisterly concern devoid of caste or class considerations. Sona's sympathy for Shiliya and Shiliya's support to Sona are also to strengthen each other. The old lady's voluntary help to Jhunia during her delivery in Lucknow is another example of community feeling. Even Dr. Malati's free campaigns in Bellari village to awaken the uneducated womenfolk ensue from the author's approach of voicing the voiceless. Dulari and Nouhar also stand in stead when Hori needs financial support. Premchand's women characters in *Godan* seem to have more voice, which they derive from their adverse conditions also. Even the cobbler girl Shiliya does not feel frightened to openly accept her relations with Matadin, a member of high caste. Her maltreatment by both her own and Matadin's parents does not weaken her. Her love for Matadin is a great voice that shelters her. Boycotted by society, she does not think of ending her life but seeks shelter in Hori's house where Matadin secretly sends some money to her. This gesture enlivens Shiliya's wild spirit and she crosses the river at night to share it with her one time friend, Sona. As time progresses, Matadin's love for Shiliya rewards her with a son, a new voice to live with. The boy proudly takes Matadin's name as his father. As misfortune has it, the boy dies in an attack of pneuminia. This tragedy shatters and snatches her voice for some time. But this also helps in paving the way for Matadin's return to her. Shiliya's determination, her patience and her austerity melt Matadin and he decides to be with her against all odds and criticism.

Malti, another lady character of the novel is very much a blend of various voices of self-esteem and is lit with the Western education. Realizing the new voice of education and finding it difficult to afford Saroj's expenses, she decides to remain unmarried. She asso- ciates herself with aristocratic circles and spends much of her time amid discussions of new challenges and changing conditions. Though a subject of discussion among Khanna, Onkarnath and Dr. Mehta, she is aware of her limitations though she becomes an admirer of Mehta's idealism. She finds in him a voice of the changing times. She has been won over by Mehta's philosophy and sympathizes with his economic conditions becoming a means of helping the students in need. Mehta spends a major amount on giving scholarships to students and lives a mendicant life. Wooed by Mehta's philosophy and influenced by his ideals, she starts welfare campaigns and does not feel degraded to go to remote areas to awaken the uneducated womenfolk towards a better and hygienic lifestyle for the well being of their new born babes. A detailed reading of Godan exhibits the author's moral responsibility to let not the values suffer. There are tribulations but the novelist keeps alive the moral sensibility throughout the novel. Like a veteran doctor, he detects the disease and suggests the medicine. He makes his characters experience the exigency of values. Value works as a great force and its realization by many characters enables them to feel more strengthened. In this connection, we find Hori who is an apostle of ideals, maintaining his moral up to the last. He absorbs

Heera's crime, Gobar's defiance, Dhaniya's sharp and biting tongue. Acceptance of Jhunia, shelter to Shiliya, the marriage of his daughters, the paying of all dues and his hard earning to refund Ramsewak's loan are some exquisite examples. Gobar errs once but realizes the vitality of his filial bond. He also repents for his maltreatment of Jhunia. Dhania is full of scorns and scourge yet abides by Hori and their progeny. Shiliya sticks to Matadin's love and bears his son against all odds. Matadin's repentance and the death of their son purge them of all sins and the desire to start life anew is another voice, which has to be realized. Suffering burns the crimes of most of the characters and makes them aware.

The elite class, too, on the other hand hears the voice of the upcoming generation and accepts the same though with a heavy heart. The mass strike of the workers and the burning of the mill indicate the rise of the new voice against suppression. Most of the members of this class realize that these rising voices cannot be curbed. Raisaheb's realizations of his son's defiance and his daughter's rebellion with her husband are also symbolic of a new voice. Malti's determination to go to the interior areas and organize voluntary camps to help the uneducated masses is a realization of the utility of education. Mehta's voice also does not go waste. The influence of urban life also works magically in the village where the use of words other than Hindi brings some more voice.

Maila Anchal (1954), written by Phaneeshwarnath Renu has been considered a regional novel and depicts the life of a village facing the conflict between interiority and exteriority. Though many critics who stick to their view of it being a novel of a particular region, feel that the novel is without a hero and the village itself is the chief protagonist. Such critics fail to see the light of progress in most of the characters that have their own way of looking at things and are not devoid of their yearning of becoming heroes in their own right. Marygunj is not a typical village where ignorance becomes a uniting force. Most of the characters in this novel are eager as well as aware and they listen to each other with patience. The diversity of voices and opinions, superstitions and inhibitions, love and hate, avarice and malice result in a fusillade of questions, which the novel provides an answer to. The novel derives its strength from some of the characters who are a foil to each other. Baldeo and Kalicharan, Tehsildar Vishwanath Prasada and Hargouri, Mahant Sewadas and Ramdas, Lakshmi and Rampiyaria, Kamli and Mamata are some burning examples.

The novel is based on the class struggle and masses fight for their freedom against the various social taboos and the neglect of an Indian village at a time when the nation had attained its freedom and the interior areas were struggling for their existence. The author of the novel, Phaneeshwarnath Renu, unlike Premchand has not been able to make classic characters like Hori, Dhaniya and Gobar but has unveiled the picture of a village life undergoing transition in the light of the changing consciousness of a free nation. The novelist makes his attempt to sketch the condition of the villages and the villagers as they are and not as they should be. Aware of his responsibility as a writer who can herald a new age he makes the condition of a village suffering the utter neglect and bearing the bruises of British government even after their departure. The village becomes a central figure and shouts for its place in changing times. The first chapter of the novel is a testimony of the fact that the lack of communication and transport seals the throbs of change.

The novel opens with the news of government's decision of opening a hospital in the village. This great news for the villagers surcharges their expectations of new development in their village neglected by time and governmental structure. The villagers find swimming in delight to imagine the distance between the village and the railway station Rauthat lessened and the barrier of Koshi being bridged. The gap between the rich and the poor has made the low caste people voiceless and the high class voiced. But this news unsettles the privileged class who become anxious to see the rise of consciousness among weaker section. Baldeo who is a member of the Congress Party becomes an apple of discord because of his participation in meetings and his acquaintance with leaders. Hargouri reacts caustically at Baldeo's advances saying:

> All of you will go to Kashi. Some of you should also remain for licking the leftovers. Do you think that you will become like Jawaharlal because you went to jail? Remember, you worked as a volunteer in congress office and are showing your leadership here by being a deaf among the blind. Volunteer a tail of the swayam sevak. (Renu 20)

The scorn of the privileged class provides a voice to the deprived lot and empowers them.Caste is a determining force in Indian villages. The novelist takes a dig at the way anybody is asked about his caste. Caste considerations erode the unity and bring a gap in the thinking processes of the villagers.

> Caste is a very big thing. People not believing in caste also have a caste. Saying Hindoo is not enough. Are you Brahmin? Which Brahmin Origin? Clan? Nobody asks your caste in a city. Who knows about one's caste in a town? But you are not acceptable in a village without your caste. (52)

The narrow considerations of caste, sub caste, sub- sub caste delineated in the novel hint at a division of all kinds. But we cannot deny the fact of members attaining respectable position on account of their personal sparks. They make their presence felt by dint of protest and submission at times. Baldeo and Kalicharan, the leading voices of the deprived lot are different in their approaches. A follower of Gandhi, Baldeo is admired by people because of his submissiveness and his participation in party meetings. Kalicharan, a follower of Baldeo earlier changes his belief and joins socialist party. More courageous and intelligent than Baldeo, Kalicharan lends his voice to the underprivileged and wants them to wake up. Klaicharan's voice is the voice of truth. He shows his heroism in the panchayat in driving the fake and malicious Narsimhdas and creating a place for Ramdas as the next Mahanth. Kali also shows solidarity with the villagers in the moments of crisis devoid of all caste and religious beliefs. The lower sections of society find in Kali strength though it is another reason that with some sympathy for these people, Kali is gathering a work force for his party. He confides in these marginalized groups and shows them a new sun in the Socialist party's slogan. It later becomes quite paradoxical that he does not get any support from his party members when he really needs them. He is sent to jail on false charges and escapes from there only to disprove the charges. The novelist hints at the treatment of the workers negligence at the hands of the leaders in order to maintain their false and ostentatious lifestyle. The crude reality of means being neglected once the goal is reached takes a universal theme.

The introduction of Prashant may be seen as the novelist's contrivance to show an alternative which can help people come out of the narrow walls of caste, creed and identity. Prashant has been shown as a person having various identities and numerous good qualities. A doctor by profession, he is a researcher too. He cures patients by his pills and nurses their bruises with sympathy. He works as a cementing force between the rich and the poor and soon becomes a favourite of all. His philanthropic approach lends an eye to the beauty of the village beleaguered by mud and flood, despite being soaked by the underprivileged's blood to fructify in the greenery worn by the fields. He also lends an ear to the poor Santhals whose land has been confiscated by the big guns of the village. He also enters the heart of Kamli, the tehsildar's daughter not only by his sweet syrups but also by his soft demeanour. He lends a voice to the coy Kamli for whom exposure of any kind was an imagination. A conduit for Kamli, Prashant absorbs everything and brings a remedy to her frequent attacks of fainting. Kamli's fits become strange fits of passion, which the duo dares to tell in each other's ear much against the social mores. Kamli's parents get wonderstruck to know about their daughter nursing the doctor's baby in her womb.

The doctor's character is an eye-opener to all those young and ambitious individuals who anticipate their future abroad and think that scholarship to pursue research in a foreign country will bring a vicissitude. Prashant refuses to go to a foreign country when the minister gives him the news of his selection. Spreading the map of Purnia and Saharsa, he says:

> I want to live in a part of this map. See, this is the part of Saharsa where Koshi brings devastation by its dance.

> And this is the eastern part of Purnia where malaria and black fever cause a deluge o f death. (54)

His determination to work in this neglected region is also born of his own borrowed identity strengthened by people remotely related to him. He understands his vocation and answers its calls as and when people require. Moved by the simplicity and purity of villagers, Prashant also understands their guiles. What he writes in one of his early letters to Mamata is not devoid of truth but the doctor's reading of the villager's pulse:

> The villagers appear very simple if simplicity means uneducated, ignorant and superstitious. As regards worldly knowledge, they will cheat people like us five times a day. But what is heartening is that you will be helplessly moved at their simplicity despite being cheated. (56)

The doctor also mentions how the veteran poet Vidyapati lends a voice to the illiterate, uneducated and semi-clad people of the villages. Vidyapati's songs are sung by all classes of people devoid of caste and class.As the novel progresses; Prashant becomes a voice to reckon with. His research on malaria brings him to the limelight. His sympathy with the Santhals enables him to read their documents at times and makes him believe that they and not the so-called tehsildars are the real owners of the land. Falsely implicated and sent to jail though he maintains his integrity and helps Ganesh by all means. He grows more concerned about the cruel social set up which does not let the marginalized people open their lips. He suddenly becomes more accountable in the eyes of Kalicharan when he tells him about his concern for santhals:

> Tehsildar sahib is an aristocratic member of the village. He is elder than me in age. I often go to his house because of Kamli's illness. They love me and I respect them. But that does not mean I will support his atrocities and side with him. (225)

He doctor's arrest raises questions in the legislative assembly. He becomes a special class prisoner. Investigations about his stay and identity in various parts reveal that he had neither political affiliations nor such ambition. When the doctor is released on bail, he proceeds for Marygunj. His humanitarian approach finally unseals the hard shell of Tehsildar Vishwanath Prasad who melts and accepts him as his son in law. The doctor has also been able to transform tehsildar's heart. The tehsildar's inner voice is awakened and he decides to return the mortgaged land to their real owners.

Prashant wins once again the heart of everyone in the village when he wants to return and restart working for the people who long to live and live to long for greater dreams. His being sent to jail has not dampened his spirit but has augmented his determination to work for the upliftment of the villagers. What he tells Mamata reveals his large-heartedness and his exquisite nature:

> I will restart my work here, in this village. I want to cultivate love. The plants of love will burgeon forth on the tear soaked soil. I shall undertake a penance in the lap of Mother India. I yearn to bring back smiles on the faded lips of the villagers to establish hope and faith in their hearts. (333-34)

The women characters of the novel also strengthen each other by lending support to their compatriots. Though they are many in numbers, yet some of them shine because of their personal qualities. Lakshmi represents the lot of those who become a victim of the olden practice of sadhus having a female disciple to help in the functioning of the matth. These orphaned girl children usually bear the brunt of sadhu's fastidiousness. As Lakshmi's infancy is over, she tries to overcome the oddities the ashram and carves a niche for herself. She reads the religious texts and slams the door on malicious intents of the two Mahants admonishing them to have a control over their bodily wanderings. Her infatuation for the young Baldeo lands her into skirmish with the Mahanth and ultimately she leaves the ashram to live a new and meaningful life with Baldeo. Her experiences in the ashram and her realization of her inner voice bring a release for her. She also shows her courage by admonishing the Mahanth and guarding her own fences by her string will power. At times her conscience pricks her, no doubt, yet she is able to assimilate herself against the odds and provides herself a more promising and pronounced voice. Her successor and the Mahanth's new dasi's evil designs make Lakshmi's stature more transparent and authentic.

Kamli is another leading voice who represents the lot of girls longing for a more meaningful and ambitious life are confined in the corridors of their courtyard made to guard the external influence of outside world buzzing with new voices and readying for an authentic existence. She is the transformed version of Lakshmi in many ways. Kamli has her own voice and her position is more enhance because of her being the only child of the privileged tehsildar. The novelist portrays her stature in the following lines:

> Kamla is an apple of her parents' eyes. No one can do anything against tehsildar's daughter's wishes. The mother fulfils Kamla's every wish. Her father has taught her Ramayana, Mahabharata, Nal-Damyanti, Savitri-Satyavan, Parvati-Mangal and Vishnupurana. Kamla worships Lord Shiva. Lord Shiva, Shiva made of clay. (75)

Kamli is a much-loved child of traditionally rich and privileged family. The doctor's arrival opens new avenues for her and her mother lends a continuous support to her. Prashant becomes a regular visitor to tehsildar's house and steals everyone's heart. Kamli's mother and mausi approve of her furtive meetings with the doctor and thus strengthens Kamli's yearning for the doctor. The mother stands by Kamli when she discovers the doctor's passionate desires sowed and growing in Kamli's heart. Kamli gets more voice through doctor's books during his stay in jail. The mother persuades tehsildar to accept Prashant as their son in law. This reveals the mother's generosity and her readiness to accommodate in a world of changing values. Kamli's faith in the doctor's love is not shaken despite all odds. She assures her mother that the doctor won't abandon her. What she writes in a letter to the doctor is not only a reminder of his promise but also an example of an authoritative voice:

> Your books have taught me a lot. They have provided me a great support. But now I need a new book the pages of whish should have been inscribed with Kamala. Believe me. Don't be frightened. Whatever will happen, will result in happiness. (328)

Mamata, the doctor's classmate though nurturing a fancy for him, does not become an obstacle in doctor's path of progress. She acts as a true friend and comes down from Patna to secure a bail for Prashant. She also visits Marygunj and accepts Kamli as doctor's wife. Her supporting voice gives the name Nilotpal to Kamli's baby. She wants the mother and the child to be taken to Patna for better medication facilities. She withdraws the words of her previous letters and assures Prashant that no research goes in vain. She puts a seal on his endeavours and realizes that experiments done in huge labs cannot compete with Prashant's research, which excels because of his love for earth and its inhabitants.

The novelist also shows his concern of providing unity and harmony through the villager's life style. The village has its own way of looking at things, celebrating festivals and recreating through traditional ways and also reaching a consensus in the hours of crisis. Renu establishes the voice of the villagers against the alien interferences and also makes it clear that all that glitters is not gold. He rather reveals the loopholes in the functioning of a structured system and seems to advocate the alibi that determination to do something is an important ingredient in the well being of the world. The novel also attracts the voice of the outside world by its use of typical local dialect, derivatives, compound words and connectives that provide a relief to the somber atmosphere of the book.

Mulk Raj Anand's *Untouchable* (1935) is out and out a novel written to provide voice to the voiceless. Based purely on the rigid social structure, the novel narrates the foibles in the central character Bakha's heart. A well-built child of nature and a young sweeper, Bakha undertakes this profession because of his forefather's maintaining it over the ages. The novel also satirizes the system that allots profession on the basis of caste. Bakha represents a community well known for clearing the garbage and excretion of the high caste. We can find an example of neglect shown to these people by the poet's description of the way live in the 'outcastes' colony' and outside the boundaries under the shadow both of the town and the cantonment. Bakha is different from the children of his age. Though not happy with his father's instructions, which bore a subtle protest in him, he never shirked his work. He was a man of principles who preferred his duty first to any other game played by his cronies. His imagination made him an able child who had many dreams to realize and eager desires to fulfil. Ages of suppression and denial of rights seemed to shock him yet his wishes would glitter him.

> The anxiety of going to school! How beautiful it felt! How nice it must be to be able to read and write! One could read the papers after going to school. One could talk to the sahibs. One wouldn't have to run to the scribe every time a letter came. And one wouldn't have to pay him to have one's letter written. (32)

Bakha suffers because of his being an untouchable and has to announce his arrival lest he should touch the high caste. He boils and burns when he's alleged to have touched the Hindu merchant and defiled him. No one is ready to her his plea and he is slapped. Ragged, torn and brazenly insulted, Bakha is burning with the desire of revenge and curses himself, "But why couldn't I say something? Couldn't I have joined my hands to him and then gone away? The slap on my face!" (43).

He is unsettled to hear what his sister tells him about the priest of the temple. The priest had hurled abuses and warned Bakha and his sister by his usual trick of temple being defiled because of the untouchables' entry. Sohini's voice dies under the lurking fear of the priest's announcement. It's ironical that the priest's lustrous gaze and later his touching Sohini's breasts do not pollute him but the temple that shields him gets defiled because of their entry. Bakha forces Sohini to tell him the truth on the assurance that he will kill him. Sohini admits of being touched yet she does not want her brother to wage a war. Bakha hates the serfdom that stops him from retaliating. The novelist beautifully draws the protagonist's conflicting voice and adds his own in the following way.

> He couldn't overstep the barriers, which the conventions of his superiors had built up to protect their weakness against him. He couldn't invade the magic circle, which protects a priest from attack by anybody, especially by a low caste man. So in the highest movement of his strength, the slave in him asserted itself, and he lapsed back, wild with torture, biting his lips, ruminating his grievances. (53-54)

Bakha is shuddered to find his father not finding any fault with the privileged class. He is infuriated when Lakha shows little concern even after hearing what happened to his son and daughter. Years of servility had sealed Lakha's sentiments and he had accepted everything resignedly. Bakha's plans to protest end in a fiasco when his father narrates his own experience about Bakha's recovery from illness because of hakim's visit though after receiving infinite abuses.

In a world divided by caste and class considerations, the voice of friendship brings a triumph to Bakha. His fascination for Ramcharan's sister and his camaraderie with Chota and Ramcharan offer some hope to him. Ramcharan pays no heed to his mother's scolds and provides Bakha a world where there are no narrow divisions but only untapped possibilities. Taking Bakha and Chota to the hill, Ramcharan shares the sugar plums with them. Bakha feels relaxed in the open on the hillocks and wants to be one with the rhythm of the cool breeze that can drive away the vacuity from his heart. The novelist seems to encourage Bakha to experience the halo offered by the outside world that could embolden him:

> It seemed to him he would be unhappy if he heard even one human voice. His inside seemed to know that he wouldn't be soothed if there was the slightest obstruction between him and the outer world. It didn't even occur to him to ask why he had come here. He was just swamped by the merest sight of the open fields that spread before him. (76)

Bakha gets exhilarated by the kind gesture of Havildar Charat Singh, who offers him tea and also gifts him a hockey stick. He also feels interested in what Colonel Hutchinson tells him about Yessuh Masih whose abode is free from all class and caste distinctions. He wonders how could there be a world where everyone could have been treated equally. Lost in imagination and reverie about such a world, he gets ennobled to hear about the arrival of Mahatma. Prompted by what people say about the Mahatma and seeing the flurry of people flocking to hear him, Bakha also rushes to have a glimpse of the noble soul. He compares himself with Uka of Mahatma Gandhi's narration and looks eagerly towards the saintly fellow. Bakha feels comforted and more voiced to hear Mahatma who wants everyone to take the solemn pledge to remove untouchability:

> All public wells, temples, roads, schools, sanatoriums must be declared open to the Untouchables. And if all of you profess to love me, give me a proof of your love by carrying on this propaganda against the observance of untouchability. (121)

What fires Bakha's imagination are the poet's words. The poet enkindles more hope in him and his community by telling them of an alternative, which could free the sweepers from scavenging. Bakha feels upped and wants to know more when the poet says, "When the sweepers change their profession, they will no longer remain untouchables. And they can do that soon, for the first thing we will do when accept the machine which clears dung without anyone having to handle it—the flush system." (126-27)

Bakha, the child of darkness beholds light in what the poet and the Mahatma hint at. One can find Bakha, the fair built child of nature, whose voice has been curbed right from the beginning, seems to regain voice towards the end of the novel. His curiosity to know what the machine is all about and his flicker of hope at the introduction of flush system bring an alternative to his predicament. The novel, though short, has been able to provide more voice to the voiceless represented by Bakha who sees his salvation in what the poet says. It is also symbolical that the novel, which starts with the description of 'outcastes colony', ends with the protagonist proceeding 'homewards'. This can be interpreted as the novelist's approach of advocating the case of the lowly and sending them home with a new song on their lips and a new hope in their hearts. E.M. Forster has very subtly remarked in the Preface to the novel in the following way:

> Bakha returns to his father and his wretched bed, thinking now of the Mahatma, now of the Machine. His Indian day is over and the next day will be like it, but on the surface of the earth if not in the depths of the sky, a change is at hand. (Forster 7)

Arundhati Roy's *The God of Small Things* (1997), which won the Booker prize, is an outstanding example of an English work written in an Indian spirit to voice the voiceless. The novel having a long line of characters—both male and female, unfolds a family story where most of the characters feel cornered because of their many wishes either remaining unfulfilled or crushed under the wheels of traditional and orthodox ideas. The novel is a bold attempt of the erudite Arundhati to throw light on the facts that a civilized society which organizes meeting and conferences to eradicate caste discriminations and ameliorate the conditions of downtrodden but shies away when it comes to put these paradigms into practice. Keeping aside the web of characters, we shall explore the conditions of two leading characters of the novel. Ammu, the tragic heroine of the novel faces the discrimination of being the girl child forbidden to go to school or college while her brother, Chacko is sent to Oxford. Suffocated in her house, Ammu goes to Calcutta where a chance meeting brings her to a young man whom she marries. She tries to raise her voice not informing her parents about her marriage. But things take a different turn as her husband wants Ammu to go to his boss' bungalow to placate complaints against him and save his job. Considering it as an infra-dig, she feels embittered and raises her voice by hitting her husband on the head. She had nothing to fall back upon but her twins and her parents' house. With a heavy heart, she returns to Ayemenem house.

Ammu's mother, Mammachi, too had a same fate and she could never raise her voice. Used to Pappachi's beating of her mother, Mammachi, Ammu inherits the legacy of females' suppressed world where there were rigid views about a married daughter having no position in her parents' house. Ammu's children also get neglected and they feel the ire of their parents' divorce. Estha and Rahel-the twins share the same fate and their voice in this world becomes voiceless. It not only affects their careers but also their habitual disposition. Estha, the boy remains quiet and grows psychologically depressed while Rahel, the girl is suspended thrice from Nazareth Convent. Arundhati is full of pity and concern when she draws the condition of Estha in the following way:

> Estha had been a quite child . . . Yet Estha's silence was never awkward. Never intrusive. Never noisy. It wasn't an accusing, protesting silence as much a sort of aestivation, a dormancy, the psychological equivalent of what lungfish do to get themselves through the dry season, except that in Estha's case the dry season looked as though it last for ever. (10)

Their inchoate childhood tormented their adult life, which witnessed nothing but divorce, transfer and torments throughout. Another remarkable character of the novel, Velutha adds more voice to the novel. A low caste paravan, he is sound not only physically but mentally too. Velutha severs his way with his father's profession and learns many skills. A craftsman who can chisel things perfectly soon steals the heart of Ammu's twins who visited Velutha's house despite the forbidding of the elders of Ayemenem house. The children's longing for a fatherly figure gets fulfilled in Velutha who feeds them the best fish curry and teaches them fishing. The children get so accustomed to him that they could recognize him even in a crowd of marchers. Velutha, a quick learner of things also excelled in mending radio, clocks and water pumps. Velutha gets a job in Pappachi's pickle factory and feels marginalized as he gets less salary because of his being a low caste. His self-respect and his party card embolden him but his father's constant harassment compels him to disappear from the village for some months. Velutha enters the heart of Ammu through children. Both Ammu and Velutha are neglected by their own parents and this brings them closer. Ammu feels voiced by

Velutha's love but the jaundiced eyes of society fulminate fire on the lovers. Both of them establish physical relation also. But society considers it as transgressing the limits and punishes both. Ammu is confined in her own house. Society forgets that both belong to marginalized class and heaps abuses, insults and abrasions on them. The man made society believes in two classes only and that too of the high and the low. Velutha becomes a victim of having crossed the barriers and he's charged with kidnapping the twins. Put in jail, Veutha is killed as a result of police atrocity and maltreatment. He does not speak a word in protest and dies to waken the sleeping lawmakers who use and abuse it as per their own privilege. His silence is more voiced than the slogans of K.N.M Pillai, who blurts something in the name of party and subverts when it comes to caste. Dejected by the circumstances and rejected by her husband, the neglected Ammu gets a faint delight to see her children happy in Velutha's company. Velutha enkindles some hope in Ammu too and she feels conscious of her bodily demands. The road to 'Age and death through its parted strands' suddenly creates in her a longing for the love she was refused. Ammu crosses the river every night to meet Velutha. Vellya Pappen, Velutha's father adds fire to the rising doubts that other members of the family have over Velutha's familiarity with the children and Ammu. We can find the novelist providing more voice to the voiceless characters through their expression of love for each other, "The lovers. Sprung from his loins and hers. His son and her daughter. They had made the unthinkable thinkable and the impossible really happen" (256). The lot of women represented by Baby Kochamma and Mammachi in stead of sympathizing with Ammu make it more explosive by adding colour and caste card. It's quite ironical that Baby Kochamma feels a sadistic pleasure and finds her denial of love for Father Mulligan satisfied in the wrecking of havoc on Ammu and Velutha. Mammachi, a victim of regular beating by Pappachi also has too less sympathy for the wounds given to Ammu by her husband. She shows her acquiescence in what Baby Kochamma says, "How could she stand the smell? Haven't you noticed? They have a particular smell, these paravans." (257).

Ammu's final attempt to save Velutha also goes waste. Her desire of making correction in her statement and also of seeing Velutha is curbed. The Inspector not only disappoints her but also insults her by using foul language. The novelist voices the false standards of decorum, sensitivity and human treatment of the police system that has been framed to guard people in times of crisis. The lines given below are ample proof of such indecorum;

> It's too late for all this, don't you think? he said. He spoke the coarse Kottayam dialect of Malayalam. He stared Ammu's breasts as he spoke. He said the police knew all they needed to know and that the Kottayam police didn't take statements from veshyas or their illegitimate children. (7)

Arundhati's novel provides more voice to Indian writing in English in her use of language and her inventiveness of words. What makes her stature dignified is the technique of telling stories. Inconsistency, a synonym of human life has more consistency since human life is not the smooth road where everyone can have a smooth ride. The road to happiness in life is bumpy and the jerks and jolts of time are the stark truths. It has to be realized that it is the individual's satisfaction, which can help in making better societies. The community feeling can be generated only when we can think of a casteless, classless and factionless society. History has been the witness that no system remains ever fixed and chinks of change are always visible only to be accepted either by an exclamation or an explosion. It is quite significant that the novel *The God of Small Things ends* with the word 'tomorrow'. This gives the indication that whatever be the consequences, hope for change still exists.

In all the four novels discussed above, the common link is that of the difference of opinion between the two generations. It is discovered that what the older generation considers loyalty to a system as a weapon to protect against odds; the younger ones view it as lack of exposure and a sort of exploitation. The delineation of these younger generations amply demonstrates the fact that the voice of protest is the only way to enable the deaf to hear. The power of protest not only exhibits the desire for release form the web of incongruities and inequalities but also unveils the truth that behind the considerations of colour and caste lies every human soul that strives to seek satisfaction and imagines to walk in a moonlit night on the stairs of stars. Change or transformation does not wait for any system or a group rather it ensues from an individual who initiates it and allows others to join the caravan.

Gobar in *Godan* feels the need to bring this change and his fleeing to Lucknow though for some other reason, is an indication of change. It's another reason that he yields to the circumstances but with a heavy heart. Gobar's faint voice becomes strong in *Maila Anchal's* Baldeo and Kalicharan. Kalichran's voice has more appeal and unable to bear the charges on him, he flees from jail to make others understand his immaculate personality. Change is in its infancy in *Godan and Untouchable* and it grows and matures in *Maila Anchal* and *The God of Small Things*. The doctor of *Mailaa Anachal* is an alternative that accommodates everyone's voices and his character seems to symbolize that one can make his voice heard even while being in a system. The doctor listens to everyone's voice and lends more voice to make them feel empowered be it Kamli, Kalicharan, Santhals, Ganesh and even the Tehsildar.

Likewise Bakha is another example that seems to herald a change. His disagreement with his father's fealty to the British government and his own desire of being looked like a sahib shows his yearning for release from the oppression and slavery. Unable though to challenge his father's subservience and the prevailing predicament, he nurses a protest in his stiff bones and glistening muscles. Bakha's silent protest is carried forward by Velutha in *The God of Small Things*. Velutha grumbles at his father's loyalty but wants to wage a war against discrimination. His party card is a licence and his many qualities get fired by the slogans of the party. Allowed not to make public his voice, he breaks the barriers by demonstrating his love for the voiceless Ammu. Sheltered in the welter of Velutha's love, Ammu bears the brunt because of her acquiescence to this rendezvous. Velutha's daring costs him heavily. He pays the price but doesn't speak a word because his actions speak louder than words.

Velutha's silent death is more voiced and leaves the message to be deciphered by mankind, which will have to hear 'Time's winged chariot hurrying near.' The chariot of time may turn turtle any moment compel humans to realize that they cannot continue to revel with the revelers every now and then. Sometimes the defeated soldiers leave more meaningful messages than the winners. Gobar, Kalicharan, Bakha and Velutha may not have succeeded in heralding a change yet they have strengthened the fact that 'Success is counted sweetest by those who never succeed.' And therein lies the purpose of all these novelists who through their delineation of these characters have opened the eyes of humans' treatment by humans and made everyone realize what man has made of man. All these novelists have remained true to their vocation and responded to the demands of time as propounded by Ralph Fox who questions if a novelist can remain indifferent to the problems of the world in which he lives? Can he shut his ears to the clamour of preparing war, his eyes to the state of his country, can he keep his mouth closed when he sees horror around him and life being denied daily in the name of state pledged to maintain the sanctity of private greed? He further says that more and more novelists are beginning to feel that eyes, ears and voice are in fact organs of senses responsible to the stimulus of the human world, and not mere passive servants of spiritual world supposed traditionally to be the domain of art. Thus, we can say that the novelists discussed above have been successful in providing voice to the voiceless and have established their own voices also.

Works Cited

Anand, M.R. *Untouchable*. London: Hutchinson International Authors Ltd., 1947.

Forster, E.M. Preface to *Untouchable*. Delhi: Arnold Publishers, 1935.

Premchand, Munshi. *Godan*. Delhi: Saraswati Press, 1936.

Renu, Phaneeshwarnath. *Maila Anchal*. Delhi: Rajkamal Prakashan, 1954.

———. *Maila Anchal*. Delhi: Rajkamal Prakashan, 1954.

Roy, Arundhati. *The God of Small Things*. Delhi: India Ink, 1997.

5

The Portrayal of Dalit Life: A Study of Baburao Bagul's Mother

— Chetna Tiwari

The Indian constitution abolishes untouchability yet it is only for namesake; the dominant castes still force dalits to perform the traditional occupation. Migration and the anonymity of urban environment have in some cases resulted in upward occupational mobility among dalits. The majority of them still continue to perform their traditional practices. Still the practice of untouchability is prevalent in most of the rural areas and the dalit faces discrimination at the hands of dominant castes. Today the dalits have tried to come in the mainstream of Indian society, and the dalit struggles and dalit movements in realities were glorious and have a great history. But they are still marginalized and despite many movements and ongoing struggles, the ruling upper caste does not consider them as people. The present paper tries to depict this reality portrayed by Baburao Bagul, a pioneer of Marathi Dalit Literature, in his short story *Mother*.

With the growing translation of works by dalit writers from various regional languages to English, dalit literature has poised to acquire a national and international presence. The dalit literature, though written in different languages, in different geographical backgrounds, shares the common themes: the common suffering, discrimination, exploitation and injustice:

> Poems, short stories, novels and autobiographies written by dalit writers provided useful insights on the question

> of dalit identity. Now the subaltern communities found a new name by coming together with the perspective 'Dalit is dignified' thereby rejecting the sub-human status imposed on them by the Hindu social order. (Mishra 2)

The motive of dalit literature is the liberation of dalits, their struggle against casteist tradition. These writers make use of the language of the outcastes and underprivileged in Indian society. Shame, anger, sorrow and indomitable hope are the stuffs of dalit literature. Because of the age-old oppression, the expressions of the dalit writers have become sharp.

Baburao Bagul was one of those Indian writers who are known as the dalit writers, as he tries to point out in his novels and short stories the divisive nature of the Hindu society. A pioneer of Marathi dalit literature, he was influenced by the works of Marx, Phule and Ambedkar. Baburao Bagul generally depicts men and women who are uneducated and lacking in any kind of sophistication. He portrays the stark reality of life and brings out the woes and miseries and economic inequality, which are the base of his experience. His writings deal with the individuals who are the victims of the social system in which casteism is a dominant factor.

Mother by Baburao Bagul is the depiction of fierce battle for life in an urban slum. The story revolves around a young, lower-caste dalit widow and her son Pandu, who faces harsh realities of life. Their life is wrought in a turmoil because their mutual understanding is breached and also because the upper caste people exploit the innocence of the child by poisoning his mind against his own mother. Their struggle to survive is so intense that there is no time for mutual understanding between the mother and the child. The story shows the pain and loss of the mother.

The story starts with the children in a school where the teacher is teaching a poem which is about a mother. The children are carried away by the soothing and melodious voice of the teacher, which reminds them of the warmth of their mother's lap, her love and care. The poem transports them to a land where only love and joy exist. Pandu starts thinking of his mother as 'Vatsalya Sindhu', which was a river of motherly love and benediction. He realizes her greatness, the love and the care she gives him and the sacrifices she has made for him. But he is soon transported back from his dreamland when one of his classmates begins to call out Pandu with bad names, abusing his mother. The dalit children are always target of the mischief of the higher caste children. dalit children have to face discrimination and even untouchability in school. Pandu is told that his mother is having relations with the overseer and she sleeps with him. Everyone around him calls his mother a slut. His young mind starts thinking that he has to face humiliation because of the acts of his mother and he is enraged:

> Pandu's face burned with shame and anger. He felt a demonic, murderous rage rising within him. He could have killed them, murder them all in cold blood. It was good to think them lying together in a pool of blood. It was short-lived joy, however. He remembered that he was an orphan, now that his father was dead, and his mother an unprotected widow. He was afraid that Dagdu, their neighbour, would pick fight with his mother, try to strip her sari....Rage gave way to infinite helplessness and he felt spent. (*Mother* 217)

His father is dead and his mother is an unprotected widow, so his neighbour Dagdu would always try to molest and rape his mother. After coming back home he realizes that he has not had his meals and on finding nothing to eat he starts crying. When nobody turns up, he realizes that his mother is quite changed these days as she doesn't come home early and has stopped caressing him. Even after returning home she spends most of her time in caressing herself, pampering her own beauty, her clothes, and the new silver chain around her neck. As he remembers her actions, he is fearful and suspects her, believing that the overseer is her lover. Still, he doesn't cry because if he does so, the neighbouring women would come and start abusing his mother.

Being a poor, helpless and above all an untouchable widow, is a curse. People start abusing and pointing fingers at her every single act. A woman has her own share of universal sufferings as a woman and the fact of being a dalit woman adds up more social, religious and cultural exploitation in the list. Pandu's neighbour, Dagdu comes to his place and started abusing his mother calling her a whore, describing his desire for her:

> The whore of a slut! You're shameless enough to make the rounds of the shops with that pimp, with your child sitting alone at home! If that was what you needed you only had to tell me—I'd have obliged. And here I've been burning with desire for you, all these years....But now.... (*Mother*)

Pandu is scared, but when Dagdu, jealous and depressed, insults his mother, Pandu loses his childlike feelings and the murderous fires continue haunting him, he feels like hurling a heavy rock at Dagdu. He is full of anger and hatred but he thinks disdainfully that whatever Dagdu has told is right. The child begins to suspect more and along with fear, even contempt and anger, slowly form in his mind for his mother. The burden of all such thoughts is so heavy and depressing that he cannot suppress his tears and starts crying, screaming and throwing tantrums. The neighbouring women, who come to show him sympathy, start abusing his mother, turning his suspicion into reality. When Pandu's mother come home and sees her neighbours at her doorstep with her son, she is sure that they must have turned even her son against her. At that moment she recalls her cruel, drunkard, and deceitful husband whose image she visualizes on Pandu's face. This cruel image intensifies her anger and she is now feeling secure in her newfound love.

With the newfound knowledge about his mother from his neighbours Pandu starts observing changes in his mother: her tightly worn expensive sari, the careless confidence, the defiance in her walk, her lips reddened. He is now convinced of her guilt. The suspicion in his eyes, constantly reminds her of her TB-ridden, suspicious, nagging husband, because of whom she had undergo extreme physical and mental torture. She will want to murder her son too when she recognizes in his eyes the same dark suspicion she had seen earlier in the eyes of his father. The memory of the days, when her husband was alive, makes her restless. She remembers the days when she used to work at the construction site, hauling bricks and cement. She was beautiful and so her husband kept on thinking that she might have sold her beauty. He kept on scrutinizing her body. Without any reason he would look for clues to prove that she was an adulterous. He even wished her to lose a lot of blood, become lame or deformed, ugly and, therefore, despite his ebbing strength he would aim at her face, her nose, head, and eyes. He even threatened to kill her when she was asleep. He blamed her for all his misfortunes and held her responsible for his estrangement from his brother who had looked at her with lust in his eyes. He was so merciless that one day when she suddenly woke up she found him heating up the iron in the fire to brand her body with the hot iron. He didn't accept her proposal to return to their village. After his death men were drawn to her but she refused to accept their proposal. They tried to rape her and their women waged a war against her.

But, when she realizes that Pandu is vulnerable and is totally dependent on her, she asks him about his health. But Pandu, unable to cope with the love she bestows upon him after so many months, refuses to answer. He is so furious that he refuses to accept the new clothes she has brought for him. The clothes remind him of the last Diwali, when on wearing the new clothes brought by his mother the neighbours jeered at him, abusing his mother that she must have done a great business getting many a rupee from each customer:

> 'Good for you!' They jeered at him. Your mother's business seems to be doing very well. What a great rush there must be. Five rupee for each customer. (*Mother*)

Dagdu almost succeeds in removing her clothes and Pandu throws a stone at his mother's tormentor. Ever since he had stopped wearing new clothes and now when he sees the clothes brought by his mother, only anger arises in him. The memory of all the abuses and the embarrassment makes him feel more disgusted towards his mother, and he runs out of the house, calling her a whore. Her mother is deeply hurt to hear it from his mouth. Since the death of her husband, all the years she had lived the life of a widow though she was proposed by many men who were wealthy and who could have provided her a happy life. But she sacrificed her happiness for Pandu, hoping that when he grows up he will support her and her sufferings would come to an end. She had spent ten long years as a widow and had tried so hard to love Pandu. She had lived only for him till the overseer came along last year. She had lost her husband and now her son had turned against her. She started crying helplessly.

She feels having been betrayed by everyone, her husband, her son and the men around her. She locks the door of her home, afraid that Dagdu would come to molest her and waited silently for her son to return. After some time she thinks that, Pandu might not return forever watching the door locked. At that moment only, the barking of the street dogs makes her sure that her son has returned and she happily opens the door. But instead of Pandu, she finds the overseer standing there. The overseer hugged her and her unfulfilled desire of ten years made her respond to him. She was so overwhelmed by it that she did not even hear her son's timid knock and cry for her. Pandu, heartbroken, ran out of the house. When she realized this she tried to go out to stop her son from going but the overseer did not let her do this. She tried desperately to let loose but like a person stuck in a quagmire, she found release impossible. The story ends thus at a note of despair and helplessness in the life of a subjugated dalit woman.

Social exclusion, lack of effective legal protection and socio, economic and social exploitation has kept the dalit at sub-human living condition for centuries. Baburao Bagul portrays the harsh realities of life in a minority's life. He shows the struggle of women in his works. His stories show the external as well as internal conflict faced by the dalit women. Bagul shows the fall as well as the rise of women characters and depicts them in their own self.

Works Cited

Bagul, Baburao. "Mother" *Indian Short Stories 1900-2000. eds.* E.V. Ramakrishnan & I.V. Ramakrishnan. Delhi: Sahitya Academy, 2005.

Mishra, Jugal Kishore. *A Critical Study of Dalit Literature in India.* http:www.sasnet.lu.se/EASASpapers/4JugalKishore.pdf

6

Hybridization of Ethos in Salman Rushdie's *Fury*

— **Devasree Chakravarti** and **G. A. Ghanshyam**

Beware the fury of a patient man.

—Dryden

Post-colonialism is a concept in literature that has been subject to various connotations. Regarded by some as an unnecessary reminder of past colonial history, it over emphasizes the influence of the colonial powers even in the present world scenario. But here the fact cannot be denied that colonialism does continue to affect the former colonies though in a more subtle manner. It is in fact "one of the points of intersection in history..." (Marcella) and as such a very important point in history, whereby cross-cultural contact resulted in giving birth to an altered and heterogeneous culture.

Heterogeneity, multiplicity and particularity, best suits post-colonial writings especially in the multicultural set up. Hybridization so engendered is a relatively common aspect of our modern world. Man has today transcended the boundaries made by man, thus creating a heady mix of multicultural and multi-ethnic society. The resultant hybridized ethos is what gets represented in world literature today and more specifically in diasporic literature, for it is the immigrant psyche, which is its most effective and most powerful symbol. "Immigrant psyche could be said to be a fall out of or an extended consciousness of colonialism" (Caldeira 23).

'Ethos' is a term denoting "the moral ideas and attitudes that belong to a particular group or society" (ALD). In diasporic literature however, ethos is an amalgamation of varied ideas and attitudes imbibed from various diverse cultures. It represents the multicultural ethos of the immigrant psyche.

Salman Rushdie, a forerunner in this genre, is an intense author who vividly portrays the sensitive psyche, pain and anguish of the immigrant in all his novels. His voice is the voice of an immigrant caught up in the vortex of a multicultural world, trying to define his identity: an identity that is the product of cultural hybridity, a character built-up of multicultural ethos, for he has not only migrated from his homeland but has "come unstuck from more than land" (Rushdie 1995: 87). R.S. Pathak has rightly analyzed Rushdie, "The novelist has made a sincere effort in his novel to explore bi-ethnicity and bi-culturalism" (Pathak 125). Afflictions common to such diverse pulls of cultures are self-alienation, fragmentation and loss.

The internal strife resulting from such chaos and confusion within, unleashes the fires of hell when all attempts at adjustment and assimilation fail. And this is precisely what Rushdie portrays in his novel *Fury* (Rushdie 2001). The novel was welcomed with the world witnessing the transformation of fiction into reality. The terror strike at the twin towers in New York reflected a world caught up in the grip of fury, which further unfolded its power in the later collective expression of fury, fragmenting the whole world in sharp divisions.

These demarcations lose their meaning in the process of hybridization. Salman Rushdie and Homi Bhabha consider this hybridization of cultures as the 'central aspect' or the focal point of post-colonialism. This hybridization or multiculturalism which is ever existent in our society has been dealt extensively by the diasporic fraternity. Bapsi Sidhwa, V.S. Naipaul and Rushdie, are all mighty exponents of this field. Although their approach may be varied, yet their concerns in some or the other way touches this integral aspect of our modern life. Rushdie considers such hybridization as being conducive to the growth of a singular world culture, which has imbibed the strains of various cultures and races into one melody. But the impractibility of the suggestion is pointed out by Feroza Jussawalla: "We are seeing increasing fragmenting and inward turning—from Hindu nationalism to Bosnian and ethnic cleansing to Hawaiian sovereignity" (Jussawalla 82). Whatever be the view point in this regard, it cannot be denied however that hybridization is an important part and parcel of our contemporary life and literature, and a cause for fragmentation either at the individual level or at the social.

Malik Solanka, the protagonist in *Fury* is one such example of a fragmented 'self'. Solanka, a migrant from India (Bombay) to England has had an early experience of abandonment and alienation from his family. "As the bonds of family weakened, so the furies began to intervene in all of human life" (251). Abandoned by his biological father, he is severed from his past by his mother who re-marries. Abused by his stepfather, and emotionally alienated from his mother, Solanka is further pushed to the edge when he migrates to England.

> ...in 1963, the eighteen-year-old Solanka had needed rescuing. He had spent his whole first day at college in a state of wild, over-weening funk, unable to get out of bed, seeing demons. The future was like an open mouth waiting to devour him...., and the past—Solanka's links with his family were badly eroded—the past was a broken pot. Only this intolerable present remained, in which he found he couldn't function at all. (20)

Unable to cope with the cultural differences, he wildly follows the dictates of western society which shocks as well as attracts him with its liberality. He tries to adjust himself, but his adjustment is merely a facade. He enters into relationships only to abandon them.

> Solanka had never thought of himself as a bolter or quitter, yet he had shed more skins than a snake. Country, family, and not one wife but two had been left in his wake. Also, now a child. (29)

Indulging himself in the world of fantasy, like he had done in his childhood, he tries to escape from his alienation. But he is a man insistently pursued by his past.

> There is Heaven when one goes out to one's neighbor and Hell when one turns back to oneself. Hell is a state of being without affectionate relationship. One may go through circle after circle of Dante's *Inferno*, down and down, and although there are always crowds, there is never relationship. (Grace Stuart)

Migration to a foreign land alienates him further, socially and culturally. His yearning to re-connect to his roots, to belong, takes the form of the dolls that he creates giving them life and a past. These dolls which had earlier performed the role of his surrogate family are his only real kith and kin:

> Malik locking his thoughts away, confiding only in whispers, only in the hours of darkness, to the dolls who crowded around him in bed, like guardian angels, like blood kin: the only family he could bring himself to trust. (223)

But even they abandon him. Commercialization of his doll 'Little Brain' distances him from his creation by taking a larger than life image. Silenced by the concerns of practical needs of life, he is unable to protest. His pent up emotions of frustration gradually transforms into anger. Losing all control over life he is plunged into despair. His desperation alienates him further from the people who love him, and so starts the process of degeneration of his psyche. This degeneration of his psyche can be represented in these lines:

> *Krodhad bhavati sammohah*
> *Sammohat smrti-vibhramah*
> *Smrti-bhramsad buddhinaso*
> *Buddhinaso-nasat pranasyati.*
>
> (Goyandka 2.63)

(From anger arises infatuation; from infatuation, confusion of memory; from confusion of memory, loss of reason; and from loss of reason one goes to complete ruin.)

His incapability to relate to real life is evidenced in the words of his first wife Sara when she says, "The world in inanimate miniature is just about all you can handle. The world you can make, unmake and manipulate" (30).

Unable to cope with the realities of life incenses him further. In one such moment of rage he loses control and stands at the very edge of disaster, saved only at the nick of time by the realization of his son's presence. His son Asmaan is the only person who gives meaning to his otherwise disordered life, and also plays the role of his conscience, "Asmaan twisted in him like a knife" (126).

Frightened by his own 'monstrosity' lurking within, Solanka flees not only from his family and his past, but also from the country, thereby distancing himself from everything that links him to life. "He had conceived, in that instant, an almost religious belief in the power of flight. Flight would save others from him and him from himself" (80). But geographical distances are not able to extinguish the flames of fury within him. In New York he takes to wandering around the deserted streets at night. His situation regresses rapidly taking him closer and closer to the verge of neurosis and complete mental break-down. Drawing a parallel between the mental fury driving Solanka away from life, and the gruesome murders of the three society girls, Rushdie shifts our focus to the collective fury of men driving the world towards insanity.

> Life is fury, he'd thought. Fury—sexual, oedipal, political, magical, brutal—drives us to our finest heights and coarsest depths. Out of furia comes creation, inspiration, originality, passion, but also violence, pain, pure unafraid destruction, the giving and receiving of blows from which we never recover. The furies pursue us. (30-31)

Throughout the novel Rushdie cites many such examples of the ever increasing presence of the furies in the world, not only fictitious but also taken from real life.

Such uncontrollable fury driving this world has its birth in the realities of life. Drawing our attention to the essence of modern contemporary society, Rushdie gives us a glimpse of the modern world as a big cauldron, where is being mixed a variety of diverse ingredients each having its own distinct flavour. This mixture or 'chutnification' as the author calls it is what describes 'multiculturalism' at its best. This hybridity, ever present in our social milieu is a resultant effect of different cultures coming in contact with one another mainly through the process of immigration. An immigrant himself, Rushdie admits to have been "an emigrant from one country [India] and a newcomer in two" (Rushdie 1995: 85), a person who belongs to too many cultures and to none in particular. This diverse pulls of 'allegiance', causing fragmentation of the immigrant's psyche is poignantly portrayed in Rushdie's novels.

The character of Jack Rhinehart in *Fury* is another example of the author's insight into the tormented psyche of the immigrant. Rhinehart's character is a stark portrayal of the level of confrontation and disorder caused by multicultural encounter. The eagerness to belong in negation of one's own identity, results in false identification and ultimately to disaster. Delineation of the immigrant's dilemma with such insight and intensity is an indication of his familiarity with it on the personal level. The search and the strive for striking one's roots is as much the character's desire as that of the author's himself, which is true of not only Rushdie but of all diasporic literature.

Rushdie's protagonist Solanka is a victim of 'unbelonging'. He yearns for acceptance as is seen in his rejection of Rijksmuseum, devoid of any representation of human life, and his creation of dolls with a life history. But his inability to find acceptance drives a wedge between him and life around him, and also causes fragmentation of his self.

> Alone, alone, all, all alone,
> Alone on a wide wide sea!
> And never a saint took pity on
> My soul in agony.
>
> (Coleridge)

His relationship with Mila helps him take his first steps in the process of recovery by filling up the gaps in his psyche. Mila brings his fantasy to life by taking on the image of 'Little Brain'. She provides him with the same kind of refuge that he had once found in dolls. But fantasy ultimately leads to disillusionment, and does not help in coming to terms with reality. It is only when Solanka falls in love with Neela Mahendra that he finds peace. "Neela's love was the philosopher's stone that made possible the transmuting alchemy. Rage grew out of despair: but Neela was hope fulfilled" (206). Filled with a hope to live life anew, Solanka's relationship with Neela gives him the strength to face his past demons and re-connect with life. The process of affirmation that started with Mila finds its completion in Neela. Love after all does conquer all, even the wrathful goddesses of fury.

But what goes back also comes around. Fury begets more fury. Having left Solanka's abode they return as his nemesis in the form of Mila, Eddie, Eleanor, Morgan and also Neela. Neela flees abandoning Solanka. Thus the furies that had emanated from him now lived through others. They took the form of his dolls with a persona that was larger than life. Begotten of fury they took its form by coming to life in the violence and chaos of Liliput-Blefescu, where Neela had fled. Malik Solanka follows her to Blefescu trying to win her back, and is given the gift of life and freedom by the last act of love by Neela. In her last act of love, she teaches him to re-connect his link with life- "The earth moves. The earth goes round the sun" (255). Malik returns to England in a last attempt at preservation of his remaining link to life, and that is his relationship with his son.

Search for identity is not a solitary journey. Identity of an individual is an amalgamation of the self with the others. Malik Solanka was a man haunted by the ghosts of his past, and tormented by the cultural diversities of his life. A product of multicultural ethos he is unable to blend in. Love frees him from such confinement and enables him to—"deconstruct the boundaries between the self and other" (Hensen 133). Life is hope, and hope is in future, his 'Asmaan'.

Through his novel *Fury*, Rushdie has successfully represented not only the victimization of a man facing an onslaught of diverse cultural influences but has also depicted the malaise afflicting the modern world. A malaise caused by the tug of war between the centre and the margins, each trying to assert their own. Collective expression of fury resulting from it can be evidenced in the rising violence, and terror of our lives. Apart from being an expression of an individual's struggle to establish his identity and re-affirm his link to life, ***Fury*** is thus also an expression of the author's criticism of modern life which has, "outstripped the heart's ability to respond." (228). Feelings, emotions, cultures are all crushed and manipulated on the altar of commercialization; and life loses all meaning, alienating men and severing their ties from life and society.

This segmentation of life, this loss of meaning in a man's life can stop only when men learn to appreciate differences and revel in them. Acceptance and celebration of life in its multi-cultural, multifaceted and multi-hued aspects is the only solution to such fragmentation of self and society. And as the author has pointed out, the answer is in the simple act of 'love'.

> Love in its essence is spiritual fire.
>
> (Swedenborg)

Works Cited

Caldeira, Nina. *Multiculturalism and the Marginalised Psyche.* New Delhi: Creative Books, 2004.

"Ethos" *Oxford Advanced Learner's Dictionary* (ALD). 6th ed. 2000.

Goyandka, Jayadayal. *The Bhagwad Gita.* Gorakhpur: Gita Press.

Hensen, Michael & Mike Petry, "Searching for a Sense of Self: Post Modernist Theories of Identity and the Novels of Salman Rushdie." *Salman Rushdie New Critical Insights.* eds. Rajeshwar Mittapalli, Joel Kuortti. Vol. II. New Delhi: Atlantic Publishers & Distributors, 2003.

Jussawalla, Feroza. "Navjot Ceremonies: The Location of Bapsi Sidhwa's Culture", *The Novels of Bapsi Sidhwa.* eds. R.K. Dhawan, Novi Kapadia. New Delhi: Prestige, 1996.

Marcella, Romeo, "Post (-) ColonialismS: "A Tale Full of Fury and Sound" as Negation of the Writing of the Self", *Obliterating Post (-) Colonialism: Towards Autonomous Writings of the Self.* Merope, 2000.

Pathak, R. S. "History and the Individual in the Novels of Rushdie." *The Novels of Salman Rushdie.* eds. G.R.Taneja, R.K.Dhawan. New Delhi: Indian Society for Commonwealth Studies, 1992.

Rushdie, Salman. *Fury.* New York: Random House, 2001. Parenthetical page references of the text are to this edition.

_______. *Shame.* London: Vintage Books, 1995.

7

"I Was Ever a Fighter, So-One Fight More": Voices of Dalits from the Margin

— G. A. Ghanshyam

In the beginning there was no centre.
In the beginning there was no margin.
In the beginning there was no margin, for there was no centre.
If there was no margin, how did centre come into existence?
Then what existed before margin and centre?
There must have been something, for there can never be nothing.

(*Rig-Veda*)

The deliberations pertaining to margin and centre attained significance in the light of the ugly social reality which marked polarization of certain social forces that constructed social structures in different ways under different labels in such a way as would bring them in the centre of these structures and serve their ends. The individual or the groups were marginalized either in the name of religion, race, region, community, cast, gender, and nationality or even ideology. But this relationship between the centre and the margin was temporary and short lived. The centre can subdue and suppress the marginalized voices, but can never silence them forever. Once they find their true voice, they cease to be marginalized.

Often a question is raised whether the marginalized can speak. It is a fact that the marginalized can not remain mute for long, they have to speak and find an outlet for their tears and fears, anguish and anger and thus, register their existence. The question of their identity has assumed different dimensions amongst the creative writers. According to Dennis Wrong the terms 'identity' and 'identity crisis' have become the 'semantic beacons of our time' for they communicate verbally the discontent prevalent in our modern life and society.

The question of identity and identity crisis plagues modern man in his quest to carve out a niche for himself in this world. But the same question assumes a much crucial and gigantic proportion for an individual for whom identity becomes a struggle to survive with dignity and equality. The marginalized, the subaltern, the dalit; call him whatever you may, one thing remains constant and that is his daily struggle for existence as the repressed, downtrodden and exploited section of society.

Gandhi called them harijans (the children of God); the high caste Hindus called them untouchables, while they called themselves as dalits. (Dalit literally means one who is downtrodden both socially and economically.) Dalits are those who have been forced to do dirty work, on whom the rules of untouchability is forced, who have been deprived of education and free trade. The practice of untouchability was formally outlawed by the Constitution of India in 1950 but in practice, the dalits are still subjected to extreme forms of social and economic exclusion, discrimination and torture. Their attempts to assert their rights are often met with strong resistance from the higher castes, resulting in inhuman torture and atrocities.

Discriminated on account of various factors the dalits are the victims of various structures that constructs society like economic, social, gender based, cultural, etc. Long suppressed into submission and silence the marginalized or dalits have since emerged out of the shadows of centuries of subjugation. Inspired by revolutionary social activists they have now given a voice to their identity through a literature of their own.

In fact dalit is not a caste, it is a constructed identity, which is a comprehensive term comprising of not only the scheduled castes, tribes and other backward classes but also takes into its purview any person, group or community that finds itself shoved to the periphery like women for instance. In other words:

> "Dalit" implies those who have been broken and ground down by those above them in the social hierarchy in a deliberate and active way. There is in the word itself an inherent denial of pollution, karma, and justified caste hierarchy. (Zelliot 267)

The term "Dalit" came into existence in the 1930s as the translation of the phrase 'depressed classes' used by the Britishers for the scheduled castes. First used by Jyotiba Phule, the term was later popularized by dalit leader Dr. B.R. Ambedkar to reflect the situation of the millions of dalits within south Asia, who are systematically and institutionally deprived of their civil, political, economic, social and cultural rights in every aspect of life. Dr. Ambedkar used the term in his Marathi speeches. Later revived by the 'Dalit Panthers' in 1973 to include neo-Buddhists, working people, landless and poor peasant women and all those being exploited socially, politically, economically and in the name of religion, the dalits are now redefining the word and with it their identity.

Literature pertaining to this specified group of people in society is referred to as dalit literature, which is in fact an attempt to liberate the suppressed voice of the downtrodden, the dalits. Dalit literature is basically the literature written by dalits in which they have expressed their pain and anguish. The non-dalit writers who write about dalits couldn't come under the category of dalit writers because they don't represent the true dalit consciousness.

Dalit literature is not a novel concept of this modern era but owes a long history. There are numerous theories about the origin of dalit literature. Buddha (6th c. B.C.); the eleventh and twelfth century writings of Vachana, Chennaiah or Kalavve in Kannada; Chokhamela (14th AD), Mahatma Phule (1828-90), and Prof. S. M. Mate (1886-1957), are hailed as its originators. These great men were deeply concerned about the plight of the untouchables and fought against all the unjust divisions in society. A huge mass of literature is created in the light of their teachings and visions.

Inspired by the writings of the Bhakti movement dalit literature was also influenced by the works of Afro-American writers. They found a resonance of their urge for self-assertion in the leading visionary of the movement, Dr. Ambedkar, who inspired and motivated the creative instinct of the people to voice the emancipatory spirit through dalit literature. And so rejecting the century's old social prejudice and practice of caste, dalit literature found a voice. Life is a continuous struggle and the subjugated, the dalits have undertaken one fight more; a fight to affirm and assert their identity.

The dalit literary movement started in Maharashtra, the home state of Dr. Ambedkar. A collective endeavour of the Neo-Buddhist elites to create a new culture of social equality, it is based on wider socio-cultural and political ideas to transcend the narrow space of the old concepts of culture and social hierarchy to new and open space. The educated dalits, belonging to the second generation, who were the beneficiaries of the reservations introduced by Dr. Ambedkar, waged various socio-political movements and agitations for self respect, dalit rights, equality, empowerment and protest. The new generation dalits began to produce a powerful body of dalit literature.

No longer in need of outside representation, the memorable characters of literature like Munoo (Mulk Raj Anand—*Coolie*), Bakha (Mulk Raj Anand—*Untouchable*), Ammu and Velutha (Arundhati Roy—*The God of Small Things*), etc. have now found the voice to express themselves.

Mostly rendered in regional languages dalit literature has been translated into English thereby ensuring a wider readership and acceptability. In 1992 *Poisoned Bread* was published which is a translation of Marathi writings by Arjun Dangle. In the same year Narendra Jadhav wrote his first book in Marathi *Aamcha Baap Aan Mahi (My Father and Us)*. His next work is a memoir *Outcaste: A Memoir* published in 2008. Apart from these several works like Bama's *Karukku*, Vasant Moon's *Vasti*, Sharankumar Limbale's *Akkarmashi: The Outcaste,* Kishore Shantabai Kale's *Against All Odds*, Aravinda Malagatti's *Government Brahmana*, Omprakash Valmiki's *Joothan: A Dalit's Life,* etc. are like the ever-flowing streams of literary creation that constantly and continuously enrich the growing genre of dalit literature.

A review of this vast and ever increasing realm of literature is a topic that is even vaster in its scope. In the present paper a few of these works will be analyzed in order to bring a focus on the specific area of literature especially fiction and represent the dalit consciousness and psyche inherent in such writings.

In its essence dalit literature is essentially a voice of rebellion that opposes as well as exposes all forms of oppression and exploitation of the weak, the minority by the stronger majority. As such the analysis will also take into its purview the works of non-dalit writers who have made an exemplary contribution to dalit literature through their works and insight into the dalit consciousness and life.

Omprakash Valmiki's *Joothan: A Dalit's Life* originally written in Hindi and later translated into English is a vivid and sensitive portrayal of a dalit youth's struggle to survive with dignity in a world that humiliates and subverts his every attempt at emancipation and progress. The work is an autobiography that reveals the toils and the turmoil of the author's life as a member of the untouchable Chura community, growing up in a village near Muzzafarnagar in Uttar Pradesh. Traditionally working as unpaid labourers on the fields, they were tortured and exploited by the powerful Tagas. Poverty, starvation, death were their constant companions in the daily struggle for survival. The story not only narrates the grim situation of their life but also reveals the spirit of endurance and courage that inspired them to dare to dream in circumstances that hardly let them survives. Valmiki's parents dreamt a future for their child that was hopeful of liberation through education. But this pathway out of darkness of ignorance towards the dawn of knowledge was far from smooth. At every step Valmiki had to face discrimination and discouragement, "Whenever I asked questions to my teachers, I was punished. They beat me up, gave me lower marks in the examinations." (Valmiki 62). Ultimately his persistence paid off but still the hurt remains and he asks with pain, "Why is my caste my only identity?" (Valmiki 134). Kishore Kale's *Against All Odds* is the story of Kale's life as the illegitimate child of a tamasha dancer. Belonging to the Kolhati community, his mother Shantabai also had to follow the community's custom of a tamasha dancer. An unwanted child for a dancer who left him in the care of her family to continue her life as a dancer, Kale had to live his life longing for hius mother's love and acceptance. The novel is a touching tale of the exploitation of the Kolhati women and one man's endeavour to educate and free them from their misery, to enable them to live their life with dignity.

Narendra Jadhav's *Outcaste: A Memoir* is another autobiographical narrative that traces the journey of a dalit family from ignorance and neglect to knowledge and prominence as an equal and integral part of society. In this transformation of the dalits an important role has been played by education that has truly proved to be the ticket to freedom. Like Valmiki, Jadhav also depicts the revolutionary changes brought in by education and literacy that eradicates all kinds of caste and social divisions. The book entails the journey undertaken by Jadhav's near illiterate parents Damu and Sonu from a small village at Ozar in Maharashtra to the city of Mumbai to escape persecution. Belonging to the Mahar community, the story unfolds to represent the struggles and hardships endured by them to ensure a proper education for their six sons. The work is not only a personal tale of endurance and success but inherent in the narrative is the struggle, hopes and aspirations of millions of people forced to live a sub-human existence owing to caste or some other kinds of class distinction prevalent in society. Jadhav, at present the vice chancellor of Pune University reminiscences in the book his struggle as a young student when he sat at a corner of the classroom scared like a rat, yet his determination and the faith of his parents finally triumphed to overcome the age old barriers of subjugation.

The novel *Uchalya* by Laxman Gaikwad describes the plight of the Uchalya community, considered as a criminal tribe in the All India Criminal Tribes Act. The novel describes the torture and sufferings of these people and especially of the women who were also tortured and abused by their own men apart from the persecution they had to face at the hands of the police when caught stealing. Laxman's father however hoped for a better future for his son and got him enrolled in School. Laxman had to face a lot of gibes and discrimination at school but an innate love for education helped him through to grow as a mature and responsible human being.

In the year 2000 was published *Kakka* by Vemula Yellaiah, which is an inward looking dalit novel portraying dalit experience in terms of poverty, disputes and violence. The events presented in the novel revolve round deprivation, violence, and the question of land, self-respect and the politics of dalit empowerment. It depicts the Madiga life in transition through three generations: the grandmother, the mother and the lead character, Kakka. The novel narrates the life of the dalits from before independence when they had to live their life as slaves. Their live does not change much even after independence and they are still victims of discrimination and exploitation. Kakka's mother faces the dual brunt of discrimination being a dalit and a woman. She is victimized by her own community and alienated to live alone with her son. The novel reflects the inhuman torture and exploitation they have to endure in order to survive and the growth of Kakka into maturity and realization that the problem of caste exists both within and outside the caste.

Shosh, a Gujarati novel by Daxa Damodara, is a first attempt by a dalit woman writer to render the dalit consciousness from a feminine perspective. The novel however does not narrate the story of degradation and exploitation based on caste but is the tale of a woman's life through various stages of being a daughter, wife and mother. A sensitive portrayal of a woman's consciousness it depicts the oppression of women in a patriarchal society. Madhavi, the protagonist of the novel, suffers from this discrimination since her childhood. Her father grudgingly accepts her birth for he had wanted a male child and later she is married to Purandar, who is more in need of her body than her soul. Alienated and deprived of the emotional security Madhavi finds solace in the friendship of Rajendra, and this relationship is suspected by her husband. Her loss of self and relationships plunges her into a neurotic state wherein she collapses into a coma. It is only her relation with her son, Rahul that saves her and assimilates her back to life. *Shosh* is a novel, which traces the inner workings of the protagonist in her alienation and depression through the conscious and unconscious corridors of her tormented mind. It is an endeavour to assert the woman's right to life as a human being unfettered by any restrictions of class or gender.

In a similar vein, Aruna represents the subaltern position of women through her two short novels, *Elli* and *Neeli.* Both the novels deal with the life of Erukula, the pig-tending community of Andhra Pradesh. The first story narrated through the flash back technique tells the story of the protagonist Elli who leaves her abusive husband and comes back to her parent's home. The story reminiscences of Elli's childhood, her marriage to a much older man decided upon by the village elders with a suitable bride price as was customary, and her struggle against violence and abuse. Her opinion or for that matter the opinion of the other women folk are totally disregarded when the marriage is fixed and also later when she is sent back to her abusive husband. In the second novel, the author presents a woman, Neeli much stronger in spirit and courageous than her predecessor. Neeli was helped by her mother-in-law to get back to her parent's home where she finds love and happiness with Duvva. Supported by the rigid and exploitative customs the society tries to enforce their superiority on Neeli and make her comply but helped by Duvva, Neeli foils all their attempts and walks off defiantly even at the cost of social boycott by the community. Both the novels narrate incidents of women's exploitation and abuse like that of Malachimi in the name of obsolete and primitive customs, and caste and class consciousness yet a transformation is evident when women will fight back and walk away from such regressive and repressive shackles of slavery.

Dalit writers have learnt to assert their concerns and their identity in a voice of their own. Mostly written in an autobiographical tone dalit literature lays bare the stark realities of our modern nation that is still grappling in the blood and mire of its century's old prejudice and old beliefs. Constituting the oppressed and the downtrodden in its gamut, dalit literature involves the subaltern voice of the woman as well. In this connection the women writers have given a vent not only to their plight as a second grade citizen in a male dominated society but have also represented the struggle and torment of the other unfortunate brethrens.

Mahasweta Devi is a name that stands for these unfortunate and subjugated people. In her writings she represents the reality of India's villages and her poor, exploited and oppressed habitants; the dalits. In her story *Seeds*, she narrates the harrowing tale of a landlord's use of power and force to extinguish the voice of rebellion amongst his poor, landless farm labourers. A tale of exploitation, rebellion and killings, the story reveals the 'return of the repressed' for revenge and retribution, and freedom.

In another of her story *Bayen,* Mahasweta Devi tells of the position of women in traditional tribal societies. Referred to as 'twice colonised' women have to walk a tight path on a two edged sword of caste prejudice as well as patriarchy. Chandidasi Gangadasi, the protagonist of the story inherits the job of burning the dead and guarding the bodies as a legacy from her father who was a Dome. A sensitive individual she feels trapped in her duty as the burner of dead bodies. After the birth of her son Bhagirath she wants to leave her job but is not supported by her husband. Later branded as a witch because of her job and her refusal to continue in her work she is forced to live apart from her family and the village like an outcaste. The torment and torture of being labelled a bayen-witch shrouds her life in misery and isolation. Death is the only leveler that equalizes all divisions and liberates her from the curse of being a witch. She is ultimately proclaimed as the mother not a bayen, not a possessor of evil eye.

Women are positioned much below in this hierarchical ladder of caste and sub-caste. Among the dalit women writers, Bama is a name that stands out. Her novel *Karakku* is an insightful and touching account of life in a caste-ridden village of Tamil Nadu from a child's point of view. The innocence of the child shatters gradually with the realization of truth and experience. Bama recreates the innocence of her childhood when unaware of social divisions and untouchability she is amused by a high caste Naickar who holds a packet of vadais brought by an elder of her community, a Paraya. Told the truth by her brother she recoils in dismay and pain.

> When I heard this, I didn't want to laugh any more, and I felt terribly sad. How could they believe that it was disgusting if a Paraya held that package in his hands... I felt so provoked and angry that I wanted to go and touch those wretched vadais myself. Why should we have to fetch and carry for these people, I wondered.
>
> (Quoted in "Labouring for the Cause of Dalits" http://www.hindu.com/thehindu/)

In her novel she depicts the hardships endured by her people not only at the hands of the high caste but also from the administration and protection agencies. Her indictment of the treatment meted out to the Dalit Christians by the Roman Catholic Church exposes the bleak situation of the dalits bound in the chains of prejudice that even conversion fails to eradicate.

What constitutes the gamut of dalit literature and what not, is a debate that continues regarding the writings of many non-dalit writers writing on the issue. But being a comprehensive term that it is, dalit literature does enclose in its scope the writings of women.

A woman is also a dalit, a subaltern, a non-entity who has to face discrimination and abuse at every step of her life. Writers like Arundhati Roy have depicted the inferior and discriminated status of a woman who is denied a life of her own. In her novel *The God of Small Things* Roy depicts the caste ridden Indian society and the subverted position of women. Through the story of Ammu and her quest for freedom and love that ends tragically, Roy depicts poignantly the atrocities committed in the name of caste wherein people in power the 'lantern' dominates and subjugates forcefully the 'mombatti'. Velutha, a Paravan has to pay the price of loving Ammu, a high caste woman with his life. All attempts at liberation are nothing but illusions, mere fleeting shadows of liberty that elude from grasp. Ammu tried to escape the confines of her life at Ayemenem by marrying a man she meets in Calcutta. Later after her disillusionment with marriage she seeks refuge at her parent's home, which is grudgingly accorded to her; even in love she fails to find security for society thwarts all her efforts to find a space of her own. She dies alone and isolated from her life and relations.

Forced to live a sub-human existence by her own people a woman has nowhere to take refuge but her own 'self'. This is a quest that she shares with the other exploited sections of the society discriminated against on the basis of various social, economic and political factors.

Mogalli Ganesh, a second-generation writer illustrates the reality behind the socio-political reformation that fails to improve the dalit situation in the country. In his story *The Tehsildar,* he exposes the prevalent angst in society among the communities that results in violence and destruction. In the story the Tehsildar in an attempt to empower the landless dalits employs reformative measures and gives them land for cultivation. The act results in retribution and destruction by the administration and police along with the high caste men.

The dalit movement is an anti-caste movement fighting for the construction of a modern secular and democratic Indian identity. And dalit literature is evolving towards this sense of collective identity and solidarity, and addressing the oppressed, the untouchables, the victims, and the oppressors. Education has proved to be a boon for the communities to obliterate all kinds of discriminations and rise above caste and any other kind of divisions that divide society and men. Dr. Ambedkar called education 'the milk of a tigress' that gives strength to the suppressed men and women of society to raise their voice against all forms of exploitation and oppression. It is education that has created dalit literature and has enabled them to assert their identity and grievances in an unbridled voice full of promise and potential.

A brief analysis of the works that constitutes dalit literature brings to our focus the fact that it is essentially the literature of the downtrodden and suppressed folk of society, which doesn't require our sympathy or pity but the right to live their life with dignity and equality like human beings. Written mostly in the autobiographical mode dalit literature is truly the maps the dalit spirit; the human spirit of endurance and courage at its core. To conclude in the words of Brecht's Mother Courage, 'The poor need courage': the life of the people left neglected and made to suffer by society need courage to survive, to endure, to fight the daily fight of survival. And the assertion of the dalit consciousness through literature is one fight more to make the society aware of its hidden, dark truths that need to be confronted in order to change and transform into a better and Equalitarian tomorrow.

Works Cited

Quoted in "Labouring for the cause of Dalits" http://www.hindu.com/thehindu/.

Valmiki, Omprakash. *Joothan: A Dalit's Life*. Trans. Arun Prabha Mukherjee. Kolkata: Samya, 2003.

Zelliot, E. *From Untouchable to Dalit: Essays on Ambedkar Movement*. New Delhi: Manohar Publishers and Distributors, 2001.

8

Voice of the Voiceless in the Poetry of Sarojini Naidu

— Gulshan Das and Meeta Ajay Khanna

Feminist literature brings forth women poets who write about their own individual experiences as women and also voice and construe the reality of other female selves. "Their shared project is to bring into being, the symbolic weight of women's consciousness to make invisible visible, to make the silent speak" (Surjeet 19). Women writers in English emerged in the literary scene with their unique writings having the hue of their feminine consciousness.

> Over the years and throughout the political instability which affected Indian society at large, along with a myriad of other influences which have affected culture, language and social patterns, women's literature in India has evolved to show common experiences, a sense of sisterhood and a range of female experiences that question the recurring face of patriarchy.
>
> (http://www.literature-study-online.com/essays/indian-women-writers.html)

Sarojini Naidu, one of the pioneers amongst women poets, came in the realm of Indo-Anglian poetry in the early twentieth century. Her poems were marked with fine diction and fiery lyricism. She wrote on varied themes and sang of seasons, festivals and life of her people. One of the recurrent subjects in her poetry was the women of India who are disconsolate because of the rampant social norms. In her poems she voices women who have marginal identities due to the socio-cultural standards of the orthodox Indian society. According to Meena Alexander, Sarojini's poems reflect the unmistakable agony of women who have nowhere in the world to go. A glance at the poems of Sarojini Naidu on women like 'Suttee', 'Dirge', 'Vasant Panchmi', 'Caprice', 'Destiny' in *The Sceptred Flute: Songs Of India* shows the poet's "deep compassion for the widow in her anguish and the secluded woman in her loneliness" (Thorner 95).

'Suttee' is one of the poems whose title itself brings back memory of the ruthless custom because of which, innumerable Indian women ended their lives after they became widows. Sarojini depicts the emptiness in the lives of such women and points out that in the Indian society the domination of patriarchy is so strong that women have to accept their place as marginal in the social set-up. They don't have the individuality of their own and are the dependent members of the society. Even though we see drastic socio-cultural changes in India that grant women certain amount of liberty which was absent in the past but still the patriarchy is deep rooted and brings forth altercation for women regarding grant of freedom and equality. Though 'Suttee' portraits the past injustice towards women but it is relevant in the present context. Even today we have such orthodox social groups who deny a widow the right to live a life of respect and dignity. According to R. P. Tiwari "The poet expresses moral indignation for she is opposed to this barbarous custom" (Narvane 103). In 'Suttee' the widow describes her absolute dependent and marginal identity in various way when she regards her husband saying 'Lamp of my life'; 'Tree of my life'; 'Life of my life'. She is unable to find reasons for her existence after her husband's death and says:

> Life of my life, Death's bitter sword
> Hath severed us like a broken word,
> Rent us in twain who are but one....
> Shall the flesh survive when the soul is gone?
>
> (*Sceptred Flute* 18)

Sarojini is criticised for glorifying sati in her poem but Ashok Kumar Bachchan remarks, "Suttee is a pathetic poem which deals with the sad predicament of an Indian widow whose husband has just died" (Pathak 90). Such a pathetic mental state was the result of the unjust attitude towards women where she was made to feel that she has no right to survive when she has become a widow. The lines such as 'love, must I dwell in the living dark?' / 'Shall the blossom live when the tree is dead?' in the poem reflect the social pressure and malevolence towards a widow.

A similar theme has been dealt by Sarojini in the poems 'Vasant Panchmi' and 'Dirge'. In 'Vasant Panchmi' the spring season brings back reminiscences of the happy days to a widow when she enjoyed the colours and beauty of spring but now she can no more be a part of the various ceremonies related to spring as "Hindu widows cannot take part in any festive ceremonials. Their portion is sorrow and austerity" (Maheshwari 55). The songs of spring are 'Poisoned arrows' in her breast; she says the 'crimson gulmohaors', 'sweet champa buds' and 'shirisha trees' pierce her heart 'with bitter memories'. She further says:

> O joyous girls who rise at break of morn
> With sandal-soil your threshold to adorn,
> Ye brides who streamward bear on jeweled feet
> Your gifts of silver lamps and new-blown wheat,
> I pray you dim your voice when you sing
> Your radiant salutation to the spring.

The last stanza of the poem is apt to quote for it describes the life of a widow without a ray of hope:

> For my sad life is doomed to be, alas,
> Ruined and sere like sorrow-trodden grass
> My heart hath grown, plucked by the wind of grief,
> Akin to fallen flower and faded leaf,
> Akin to every lone and withered thing
> That hath foregone the kisses of the spring.
>
> (*Sceptred Flute* 90)

In the poem 'Dirge' Sarojini voices the plight of a Hindu widow and describes how she can no more have the 'glimmering robes', 'gleaming glass or jewels' on her wrist, 'blossoms or fillet-pearls' on her head, 'happy symbols of the henna leaf' on her hands. The third and the fourth stanzas further state how a widow has to depart with the sacred thread of marriage that once was a significant symbol:

> Shatter her shining bracelets, break the string
> Thread the mystic marriage-beads that cling,
> Loth to desert a sobbing throat so sweet,
> Unbind the golden anklets on her feet,
> Divest her azure veils and cloud
> Her living beauty in a living shroud.
> Nay, let her be! ....what comfort can we give
> For joy so frail, for hope so fugitive?
> The yearning pain of unfulfilled delight,
> The moonless vigils of her lonely nights,
> For the abysmal anguish of her tears,
> And flowering springs that mock her empty years?
>
> (*Sceptred Flute* 66)

In 'Corn Grinder', Sarojini begins the last stanza with a question to a young bride:

> O little bride, why dost thou weep
> With all the happy world asleep?
> The bride then answers that her husband has died:
> Alas! alas! my lord is dead!
> Ah, who will stay these hungry tears,
> Or still the want of famished years,
> And crown with love my marriage-bed?
> My soul burns with the quenchless fire
> That lit my lover's funeral pyre....
> Alas! alas! my lord is dead.
>
> (*Sceptred Flute* 10)

'The Purdahnashin' deals with the decadent and oppressive Muslim custom of 'purdah'. Sarojini describes the life of women behind veils and points out that all the luxury and the security of purdah are deceptive in essence. Meena Alexander remarks "The work is haunted by a voice telling too of other female selves, resonances of subjectivity that are both imprisoned psychically and endure mutilation" (Thorner 94). Sarojini conveys that though purdah is considered as a shield to protect women from adversities of the outer world but the harm done to women in *harem* by 'Time' is irreparable. The purdah cannot shield her from the inner sorrow she experiences spending life in the confines of the veil and being denied of freedom. Sarojini reflects the ravages of time on the face of the purdahnashin and the depressing impact of purdah on her heart and soul. She writes:

> But though no hand unsanctioned dares,
> Unveil the mysteries of her grace,
> Time lifts the curtain unawares,
> And sorrow looks into her face....
> Who shall prevent the subtle years,
> Or shield a woman's eyes from tears?
>
> (*Sceptred Flute* 53)

A.N. Gupta and Satish Gupta comment that 'purdahnashin' portrays "the picture of a veiled Muslim beauty, evoking all the grace, colour and pathos of her life. With the sympathy of a woman, as well as a poet, Mrs. Naidu paints the picture of her fellow-women behind the purdah. It protects them from the temptations of the outer world. It also shuts them off from its interests..." (Gupta 194).

The 'Village Song' is a remarkable poem which throws light on how a daughter wants to break free of the bonds of patriarchy her mother is trying to endorse and shows resistance for marriage. The mother is reminding the daughter of her social and conjugal responsibilities but the daughter is not convinced to enter that world and escapes to the forest where she recognizes herself as a free being without any oppression and subjugation. The poem, according to Meena Singh, "focuses on the two women's growing sense of alienation with mainstream life" (Surjeet 70). The poem is in the dialogue form and opens with the mother's question to her daughter:

> Honey child, honey child, whither are you going?
> Would you cast your jewels all to the breezes blowing?

> Would you leave the mother who on golden grain has fed you?
> Would you grieve the lover who is riding forth to wed you?

The daughter's answer to her mother in the second stanza conveys her thoughts:

> Mother mine, to the wild forest I am going,
> Where upon the champa boughs the champa buds are blowing;
> To the koil-haunted river-isles where lotus lilies glisten,
> The voice of the fairy-folk is calling me, O listen!

Seeing the daughter's indifference towards marriage the mother again tries to tempts her saying:

> Honey child, honey, child, the world is full of pleasure,
> Of bridal-songs and cradle-songs and sandle-scented leisure.
> Your bridal robes are in the loom, silver and saffron glowing
> Your bridal cakes are on the hearth: whither are you going?

Not submitting to her mother's persuasion, the daughter expresses her absolute rejection of the conjugal and filial responsibilities thus in the last stanza:

> The bridal-songs and cradle-songs have cadences of sorrow,
> The laughter of the sun today, the wind of death tomorrow,
> Far sweeter sound the forest-notes where forest streams are falling
> O mother mine, I cannot stay, the fairy –folks are calling.
> (*Sceptred Flute* 11-2)

In the above poem there is no mention of the girl's father and it may be assumed that the daughter was brought up by the single parent and that was her mother who was a widow. The girl being aware of the difficulties of carrying on the maternal responsibilities and the harshness of the society towards a widow, decides not to marry for she thinks that 'the bridal-songs' and 'the cradle-songs' throb with sorrow. Sarojini has showed her empathy towards the gloomy lives of the Indian widows in her poems 'Corn Grinders', 'Suttee', 'Vasant Panchmi', 'Dirge'.

It is interesting to compare 'The Village Song' with Sumangalamata's poem, 'The Women set Free' translated from Pali by Uma Chakravarti and Kumkum Roy in their anthology *Women Writing in India*. It reflects that religious escapism was the only way out for many women who were aggravated with a life inside the home. They chose to join the Buddhist sangha (religious communities) in their attempts to break away from the social world of tradition and marriage. Thus it was way back in 600 B.C with the advent of Buddhism in India, there emerged poems and songs about what it meant to be free from household chores and conjugal responsibilities. She writes:

A woman well set free! How free I am,
How wonderfully free, from kitchen drudgery.
Free from the harsh grip of hunger,
And from empty cooking pots,
Free too of that unscrupulous man,
The weaver of sunshades.
Calm now, and serene I am,
All lust and hatred purged.
To the shade of the spreading trees I go
And contemplate my happiness.

(http://books.google.com/books?)

Sarojini was one of the notable women a poet, writing in English, who apart from dealing with social ills relating to women also reflects the feminine psyche on topics that were considered as taboo in the conventional Indian society. Her love poems express the shades of human love having a unique feature of feminine sensibility. Sarojini's 'Destiny' has the theme of love in which the poet expresses the indifference of the lover. Here again one can see the submission of a woman to the will of her lover who leaves her with a broken heart:

Love came, with his ivory flute,
His pleading eye, and his winged foot:

"I am weary," he murmured:" O let me rest
In the sheltering joy of your fragrant breast,"
At dawn he fled and he left no token....
Who cares if a woman's heart be broken?

(*Sceptred Flute* 201)

In 'Caprice' Sarojini once again expresses a woman's disappointment in love:

You held a wild-flower in your finger-tips,
Idly you pressed it to indifferent lips,
Idly you tore its crimson leaves apart....

You held a your finger-tips,
Lightly you raised it to indifferent lips,
Lightly you drank and flung away the bowl....
Alas! It was my soul.

(*Sceptred Flute* 200)

Lines above resemble the voice as seen in Monika Verma's poem where the poet experiences loneliness in love:

Gold-mulched hours
Those days of rain,
I remember you, my love
Beside me,
Held in your arms, loves,
But now the somber clouds
Hide
my gold-mulched hours...

(Verma 139)

Sarojini's poems on love have the element of decency though they clearly convey the yearning in love. In 'Ecstasy' she says:

Shelter my soul, my love!
My soul is bent low with the pain
And the burden of love likes the grace
Of a flower that is smitten with rain:
O shelter my soul from thy face!

(*Sceptred Flute* 99)

A different view of feminine sensibility is seen in the line written by Kamala Das:

> You called me wife,
> I was taught to break saccharine into your tea and
> To offer at the right moment the vitamins. Cowering
> Beneath your monstrous ego I ate the magic loaf and
> Became a dwarf.
>
> (Das *The Old Play House* 66)

Sarojini's poems that express the emotions aroused by repressed desire, unrequited passion and the yearning for the male beloved do not bear rough facet as seen in the poems of new poets like Kamala Das. Poems like 'Ecstasy' and 'Caprice' written by Sarojini "is a search after bliss in transcendence and in the personality being completely merged in the beloved" (Gupta 67). Kamala Das's poem 'The Old Play House' on the other hand one comes across "a very clear consciousness of a separate ego (personality), and of maintaining this separateness as a matter of right and also perhaps as a matter of realization of one's own personality" (Gupta 67).

A glance at Sarojini Naidu's poetry on feminism conveys that she has given voice to the varied experiences of subdued womanhood of India in her writing. Ranging from personal to the social aspect her poems throw light on oppression, disappointment and emptiness in the lives of innumerable women of past and present. Regarding the poetry of Sarojini, Meena Singh Surjeet says aptly:

> Sarojini's poetry cannot be viewed as a battleground for the war of the sexes, for she could never have conformed to any form of radical or militant feminism. Yet it does reflect very silently and very subtly, a deep and abiding concern for potentially intrinsic relationships that can be soured and undermined in a meaningless struggle for power. (Surjeet 73-4)

Works Cited

Das, Kamala. Quoted in Chetan Karnani. *Eminent Indian English Writers: An Assessment.* Jaipur: Rawat Publications, 2001.

Gupta, A.N. & Satish Gupta. *Perspective on Sarojini Naidu*. ed. K.K.Sharma. Ghaziabad: Vimal Prakashan, 1989.

Gupta, Rameshwer "Sarojini Naidu and Her Poetry: An Over View" *Sarojini: The Poetess*. Delhi: Doaba house, 1986.

http://www.literature-study-online.com/essays/indian-women-writers.html. Accessed on 14.8.06.

Maheshwari, Vinod Kumar. *Perspectives on Indian English Literature*. New Delhi: Atlantic Publishers and Distributers, 2002.

Naidu, Sarojini. *Sceptred Flute: Songs of India*. Allahabad: Kitabistan, 1958.

Narvane, V. S. *Sarojini Naidu: An Introduction to Her Life, Work and Poetry*. New Delhi: Sangam Books, 1980.

Pathak, R. S. *Indianisation of English Language and Literature*. New Delhi: Bahri Publications, 1994.

Surjeet, Surjeet, Meena Singh. *Six Women Poets: A Cross Cultural Study*. New Delhi: Prestige Books, 2003.

Thorner, Alice and Maithreyi Krishnaraj."Sarojini Naidu: Romanticism and Resistance" *Ideals, Images and Real Lives: Women in Literature and History*. Mumbai: Orient Longman Ltd., 2000.

Verma, Monica. Quoted in A. N. Dwiwedi. *Papers on Indian Writing in English*. Delhi: Amar Prakashan, 1991.

9

Casting a Potent Spell: Mahasweta Devi's *Bayen*: Testimony of a Bewitched Mother

— Indrani Singh Rai

Have we ever tried to seek the faces of 'other' India? We meet such a face in Mahasweta Devi's *Bayen*. Mahasweta Devi is one of those writers who have always aspired to uncover and explore something challenging and new; never accepting the existing ideals. She has made important contributions to the literary and cultural studies in this country. Her empirical research into oral history as it lives in the cultures and memories of tribal communities was a first of its kind. In the late '70s, she turned her attention to the marginalized tribal and untouchable poor of Eastern India, particularly Bihar and West Bengal. She bears a stern testimony to the harsh reality of their lives.

Witch-cults seem to have acquired a place of significance in contemporary India. Yet faith in witch-cults has always existed in tribal societies. This belief in witch-cults makes a mother, a witch-mother in *Bayen*. The story introduces us to the rural India where the monstrous exploitative mechanism, stretching its ugly tentacles all over, reduces the human being to the level of mere beast. The practice of witchcraft, based mainly on the ignorance of the people and the vested interests, has been there from time immemorial. Predominantly, the women of the oppressed sections, who are alleged to have been possessed by evil spirits, practice necromancy, that is, rising of the dead. Especially in the Santhal regions of Bengal, witch-hunting or witch- branding, a social evil, ever growing, is a cancerous ulcer on the face of rural life. It is used as an excuse by the vested interests of the feudal lords to kill innocent people and grab their property.

Even in present days, people believe in the realities of witchcraft and 'witchcraft persecution', which began in Europe about the close of the Middle Ages. It has been prevalent among uncivilized peoples of the world.

The protagonist, Chandidasi Gangadasi, is a professional gravedigger. Her work is to bury the dead children and guard the graves at night as she is the progeny of the illustrious Kalu Dome, who has been assigned to look after "all the cremation grounds of the world"(*Bayen* 88). Obliged to continue the conventional profession, which, in fact, does not befit a woman with a tender heart like Chandi, she is caught in the trap of tradition. She carries out her obligations as a mark of reverence for her forefathers. There is a sense of purpose in her acceptance of the job. She has sacrificed herself knowingly for the sake of the larger good of the community to which she belongs.

So long as she remains unmarried, there is no real anguish in Chandi. She never experiences any inner conflict whatsoever. As a responsible human being, she shows boundless enthusiasm for her work. She feels proud of being a gravedigger and is conscious of her social status among her own tribe. When Malindar Gangaputta, an employee in the morgue proposes to her, she accepts the proposal and proudly declares:

> I'm Chandidasi Gangadasi. My father, the late Patitpaban Gangadhar. I bury dead children and guard the graves... Kalu Dome's my forefather. I'm at the top of the Domes here. (*Bayen* 89)

They get married and have a son Bhagirath. Chandi has essential human qualities—an intense love for life and a sense of sympathy for the suffering humanity yet she is not happy. The privileged, belittled by the prominence of her household, wait for an opportunity to strike—the way they always do. They begin thinking that she is responsible for the death of the children in the village. They encourage villagers to pelt her with stones. She feels wounded as people suspect her of having an evil eye. She tries to break free of the obligations of her profession now thrusted on her by the feudal society. She moans:

> It hurts to do the job these days, the job handed down to me by my ancestors, my hands rebel... why can't you see it, Gangaputta, why I think throwing up the job again and again? When I guard the graves through the night, my breasts bursting with milk for my Bhagirath back home, all by myself. I can't stay from him. (*Bayen* 91-92)

Now that she has a son Chandi feels distraught with her profession of cremating dead children. Yet she cannot give it up. She pleads time and again with her husband to take her away to a place where she can lead a more contented life looking after her little son. Malindar, despite his enthusiasm and love for his wife, turns out to be a little more than a conventional husband. Though at times he protests vehemently against those who speak ill of Chandi, he fails to see what really is eating her up. Surprisingly, though deep down in his heart he has compassion for her plight, he is miserably powerless in the face of societal forces. He never ventures to protest against the tradition which is all set to wreck havoc on his family. He learns to make compromises at every stage. Chandi reveals her frustration speaking with her little sleeping son:

> Bhagirath, your father hasn't two minutes to spare to listen to my woes. Won't you listen to all that hurts within me? (She strokes the sleeping child) Before you were born, I never knew I'd feel like this. Now it hurts so bad when I bury the little ones under the banyan tree. O my son, do you feel your mother's woe? Men in general are so insensitive. Their children die. I bury them. And they say I have the evil eye, if I stare at a child, it's sure to die. (*Bayen* 90)

Chandi's grievances go unheard. Obliged by the sense of duty, she accepts to perform the last rites of a dead child of her relative, who at first had blamed her for their misfortunes. Thus, Chandi, while discharging her duties, is caught unaware and branded a witch. She is mercilessly separated from her son and family and is denied entry into the village. She has to live as a pariah away from her home and community as her presence is considered ominous. Chandi is from 'other' India where people, ignorant of the radical changes brought about by different movements in the mainstream society accept the verdicts of their community as norms.

Chandi is branded a 'witch,' her fault being her refusal to do the job. She has broken the precedence and has to pay a price for her defiance of the age-old conventions. She urges her husband to avenge the injustice meted out to her. She cries out in pain "...before your very eyes, I'll jump before the running train with Bhagirath in my arms" (*Bayen* 94). She is not the typical female rebel of the modern world but a sensitive being pulsating with the essential human virtues of tenderness, sympathy and compassion. Her fight for status and identity is prompted by her inner necessity to protect the higher principles of life. In fact, hers is not a social or political resistance but human resistance to all forms of tyranny. The men—hypocrites and counterpart of the urban exploitative class, afraid of losing advantages—plot against her. Shashi, a close relation of Malindar, accuses Chandi of being responsible for the death of his child. She feels pity for Shashi's predicament and decides to do the rites of his child. She firmly declares, "Go, I'll come. And let the community know that this will be the last time that I'll be on the job"(*Bayen* 95). Chandi had fed, bathed Tukni, Shashi's child, before Bhagirath was born. When she buries the child, she feels bereft and distraught. At the night when she is with her son, the tug of mother love compels her to act when she hears the cries of the jackals in the graveyard. She leaves her suckling son and goes to the cremation ground to ensure a peaceful sleep of the dead Tukni in the grave. Bending over the newly dug grave, Chandi with great affection says:

> There's nothing to be scared of, Tukni dear. I've loved you... It's me on guard, little mother. You needn't get a scare. I've planted thorny bushes all around you, you can be sure. (*Bayen* 95-96)

Her motherly affection is ignored by her village people including her husband. Chandi is defenseless when her husband becomes a party to the conspiracy. Her alienation from the society is total. Asked why her sari is dripping with milk and for whom the lullaby is, she pleads, "I'm no Bayen. I've a suckling child, and that's why my breasts ooze milk all the time. Gangaputta you know it's true. Why don't you tell them?" (*Bayen* 97). Surprisingly, Chandi, who fearlessly moves among the graves, driving the jackals away from the dead souls, fails to protect herself from being victimized by people whose humanity has been crushed over by superstition, a form of domination of the vested interests. She loses all her autonomy. She must either conform to the existing morals or become mad and marginalized.

Branded a witch, Chandi's presence is considered inauspicious. The villagers are scared to look at her because they feel her looks may bring them misfortune and even death. The witch, as an evil-doer, is believed to have become the enemy of the state, the individual, and of her own salvation. Thus, she is driven out of the village. She is provided with the essential commodities from the community depending on their whims; disregarding her requirements. The inhumanity of the superstitious people, forces a fellow being to the level of an animal. It is effectively depicted in Malindar's revelation of Chandi.

> They set up a hovel for her beside the railway track, every Saturday they leave a hamper of food for her at her doorstep. Once a year they give her two saris and two gaamchhas. (*Bayen* 98)

Condemned to lead a solitary life, Chandi is deprived of the right to motherhood. Her son, Bhagirath, is forbidden to enjoy the motherly affections. Though she is separated from the humanity yet she is not devoid of human qualities. Her heart is full of love for her little son. The lullaby she sings for her imaginary child is no way different from that of any mother for her child. It is the mother in Chandi that sings the lullaby. Her transformation from mother to the witch-mother not only sharpens her awareness, which in a special attribute of the human beings but also serves as a means for her self-realization. Chandi bears no grudge against her persecutors.

She learns to love whatever is human. What she is denied in real life, she tries to create through the power of her imagination. She ruminates:

> I don't have anybody any more, nobody. When I hadn't become a Bayen, I had everybody. (Puts down the pitcher, and rocks an imaginary child in her arms) I used to rock him like this, suckle him, all that milk, a real flood, the milk from the breast spilt on the floor. (*Bayen* 83)

Chandi, an intellectually inferior woman, never tries to suppress her inner desire for freedom. The seeds of conflict within herself between a committed mother and professional gravedigger as well as the larger confrontation between the womanhood and the forces of male dominated society are sown. She is a woman of complete integrity. She yearns for freedom unfettered by the social constraints. In fact, with the strong moral fiber of a true rebel, she violently resents any kind of encroachment on her freedom. What makes for tragedy in her life is her being a wife of an insensate husband. Mahasweta Devi's mothers are always as much the victims of indifference of their household as of the society in which they live.

Chandi considers her son Bhagirath, a missing part of her soul and Bhagirath sets out to learn of his mother, the victim of decadent social conventions. When he notices his father speaking to a witch, he can not resist himself. He asks his father:

> Bhagirath: Father?
>
> Malindar: Yes?
>
> Bhagirath: Father you...you spoke to the Bayen?
>
> Malindar: So what, son?
>
> Bhagirath: Isn't the living man who speaks to the Bayen doomed to die? My second mother tells me, Bhagirath come back straight from school, run whenever you hear the canister clanging otherwise she'll suck lifeblood. And you spoke to her? Won't she kill you off?
>
> Malindar: No, dear, she won't kill me... she's your mother.
>
> Bhagirath: My mother? The Bayen my mother? What sort of a mother?

> Malindar: You were born of her womb, my son... she showed you the world, she suckled you, and then she became a Bayen.
>
> Bhagirath: But why did she become one?
>
> Malindar: ...she's no longer human.
>
> Bhagirath: My Mother? Without clothes? Without food? Without oil on her hair?
>
> (*Bayen* 86-87)

The bond between a mother and her son cannot be ignored for very long. Bhagirath, though cautioned, visits his witch-mother and compassionately tries to restore his mother's relations to humanity. Infact, the natural instinct that binds a mother to her child is impossible to ignore by any human institution for very long. The natural relationship between a mother and her son, which has been severed by the society, is yet again established. Bhagirath wants to see his mother's face but he is scared because his mother is not the usual mother, she is a Bayen. So he decides not to look at her face, "I'll just see her face on the water. There can be no harm if I don't look on her face. I'll look at the shadow upon the water. The other day I didn't" (*Bayen* 99). Yet he cannot restrain his inner urge to have a look at his mother as is evident in the direction.

> She is about to turn around. Bhagirath notices the shadow in the water wavering. He raises his face, and for one long second they stare into each other's faces, before the Bayen turns her face away, Bhagirath stares on. (*Bayen* 100)

But Chandi fears the confrontation more than her son for she thinks that "there's a poison in the air into which I breathe, there's poison in my touch" (99). She seems to be convinced that she is really a Bayen. She is shocked to hear Bhagirath's quires, "Don't you have another sari? ... Would you like to have a whole sari, not in shreds? Want my dhoti?" (*Bayen* 99). And "Why do you cry?" (*Bayen* 100) She forbids his coming there:

> Oh, my God! What do I do now? (Her voice chokes with sobs.) What do I do? (She wipes her tears away, takes a deep breath, hardens herself to speak with greater firmness.) The Gangaputta's son should never again come

> to the trackside in the evening. I promise I won't cry again... Let him go home swear that he'd never come here again to look even upon the Bayen's shadow. (*Bayen* 100)

Chandi shudders with the realization that the mother in her is still awake and speaks to Bhagirath earnestly. She blames Malindar for not keeping an eye on the son. Nevertheless, the natural commitment that binds a mother and her child together is impossible to ignore and the sacrifice on the part of the victims of oppression is inevitable to defend.

Chandi is seen again in action. Having seen villainous Gaurdas and his gang spread the bamboo poles on the track to stop and loot a train, she rushes to the spot and gets killed trying to avert the accident. Her sacrifice pulls down all the superstitions, prejudices woven around her as a bayen. She is vindicated as mother and a human being. Her act of sacrifice not only exposes the exploitative system but also creates a sense of urgency to end it.

Chandi's death is not only a protest against her society but also an affirmation of the undying springs of human love. The shameful social system which so forcefully separated the mother and her suckling son in the name of witch cult can hold no longer. Ignoring the age-old social ethics, Bhagirath gives the mother-child bond a concrete shape as he comes to acknowledge the dead as his mother:

> Let me tell you all. You can write down...she's my mother...Yes, sir. (The guard takes it all down).... My mother (pauses for a while, then very distinctly)...my mother, the late Gangadasi Chandidasi.... Not a Bayen. She was never a *Bayen, my mother.* (*Bayen* 103)

Bayen is an incredible saga of the exploitation resulting from the political, social and economic marginalization on the psyche of a sensitive individual who is essentially a mother branded a witch.

Works Cited

Devi, Mahasweta. "Bayen" *Five Plays by Mahasweta Devi.* ed. Samik Bandyopadhyay. Calcutta: Seagull Books, 1986.

10

Speaking from Below: Marginalized Women in the Films of Deepa Mehta

—James R. Aubrey

Although this is a literature conference, I will be discussing cinema. Although a film often originates in a written screenplay, or even a work of literature, a film's success depends largely on oral performances by actors. Thus the study of cinema, especially popular cinema, is often undertaken by professors in departments of communication; but it also is true, at least in the United States, that more than half of university-level programs in cinema studies are housed in English departments. This is partly for political reasons, because film programs often aren't large enough to have their own departments and have to be co-located with some other discipline, administratively, but it's theoretically appropriate because cinema is a language art.

Where I teach in the US, at Metropolitan State College of Denver, Colorado, cinema studies is treated as an interdisciplinary medium and is shared among the departments of Art, Communication, English, Music, and Modern Languages and administered by an associate dean of Letters, Arts and Sciences. I am explaining only because this conference did not call for papers on cinematic forms. I hope it's not the case here, but sometimes cinema is marginalized as an art form, considered not worthy of study, or at any rate not so prestigious as the study of literature. I like to argue that cinema was the dominant art form of the twentieth century, but some times it is that very stronghold that calls its status into question;

popular culture is suspect in the academic world. However, over the last several decades cinema studies has become widely accepted as a facet of English studies in the West, and similar developments are probably under way in India, for I read in the *Times of India* for July 21st that three films directed by Satyajit Ray have been added to the Elective English syllabus by the Central Board of Secondary Education.

My purpose today is not to defend cinema studies but to relate the films of Deepa Mehta to an aspect of cultural theory that is usually applied to literature and to history, namely, subaltern studies. I am not deeply schooled in this critical approach, but its perspectives put Mehta's work in an interesting light, I believe.

Most of you will be aware of the work of Gayatri Chakravorty Spivak, one of India's best known literary critics and a member of the so-called "Subaltern Collective" in Kolkata. Spivak has become famously associated with a question she first asked in 1985 and then re-examined in the central chapter of her 1999 book *A Critique of Postcolonial Reason*, the question is, "Can the subaltern speak?" Just asking the question implies that they cannot, and answering it seems to require volumes of discourse about historical oppression, individual psychology, social identity, and textuality.

The British term *subaltern*, meaning low-ranking, was adopted by the Marxist critic Gramsci to refer to Italian peasants; in more recent usage, it has referred primarily to the Scheduled Castes in India, but it also can be used to refer to any oppressed group. In a recent lead article by Rahul Gairola in *Comparative Literature*, Hindu women generally are referred to as "subaltern" (Gairola 1). If subaltern points of view are customarily silent, partly because their situation presents them from being represented to themselves, I would point out that cinema has a unique potential to give them voices.

In films, subaltern viewpoints can be represented not only visually, by characters on the screen, but also on the sound track. The subaltern can speak. And if a female subaltern character re-negotiates her position from the below, that is, from the margins of power, she can provide a representation, a model from which the female spectator can form a sense of personal agency and possibly re-form her personal identity. Thus cinema is a powerful medium for social change because it can provide living, speaking models of innovative behavior; and the films of Deepa Mehta seem deliberately designed to promote such change.

Mehta is a woman of Indian origin, born in 1950, who moved to Canada at age 23. She has provoked controversy for a decade, now, largely because of her attraction to stories of women whose behavior situates them on the margins of traditional communities. Given her residence in Toronto, she is already on a diasporic margin of the Indian community; Mehta's artistic decisions have further marginalized her by placing her films well outside the mainstream of the Indian movie-making community, as well. Her 2006 film, *Water*, though set in India, was filmed in Sri Lanka and nominated by Canada for an American Academy Award. Mehta's original plan to shoot *Water* in Banaras had to be set aside when her set was destroyed by Hindu fundamentalist protesters in 2000—an event that echoed the attack on a Bombay theatre showing her film *Fire* in 1996. Her experiences with hostility to her projects have probably increased her interest in women who feel exiled from their own communities, but women on the margin have figured prominently in her films from the start, even with the movie *Camilla*, in 1994, in which an eighty-year old violinist runs away from her overbearing son with a young woman who is leaving her husband.

However, Mehta is best known for her so-called "Elemental Trilogy": *Fire*, *Earth*, and *Water*. The first, *Fire*, was released in 1996 and provoked a theatre burning in Bombay, which greatly shocked Mehta at the time. *Fire* is a story of love between two sisters-in-law, thus well beyond the margin of what is socially permitted in India's patriarchal, hetero-normative culture. Radha, played by Shabana Azmi, is married to Ashok, a man who has been seeking enlightenment through celibacy for thirteen years. His younger brother, Jatin, is more interested in his Chinese mistress than in his new wife Sita, played by Nandita Das. The two women develop affection for each other and skepticism for the traditional ideas of duty that bind them to their husbands. In a scene that offended some religious people, after Sita has been fasting until moonrise to insure the long life of her husband, she is not supposed to drink until he comes home. Of course, he is out with his girlfriend, so Radha breaks with tradition and offers Sita her blessing instead of his, and gives Sita the ritual drink of water. In a later scene, Ashok discovers them in bed together, bringing the situation to a crisis. Sita determines to leave her indifferent husband, but when Radha tells Ashok she is leaving him, and refuses his demands that she touch his feet and beg forgiveness, he becomes angry and starts to force kisses on her. Radha's sari accidentally catches fire from the stove; however, she manages to escape the fire unharmed, like the goddess Sita in the *Ramayana*, whose purity protects her—another controversial reference to religion. In the final scene, Radha and Sita meet and embrace in public, about to begin their lives together. The pressures on the women to conform to social norms have been considerable, and occasionally enforced by violence, but the outcome of the story suggests that there is room at the margin for women to negotiate traditional boundaries or even expand them, making seem acceptable a kind of behavior that has traditionally been viewed as socially unacceptable. As representations of the lesbian subaltern, Radha and Sita are showing the way.

The second film of the trilogy, released in 1998, has two-part title—*Earth: 1947*; the DVD is marketed as just *1947*. The setting is Lahore just before Partition, as characters with diverse religious affiliations become alienated from each other in the climate of tension and violence, with tragic consequences—not unlike the partition of India that is underway at the time. Hassan, a Muslim masseur played by Rahul Khanna, and Shanta, a Hindu nanny to the crippled daughter of a Parsi family, gradually develop strong feelings of affection for each other. Their first night of sexual intimacy is followed by an exchange of vows to marry and move to Amritsar, but they have been observed by Del, the Ice-Candy Man, who wanted to marry Shanta, himself. So, motivated by both jealousy and anger over the murder of his sister by Hindus, Del takes advantage of a Muslim mob's anti-Hindu rage to have Hassan murdered and Shanta abducted. The film does not show what happens to Shanta but offers three contradictory reports by voice-over—that she was killed, that she married her abductor, or that she ended up in a brothel. Any of these outcomes would constitute a punishment for a woman willing to leave her community to marry across religious lines, which has made personal choices as a free agent rather than guided by her community's religious norms. That the boundary between the religious communities is the site of violence in the film is meant as a comment on the political situation, of course, but it is also a reminder that women are often the victims of such strife.

The third film in the Elemental Trilogy, *Water*, has its own history of association with violence, this time even before the movie was made. Rumors about the film led conservative Hindus to destroy Mehta's sets in Banaras on the first day of filming, in the year 2000. Five years later, in 2005, she completed the film by shooting in Sri Lanka under an assumed name and a different working title. When I left the US in July of this year, *Water* was enjoying a long run in Denver's art-house theatre, and it was recently nominated by Canada in the 'Best Foreign Film' category of the American Academy Awards. It's available on DVD in the US, but it seems not yet to have been shown in India. The photography is lyrically beautiful, in marked contrast with the content of the story, which is disturbing.

The story begins in 1938 as two parents deposit an eight-year old girl at widows' ashram, because her husband has just died. The girl, named Chuyia, doesn't even remember the marriage and has no idea what is happening to her. She knows she has been abandoned, of course, and we are led to feel sympathy for her and antipathy for the elderly matron of the ashram, who we learn is sending one of the young adult widows across the symbolically divisive river to visit a wealthy brahmin for paid sex. The ashram has come to depend on this income, and the guileless widow, Kalyani, played by Lisa Ray, seems to accept her lot.

One day while Kalyani and Chuyia are out in public, she is noticed by a handsome young man named Narayan, played by John Abraham, who finds out who Kalyani is and proposes marriage. The other widows are astonished, for according to traditional guidance in the *Dharmashastras*, quoted in the film, a widow is expected to honor her dead husband by leading a celibate life. First they cut off Kalyani's hair, and then Narayan discovers that she has been sexually servicing his own father, but he still determines to marry her. Unable to bear the shame attendant on his discovery, however, and probably unable to imagine he would forgive her, or even to imagine herself with subjective agency to decide her future, independent of tradition, Kalyani drowns herself.

The story is framed by texts, at the beginning with quotations from the Hindu scriptures that are sometimes used to justify marginalizing widows, and at the end by a statement that, even though the situation has improved in India since 1938, there were 34 million widows in India in 2001, "Many continue to live in conditions of social, economic and cultural deprivation as prescribed 2000 years ago by the Sacred Texts of Manu." Thus Mehta leaves the impression that Kalyani speaks for Indian widows, generally, and that they remain oppressed.

I have been told that the film's representation of widowhood is distorted, that the problem may persist in Bengal but in the rest of India (Lamb). You probably know better than I how pervasive the problem is or is not. Even if the situation has been over-dramatized to some extent, Mehta's purpose is to call attention to one of the effects of privileging males in India's culture: in so far as wives are viewed primarily as investments in a patriarchal account, they lose their economic value—and consequently their sense of self-worth—if the husband dies.

During the years that the making of *Water* was interrupted, between 2000 and 2005, Deepa Mehta made two other films that are very different from her Elemental Trilogy, both set in Canada: *Bollywood/Hollywood* and *The Republic of Love*. Because these films are usually classified as romantic comedies, it is often not recognized that *Bollywood/Hollywood* also addresses serious social issues, again involving marginalized women. On one level the film is simultaneously an appreciation and a send-up of Hindi popular cinema; on another level, this film also represents traditional women as a subaltern group—a view that Spivak encourages with her observation that "representation of the Indian woman, and the way femininity operates within patriarchal Indian society," with "'woman' (as the Othered subordinate to 'man') . . . [,] effaces the consciousness of actual Indian women" (Richter 19). By representing a woman who consciously moves from the powerless and silent margin toward the speaking centre of family power, *Bollywood/Hollywood* encourages the female subaltern to speak.

Like many Hindi movies, *Bollywood/Hollywood* is a love story of two unlikely partners whose unauthorized attraction for one another eventually obtains parental approval, but how the couple gets to that point is anything but typical. As the title promises, there are many superficial similarities to Bollywood, including song and dance numbers, two fistfights, a transvestite character who seems to be Toronto's answer to the *hijra*, and lots of family pressure on the son to marry a suitable girl.

The boy, Rahul, is played by Rahul Khanna; the girl he marries in the end, Sunita—or Sue—is played by Lisa Ray. His family adores her, particularly because their son's previous choice of fiancée was, in their view, so obviously wrong: a white American pop singer, named Kimberley. In Bollywood fashion, Kimberly dies to clear the way for Miss Right. Even more Bollywood-like is the preposterous manner of Kimberley's convenient demise: she is killed in a "levitation accident" while practicing her New Age meditation, when she loses her concentration and falls to her death. "Probably she became a chappatti," says the grandmother, with evident glee.

What the parents don't realize about Sue's character is that she is working as their son's paid escort, a companion for hire. She tells him that there will be no side benefits to their contract—"no sex"—but he wrongly assumes that she is a prostitute. We learn that she is not, but Sue is clearly working close to the edge of the sex trade. Rahul's parents like her so much because she's charming and she's Indian—characteristics that we are shown any woman of dusky complexion might put on like a mask in order to pass a traditional marriage interview. Even though Rahul is the protagonist, many scenes are shown from Sue's point of view, such as a sequence where she coaches Rahul's younger brother on how to deal with a bully, and another where she dances in her bedroom to a scene from *Rangeela*. Such scenes endear her to us, or as film theorists might say, they suture the spectator into her narrative. We in the audience also like her for her candor and her intelligence and her sense of humor; so we approve as we see Rahul's mother and grandmother taken in by Sue.

Rahul, who has hired her to reduce the pressure on himself to find someone to marry, is annoyed to find that his family likes her, but his opinions are already suspect. From the opening scene at the deathbed of his father, Rahul has been made to seem overly submissive to family concerns as well as censorious toward others, prompting us in the audience to feel that he should become more liberal minded. At one point, when he invokes tradition, Sue tells him, "Only fools don't ever question tradition." His viewpoint is further called into doubt by his fundamentally wrong assumptions, including his assumption that Sue is Spanish rather than Indian. His traditional ideas are made to seem particularly absurd as he coaches her on how to behave like an Indian: "Just say, 'Namaste,' and always look down if someone is talking to you." At one point she asks him, "What century is this?"

When the grandmother sceptically asks her what she is doing frequenting nightclubs by herself, Lisa disarmingly says, "Dancing. The usual. You should come along some time." When Rahul asks her how she got into the business of picking up guys in bars, she explains, with a representation in flashback, that her parents tried to get her to marry a professional wrestler named "Killer Khalsa"—someone totally, even laughably unsuited to her temperament. When Mr. Khalsa hints that his hidden muscle is as big as his biceps, Sue removes her head covering and breaks into laughter, telling her suitor that it's too bad his brain isn't as big as his muscle. Her father tells her, "Don't you talk like that!" but the subaltern will speak. Sue shows us, from her point of view, in her words, that arranging to meet men on her own terms is her way of rebelling against her parents' wish to arrange her marriage.

When Sue's father catches her sneaking into their house through the kitchen window after an evening of pretense at the *sangeet* for Rahul's sister's wedding, it is Sue's father who is made to seem in the wrong. Looking disheveled and fat in his underwear, he points out that Sue is not dressed appropriately in her sweater and skirt. He tells her that it is after midnight and says that he would beat her up if they were still back in the Punjab, but he must not do so because they are in Canada, where he would be arrested and thrown in jail. Then he rants about how he misses India. Sue tells him that he sounds drunk and thus cues us also to see his accusations as unreasonable. Finally, Sue's mother intervenes and sends Sue to her room. After she calms the father down, the mother explains to Sue, "Men can rebel; women cannot." Sue replies that she's going to move out of the house. In effect she is declaring her independence, vowing to live her adult life on her own terms.

Thus the film makes the mature, sophisticated, public woman seem to be the innocent party; the tradition-minded, concerned father is made to seem harsh and overbearing. Rahul, who protests that he can't help being middle class, is shown to need to outgrow that very attitude, to overcome his prejudices against Sue and trust her—and ultimately declare his love for her with a self-initiated marriage proposal. Her status as marriageable in spite of her having situated herself on the social margin indicates that tradition-based moral judgments are inadequate because they exclude admirable women such as Sue, who refuses to remain in a subaltern status and moves from the margin toward the autonomous centre.

Like Mehta's elemental tragedies, this comedy suggests that the traditional Indian wife is a marginalized woman. She lives at a distance from the centre of traditional family power, her husband. In the Elemental Trilogy, that power is linked the characters of an abuser, an abductor, and a dead man. Good marriages remain in the realm of possibility, but they would be unorthodox in some way; and they don't seem attainable, finally, in any of the three films. As for the main female characters in the Elemental Trilogy, each is exiled to the social margins for being in a love relationship that is not sanctioned within the marriage tradition. Likewise, in *Bollywood/ Hollywood*, marriage happens because Sue refuses to participate in traditional marriage arrangements and takes charge of her own life, not as a figure on the margin of the family and of society, but as an independent agent who insists that the boundaries of marriagability be expanded to include her. We can imagine that she will be an equal partner in her marriage to Rahul; indeed, in the final scene, they are in a car, but she is driving. So it would seem not to be the institution of marriage that Deepa Mehta objects to, but certain traditional practices associated with it.

In the cinema of Deepa Mehta, then, women are represented as speaking from the margins of power and, with varying degrees of success, opting out of the hierarchical, traditional system that has kept them on those margins. Perhaps we should not be so surprised that Mehta's detractors consider her a threat to traditional values, for Mehta's films are quite subversive. In Mehta's films, we have an opportunity to hear the subaltern speak, and what the subaltern are saying is that they want change.

Works Cited

Gairola, Rahul. "Burning with Shame: Desire and South Asian Patriarchy, from Gayatri Spivak's "Can the Subaltern Speak?" to Deepa Mehta's *Fire*. *Comparative Literature*. 54.4 (2002): 307-24.

Lamb, Ramdas. Interview with the author, 31 July 2006.

Mehta, Deepa. *Bollywood/Hollywood*. Cinebella, 2002.

_______. *Camilla*. New Yorker Video, 1998.

_______. *Fire*. New Yorker Video, 1996.

_______. *The Republic of Love*. Film Movement, 2004.

_______. *Water*. Mongrel Media, 2005.

Richter, David. Introduction. *The Critical Tradition: Classic Texts and Contemporary Trends*. 3rd edition. Boston: Bedford/St. Martin's, 2007.

Spivak, Gayatri Chakravorty. *Critique of Postcolonial Reason: Toward a History of the Vanishing Present*. Cambridge, MA: Harvard UP, 1999.

11

Peripheral Nature of Dalit Psyche

— Oorja Rajan Sinha

Dalit psyche is what our litterateurs refer to as the 'marginal psyche' in our caste-based pluralistic set-up. As a matter of fact, 'marginal psyche' is not the proper term to define, for it looks somewhat paradoxical to talk of the larger population occupying the margin rather than the centre-space. However, the use of the term 'marginalized' brings out a very important meaning of the phrase: it says that what should be centrespread has been pushed to the margin. Such statement implies that the importance of the larger community has been undermined, that the community is denied social justice and, finally, that the community must shift from the periphery to the centre.

The use of the term 'dalit' is more significant because it describes in its import the conditions of living of those to whom it applies. The work "dalit" literally means "downtrodden". It refers to the downtrodden—that is, to the body of persons who have always been looked down upon, repressed and oppressed. It we look back in history we come to know that it is the people from the lower order of caste-based society who were always subjected to disgrace, torture, inequality, and poverty etc. to such an extent that they could live and earn their livelihood only if they subjugated themselves to the service of the people from the higher order. The high-caste population not only enjoyed power and privileges at the cost of the lower caste people but also indulged in excessive behaviour to demoralize and even enslave the latter. As a result of the high-handed attitude and behaviour of the high order population the low caste people completely lost their identity, suffered from isolation and a defeatist mentality. They were segregated as the unholy lot called 'achhut' or the untouchable. Even the shadow of an achhut was considered unholy. So that others may not even inadvertently ever come in physical contact with such persons or their shadows certain sanctions were imposed upon them—for example, that they shall wear a black thread round their necks, that they must walk on the road with a broom tied to their waists, and that they must tie loose their necks earthen pots for spitting into while walking on the road. In a sense, they were allotted derogatory identification marks after their estimable identity had been denied. Their morale was so broken that they accepted without murmur anything that came their way; in other words, they had come to believe that all was predetermined and that, therefore, they had no option but to submit to all that happened with them. Such state of affairs persisted for centuries. However, an undercurrent of change was surging through. It was only in the latter half of the past century that the dalits began to unite in protest against the so-called superior caste people and started their struggle for self-assertion.

Actually, the appellation 'dalit' is of recent origin. The term is preferred to any other term because it can be used to identify a certain community and mark off a certain kind of literature. Dalit literature made its beginnings only in the seventies and eighties, of the last century. Dalit writings first appeared in Marathi, then in Telugu, and thereafter in other languages of the land including Hindi, Gujarati and Punjabi. The reason for dalit literature growing fast is that dalit psyche is not in the making; it is well-formed, its contents being definitive. If you know dalit psyche you can rightly predict the trend of dalit literature. This means that we do not have to reconstruct the psyche in terms of dalit literature that we come across. To understand the psyche properly we have to have full knowledge of the social history of Hindu society and certain changes that were taking place in and outside the country. A close study of social history will tell us about the wily theories, which the Brahmins propounded and propagated regarding the status of dalits. It will reveal the spiteful attitude and cruel behaviour of the high-caste people towards the dalits. Being conversant with all this we would be able to know as to why and how dalit psyche was emptied in the remote past to fill in it such stuff as the sense of guilt, the feeling of inferiority, the feeling of dependence, the feeling of dejection, etc. and the attitude of compromise, surrender and defeat.

The primitive psyche was thus full of emotional content. But it lacked in ideas. It was bereft of ideas such as freedom, self-identity, equality, justice, community of life, and organizational unity. All this was so because dalits were denied the right to education and put to such difficult conditions of living that they hardly had any leisure to think of their betterment. Another reason was that they were led into believing that everything that happened was pre-determined—that is to say, nothing could be done by way of intervention or redemption. A dalit, therefore, being a helpless creature, was condemned to live in a state of hopelessness.

However, in modern times, dalit psyche seems to have transformed altogether. It is devoid of all such emotional content that had formed the stuff of the primitive mind. It has in it ideas regarding ways and means of exposing the conspiracy and hypocrisy of the upper caste and also the ideas regarding countering their tricks and arguments. Naturally then, the psyche has in it the feeling of self-assertion.

There are, of course, other elements of dalit psyche, but we may not recount them at present. We had better raise now the question as to how it is that the psyche that suffered from a defeatist mentality in its olden days has developed now as much to be able to display an attitude of self-assertion. We may further ask as to why the development of the psyche did not take place at even pace. These two questions are important inasmuch as their answers are bound to record the influences upon the dalit mind from the early days to the present, and also inform us as to what frustrated and what facilitated progress of society and development of the psyche. Therefore, a brief history of Hindu society is called for.

The caste-based Hindu society came into being after 'Chaturvarna' or the system of fourfold classes degenerated into the system of fourfold castes arranged in a hierarchy. In chaturvarna, the principle of division of society into brahmin, kshatriya, vaishya and shudra was action or potentiality; and so the system admitted the possibility of a shudra becoming a king or a kshatriya becoming a brahmin. But the system of the fourfold caste was rigid and it rested on the notorious principle of high and low birth. This principle is obviously discriminatory as it does not treat all human beings on equal footing. In the caste-based society the brahmin was considered as the most venerable and the shudra was held as the most contemptible. Such principle cannot gain validity either in logic or moral law. Yet the principle not only survived but was used as a weapon against the shudras. Obviously, this was due to the conspiracy that succeeded against the shudras. The brahmin first exploited the religious myth that the brahmin was born out of the mouth of Prajapati or Brahma, the kshatriya from the arm, the vaishya from the waist and the shudra from the foot. Thus, the shudras were relegated to the lowest position. Later, the brahmin advanced the philosophical theory of rebirth to say that the status and conditions of life that any individual gets in his present life is due to his actions of virtue and sin committed by him in his past life.

The religious-minded, meek and illiterate lot came to believe easily that the holy system of caste was ordained by God, that they were the lowest in order or status because they had lived a sinful life in their previous birth, and that their salvation lay in performing their duties religiously. They also believed that their duties were defined by the knowledgeable people of the supreme caste. It appears that the demands of the non-shudras—howsoever unreasonable or morally objectionable such demands might be—were craftily added to the list of duties prescribed for the shudras. That is how it became the duty of a shudra to be always conscious that he was an untouchable and therefore he must keep himself and his shadow at such distance from other people as would debar the possibility or contact. It he failed to perform his duty deliberately or due to inadvertence he must suffer punishment. Disobedience or dereliction of duty on the part of the shudra was never condoned. In such state of affairs, the psychology of the shudra was so formed that if he was disgraced and treated with cruelties he would curse his fate rather than the person who caused him offense. Thus, we can see that the psyche of the shudra consisted of fatalism, acceptance and the feeling of dependence.

Thus, orthodox Hindu society robbed the shudras of their freedom without letting them know that they were being enslaved. It had already denied equality to all by its thesis of social gradation. The notion of superiority/ inferiority permeated through every caste and since the shudras performed numerous tasks they were divided into many sub-castes, some considered superior to the rest. The high-caste people exploited the population of the lowest order for their benefit and entertainment, but kept the latter away from themselves. They called them 'achhut'. However, they knew that if they treated all of them as untouchable they would only be making their lives difficult. Therefore, they classified the shudras into touchable shudra and untouchable shudra. The category of touchable ones included barbers, weavers, milkmen, carpenters, goldsmiths, blacksmiths, etc. The untouchable shudras were the sweepers and the cobblers. Unfortunately, the shudras could not see through the game of the brahmin. Therefore, instead of rejecting such discrimination they succumbed to the notion of superiority/ inferiority. A barber or carpenter rated himself superior to a cobber or sweeper, and the latter also believed that they were inferior to the former. Under the circumstances, the idea of brotherhood could not be anything but a daydream. Thus, the dalit psyche seems to have drained completely as it did not possess either power or will even to talk of equality and fraternity.

During the Middle Age the psyche seems to have been stirred by socio-religious movements of Shaivism and Vaishnavism. The saints from the lower rung of Hindu society such as Kabir, Nanak, Namdeo, Dadu, Tukaram and Ramdas kindled some hope because they objected to the primacy of the brahmin and opposed the caste-consciousness which led to discriminatory behaviour. But, Tulsidas supported the view of the orthodoxy in his *Ramcharita Manas*, a book that is as popular and regarded as venerable. He wrote to say that it is better to worship a brahmin devoid of grace and merit, rather than a shudra who possesses merit and learning.

The 'Dalit' saints opposed casteism but none ever put up a fight. The reason is that it is not in the nature of a saint to contend or rebel. Therefore, unfortunately though, orthodoxy prevailed, but it could not mitigate the consciousness that Kabir, Nanak etc., had aroused. In the nineteenth century such awareness further deepened due to several factors:

Institutions like Arya Samaj, Brahmo Samaj, Ramkrishna Mission and Theosophical Society worked to bring the elements of religious awakening to contemporary social consciousness, so that the ideas of high or low birth and untouchability could be rejected. Then, there were social reformers and freedom-fighters who condemned caste-discrimination and untouchability. The social reformers looked upon these as social evils that needed to be eradicated for removing social tensions and bringing peace and prosperity to the society. And, those who struggled for Independence realized that for achieving the goal it was necessary that the people came closer to each other to fight against the British Government. English education also helped. It facilitated access to many new concepts like democracy— liberty, equality and fraternity; class-struggle— that is the exploitation of the poor by the rich and the latter uniting to defeat the rich; nationality—that refers to membership of a nation and not of caste; and human rights. The role of Christian missionaries in providing better conditions of living to those who embraced Christianity is also an important factor.

However, caste-discrimination and untouchability could not be eliminated. The reason is simple: You cannot simultaneously accept the given framework of caste hierarchy and dismiss the practice of untouchability. That is why Swami Dayanand failed in spite of his emphasis on the thesis that the principle of social division is not birth but karma. Gandhi also failed for the same reason despite the interpretation of shudra as 'harijan'. His view could, at best, elate but not elevate them. Since after Independence, things are changing. There have been changes in the politico-legal field, which have a bearing on the question of safety and empowerment of the downcast people. There have been changes in the socioeconomic field also, which somewhat facilitate intercommunication and interdependence between people of high and low divisions. Yet, all this is not enough. It is to the credit of Dr. B.R. Ambedkar that he was the first person to advocate demolition of caste as such. Rejection of the nation of superiority/ inferiority of one caste against the other cannot serve the desired purpose of achieving equality and brotherhood. The reason is that caste-nomenclature is so deeply ingrained in the public mind that if in some context you talk simultaneously of a brahmin and a shudra you communicate to the public mind the idea of one individual being of higher rank than the other. The idea of demolition of caste is vital to the success of democracy: for, the ideal of democracy is equality among all, whereas the ruling principle of caste-discrimination is inequality.

Dr. Ambedkar must be further complimented for his thesis that political reform will be in fructuous without there being social reform and that economic inequality is due to social inequality. Therefore, social reform or reconstruction is the first priority. Reform of the orthodox society cannot be limited to rejection of its principle of superiority or inferiority. All must stand on the same footing; and the social ladder, because it gives the idea of high and low rungs, must be broken completely. This means that casteism must be abolished. It further means that bringing about changes within the society is not enough; the society needs to be reconstructed after its present foundation is broken. Now, the question is, 'How to accomplish the task?' The answer from the dalit side would be to expose the conspiracy and hypocrisy of the people from the so-called superior (or higher) caste, and counter their arguments and confront their actions. The dalits need to be confident, stand united, assert their rights and not give in.

Dr. Ambedkar pleaded what he practiced. He knew that demolition of the structure of Hindu society could not be a one-man show, so he embraced Buddhism, a religion that does not recognize any caste in its social order. Dalit psyche, as we know now, is the collective unconscious of the downtrodden, which is mature and consummate. It is constructed primarily out of the ideas and experiences of Dr. Ambedkar and his followers. Thus, the stuff of the psyche consists of certain ideas and emotions.

The division of society into castes of high and low order is ill-conceived, immoral and indefensible. Such division denies that all are free and equal. Casteism cuts across humanism; it leads to repression and oppression, denying the low caste peoples the rights and privileges to which they are entitled by virtue of being humans. Therefore, in the interest of humanity and the well-being of human society the caste system must be demolished. Those who have suffered the cruelty of caste-discrimination must rise in anger and stand united to deal with it; they must confront and not conform.

Dalit psyche harbours the feeling of unity that dalits are one. Dalits resent and detest hypocrisy and excessive behaviour of the upper caste and nourish a feeling of intolerance towards them. They are given to rebelliousness that expresses the strong feeling that injustice shall be countered both by word and deed. Then, there is the feeling of self-assertion as well, which negates the possibility of their morale going down amidst adverse situations.

There is yet one more aspect, which perhaps can be treated as part of dalit psyche. Dalit writers define dalit literature as a body of writings by dalits only. They hold that pro-dalit writing by a non-dalit writer will lack in authenticity. They assert that sympathizing and experiencing are two different things, for one who undergoes painful experience only knows what pain means and what it means to feel pain. It is perhaps because of such attitude that dalit literature tends to be more caustic and full of punch.

Works Cited

Ambedakar, B.R. *Annihilation of Caste*. Jullundhar: Bheem Patrika Prakashan, 1968.

Kardam, Jaiprakash (ed.). *Jati: Ek Vimarsh*. 2nd ed. Delhi: Navbharat Prakashan, 2004.

Keer, Dhananjay. *Dr. Ambedekar: Life and Mission*. Bombay: Popular Prakashan, 1962.

12

Translation and Its Significance for Marginalities—Local and Regional Literatures and Identities

— Prashant Mishra

Translational activities contribute to the enrichment of both the source languages and literatures and the target languages and literatures. In the context of India, translation will not only contribute to the growth of Indian languages and literatures but also the world languages and literatures. It is a reciprocal relationship between the main and the marginal voices and identities. Translation of global works into Indian languages will acquaint and contribute to the growth of literary competence and consciousness about the genres, forms, movements and experiments and innovations that have been taking place in the literatures of the world.

Whereas translation of Indian literature into English and other global languages of wide coverage will contribute to the expansion and widening of the world literatures and languages, translation of Indian literatures—local and regional—will enrich and expand the thematic, socio-cultural, aesthetic and linguistic horizons of the world literature. It will also make the world literature more plural, multiple, and heterogeneous. By contributing to the growth of each other, both the source literature and the target language literature will acquaint each other with the uniqueness and innovations inherent in them and will further contribute to the sharpening of creative sensibilities. Translation, in this way, will make creative activities for both the marginal and the main voices more flexible, dynamic and pluralistic. The present paper reflects on the significance of translation studies for the marginalities—local and regional voices—which have been ignored due to spatial limits and the many prejudices fabricated about them.

India is a vast reservoir of linguistic diversity. According to 2001 census, people in India speak 234 mother tongues which are grouped under 122 languages. Many of these languages are local and regional which descended from the same progeny. These languages, therefore, inherited many syntactical, morphological, phonological and lexical features from their parental languages. These shared features among the local and regional languages contribute to mutual intelligibility, dynamism and flexibility in their uses. The interaction between the linguistic communities who live in the adjoining localities or regions makes possible for these languages to unconsciously converge with each other and to flourish by generously exchanging words and phrases from each other. The linguistic communities who live next door to each other unconsciously and spontaneously mix codes and sometimes even switch from one code to another.

The co-existence and presence of many neighbouring local and regional languages and their proximity and mutual enrichment becomes a blessing for translation activities. Referring to this phenomenon, Mohanty rightly pin pointed, "Languages in two neighbouring states (for example Orissa and West Bengal, or Orissa and Andhra Pradesh, West Bengal and Assam) bear a tendency to be flexible. The flexibility and fluidity of languages, because of physical contiguity and proximity not only permit an easy flow of words from one linguistic system to another, but also unconsciously initiate the process of translational practices" (Mohanty 167).

Translation activities in adjoining local and regional languages will be easier in comparison to those which are remote from each other and do not share cultural, regional and experiential background. Translation from a marginal local or regional source language text to another adjoining local or regional target language text will contribute to the mutual enrichment and expansion of the vocabulary, language and literature of these languages.

The works of local and regional writers remain restricted to small localities and regions where the source languages are spoken and understood. The voices and aspirations of these writers too remain unheard to the large population that dwells outside their regions and do not understand their languages. Consequently the beauties of their works remain in oblivion from the sight of the majority who do not come across it. These works remain like flowers that bloom in wilderness with no one to admire their beauty. Therefore, translations of these marginal writers into a global language like English acquire significance. According to Charu Sheel Singh:

> Translations are definitely globalizing mental colonies but it is vital to preserve the sanctity of the local and the regional. Eliot called himself a cosmopolitan in literature thereby losing touch with the local. William Carles Williams said that Eliot does not show any respect for time and place. Northrop Frye remarked in creation and Decreation that in order that a creative work of art might preserve its universal value, it is essential for it to respect the local and the original . . . our existence as a nation depends upon transcreation of the textual traditions both in the mainstream and in the substream. (Singh XV)

Translation of a local source language text into a standard target language will not only create greater literary space for these writers but also create a bigger market, readership, and academic space for them. As is evident from the large body of translations undertaken on Rabindranath Tagore, Tagore now no longer remained a regional poet of Bengal but has become a national and international figure. People who read Tagore's renderings into English regard him as an Indian English writer in spite of knowing that his works were originally written in Bangala. Though Tagore's English *Gitanjali* included only 51 songs than the original Bangala *Gitanjali* that contains 157, but the English *Gitanjali* not only won him Nobel Prize in 1913 but created scope for his other works to be translated into English and other languages and brought him from anonymity to universal recognition. Subhas Sarkar rightly says:

> What is really interesting about Tagore's translations into English is that they started as a literary diversion and yet catapulted him to the world fame, not as a writer of Bengali poetry but as a writer of English poems.Even Buddhadeva Bose, in his *An Acre of Green Grass*, once remarked that 'the English *Gitanjali* has been rightly praised by the world: it is the quintessence of Rabindranath and a miracle of Translation. . . He ever described it 'as more than a great work in English; it is the work of a great English poet.' (Sarkar 160)

Similarly Dilip Chitre's translation of some selected poems of Namdeo Dhasal, a regional Marathi dalit poet included in an Anthology entitled *Namdeo Dhasal: Poet of the Underworld* introduced Dhasal to the world of man of letters, critics and people. Dhasal's poetry was, otherwise, confined only to Marathi readership. It is Chitre's translation that exposed Dhasal's Marathi Dalit Muse to the world.

Translation is not only a process pf transformation of source language linguistic units into target language linguistic units but it also involves transformation of socio-cultural ethos of the source language text into target language text. Firth (1957), Halliday (1973), Leech (1983) and other functionalists regard a text as a semantic unit that consist of words and sentences which function in various socio-cultural situations. Since various local and regional texts are representatives of the socio-cultural ethos of the marginalities—dalits, tribals and rurals etc., translation in this context, not only implies transference of words but also transference of source language culture into target language culture. Translations of the text of marginalities bring their culture to the main which earlier was pushed to periphery and even mocked at by the dominant groups and their culture.

Postmodern and postcolonial theories and studies exposed the oppressive and hegemonic impacts of the majoritarian attitudes and unveiled their hollowness and evil consequences. In this context, glorification of meta theories, dominant culture under the colonial projects of expansion, domination, enslavement have been challenged and marginalities and their cultures, literatures, the knowledge systems have started drawing attention of the scholars and critics. In this changed context, translations of marginal voices—dalits, tribals, etc., gained momentum. According to T. Sai Mouli, "Dominant cultures have always enjoyed glorification. But in the changed context less known cultures and languages demand more attention, exploration and exposure. It is here translation studies assume greater significance" (Mouli 60).

Many works of marginalities produced in local and regional Indian languages are in the form of grievances and protests against the pains and wrongs inflicted on them by the majority in the name of caste, colour, creed, region and gender etc. Be it dalit literature or feminist writings or tribal or subaltern literature, we notice protests against the racial, casteist, patriarchal and elitist bias that contribute to their wretchedness, impoverishness and marginality in society. However voices of protests become stronger when they get translated from local and regional languages into English and other privileged languages. Through translations, these protests reach bigger sections of the society and find a powerful platform. These voices of protests translated into standard languages of the exploitative forces subvert the perception of the colonial forces and humanize them to feel the pangs of the marginal and the subaltern. But for the translations of the marginal texts, these voices would have never reached the majority who earlier thought differently and inhumanly and exploited the marginal ruthlessly. These translated voices of protests of the marginal—may be dalits, adivasies or women counter the selfish narratives of the colonial forces—which may be Europeans, elites, patriarchy, nationalists and upper castes. Praveen Gadhvi who is a distinguished Gujarati dalit poetess raised her voice against the discrimination, deprivation and marginalization of the dalit. She translated her poems from Gujarati into English and published them in the collection entitled *The Voice of the Lost*. Lamenting about the denial of identity and respects to dalits by the discriminatory caste system practiced by the upper caste people, she complains:

> She had no village,
> She had no religion,

She had no language,
She had no dignity,
She had no modesty,
She was guilty,
Because she was untouchable by birth

(*Barter System 33*)

She translated her poems from Gujarati into English to use a more powerful medium to raise her protest against the bane of untouchabililty. Thus, the translations of the marginal writers, who questions the exploitative, selfish and undemocratic narratives of the colonizers, contribute in creating a just world order and in granting democratic human rights to the subaltern and in this way heralds independence, freedom and sovereignty to the local narratives and view points which otherwise remain confined to restricted locality and people. Translation, thus for the marginal become a counter strategy to challenge the hegemonic designs of the colonial powers.

Works of indigenous writers, regional and local writers do not come to the fore because they are not codified in a prestigious language like English which is a global language and has a vast geographical coverage in the world. In comparison to the Indian writers writing in English, these writers of the native local and regional languages whose works reflect the marginalities in different aspects, who dwell in the secluded spots and are scattered over lands, have a rich cultural literary traditions developed over centuries of cultural advancements in the form of folk literature. The Indian writers in English do not enjoy such acute cultural sensibility due to their elitist and urban background. Even if some of them possess the native cultural ethos, the expression of their cultural ethos through the medium of a foreign tongue do not provide their writings the local and the native flavour and fragrance that we notice and enjoy in the local and regional literatures. Due to their elitist, urban and even alien associations, as some of them work abroad, their works do not provide the first hand descriptions of Indian experience and cultural ethos. These local and the regional writers are the sons of the soil who possess the real historical and the cultural sense due to belonging to a very long cultural tradition, a tradition of more than 5,000 years of literary writings in India. In spite of possessing and inheriting a long temporal literary tradition, these local and regional writers due to spatial constraints and demographic smallness of the local and regional languages in which they write become marginal writers. In the 'Translator's Introduction', Alok Mukherjee who translated Sharankumar Limbale's *Towards an Aesthetics of Dalit Literature* hinted at his motive in translating the book and writes:

> Since most dalit writing, and discussion of this writing, have been in the various regional languages of India, very little of either is accessible in English. This is a major gap, given that much of the theorizing in India and abroad about Indian literatures, culture and society, whether from Marxist, postcolonial or subaltern perspectives, has been in English.... Dalits are an important political and social force in India. Their literary and critical writings constitute a major challenge to, and questioning of, the theorizing about Indian politics, society, culture and literature by intellectuals from upper caste Hindu and other dominant communities, and by non-Indians. To fail to pay attention to this challenge and questioning, is to engage in a hegemonic discourse that excludes the realities and experiences of nearly a quarter of the country's people.... As a small effort to fill this gap, I have translated Limbale's book. (Mukherjee vii-viii)

Translation for dalits and all the marginal functions to make accessible in English and other standard languages what is available in their local and regional languages. Translations of local and regional language writers into English paves the way for the globalization of these studies and brings them from margin to the mainstream. The works of local and regional writers remain confined to only particular restricted regions where people knowing these languages are able to read them. Due to efforts of National Book Trust and Sahitya Academi, works of award winning writers get translated into English and other languages. Sahitya Academi's journal *Indian Literature* too publishes translations of local and regional writers in English and contributes to the expansion and scope of these writers and their literatures. But these are meager efforts in comparison to the vast number of quality works produced every year in Indian languages. Sujit Mukherjee rightly complains when he says:

> Through the medium of English we find it possible to discuss French or German or Russian literature, but the same is not true of Indian literature which continues to be without a literary forum in India that could be shared by the largest number.... The literary compartments in which we live in India—with windows wide open to non-Indian literatures but doors closed to the work of neighbouring Indians—tend to grow rather than diminish in spite of organized attempts at bringing together writers, critics and readers from different languages. (Mukherjee 15)

To sum up, translations of the works of marginalities—local and regional writers—will contribute to their expansion, globalization, standardization and decolonization. Translation will bring their works from margin to the main, periphery to the centre, anonymity to recognition and local to global. Renderings of the local and regional works of the marginalities into English and other standard languages will unveil the beauty of their works and bring their glorious literary and cultural traditions before the world that was earlier oblivious of them and consequently developed hostile attitude towards them. Translation of the marginalities will deconstruct the selfish metatheories fabricated about these communities to exploit and rule them. Translations of the marginal literatures will make these literatures a part of the world literature and will make the spectrum of the world literature rich, varied and kaleidoscopic.

Works Cited

Dhasal, Namdeo. *Namdeo Dhasal: Poet of the Underworld Poems of 1972-2006.* trans. Dilip Chitre. Chennai: Navayana, 2007.

Firth, J. R. *Papers in Linguistics:1934-1951*. London: O.U.P., 1957.

Gadhvi, Praveen. *The Voice of the Last*. New Delhi: Yash Publications, 2008. All the quotations from her poetry have been taken from this edition.

Halliday, M. A. K. *Explorations in the Functions of Language*. London: Edward Arnold, 1973.

Leech, Geoffrey. *Principles of Pragmatics*. London and New York: Longman, 1983.

Mohanty, Niranjan. "Demystifying Translation" *Studies in Translation*. ed. M.K. Ray. Delhi: Atlantic Publishers and Distributors, 2008.

Mouli. T. S. C. "Nuances of Translation" *Spindle and the Wheel: Re-Living Text and Context in Translation Studies*. ed. Binod Mishra. New Delhi: Adhyayan Publishers, 2011.

Mukherjee, Alok. Trans. Introduction. *Towards an Aesthetics of Dalit Literature*. New Delhi: Orient Longman, 2004.

Mukherjee, Sujit. *Translation as Discovery*. Hyderabad: Orient Longman, 2006.

Sarkar, Subhas. "Tagore in Translation: A Case for Revaluation" *Studies in Translation*. ed. M.K. Ray. New Delhi: Atlantic Publishers and Distributors, 2008.

Singh, C. S. "Foreword" *Spindle and the Wheel: Re-Living Text and Context in Translation Studies*. ed. Binod Mishra. New Delhi: Adhyayan Publishers, 2011.

13

Reclamation of the Fractured Self in Namita Gokhale's *The Book of Shadows*

— Prerna Hiradhar

> Who am I? This essentially philosophical question has assumed a tangible immediacy. We define ourselves by the people that we know, by the face we see in the mirror. (3)

So says Rachita Tiwari, the protagonist of Namita Gokhale's *The Book of Shadows*, who once taught English literature at Jesus and Mary College Delhi, and wouldn't she know it! For, the next moment she acknowledges "all the parameters have changed" and "Even the face I might meet in the mirror is no longer mine." (3). And this because she has been left permanently disfigured from an acid attack by her dead fiancé's sister.

"Who am I?" A question we ask ourselves umpteen number of times, seek to answer and continue to search for answers to. Just an individual? A person with a particular face, name, character traits, value systems, perceptions, attitudes—the sum toto of parentage, family, community, society and environment? One who seeks a balance between one's perception of who he or she is—what one wants and the inner world plus the realities of life—the external world as one goes about the business of day-to-day living with hopes of fulfillment of aspirations, expectations and happiness ? This question thus forms the very essence of a person's existence and so the focus on 'self'.

The Concise Oxford Dictionary defines 'self' as a person's essential being that distinguishes them from others, especially considered as the object of introspection or reflexive action, and so is a person able to identify with himself and the exterior world through his self-identity and self-image.

Carl Rogers defined self as an organized consistent, conceptual gestalt composed of perceptions of the characteristics of the 'I' or 'me' and the perceptions of the relationship of I and me to others and to various aspects of life, together with the values attached to these perceptions. 'I' is the personal self—the self one believes oneself to be, strives to be and consists of individual's psychological processes—perception, learning and motivation. 'Me' represents the social self—the way a person appears to others and the way the person thinks he or she appears to others. There has to be a balance between the two. People thus develop an established set of relations with their environment, learning how to deal with life and each other, how to fulfil their roles and what to expect next. If only life could be so predictable!

And yet, change is a necessary way of life. It is all around us—in the seasons, in biological processes, in the social environment, etc. The change operates through individual's attitudes to produce a response that is conditioned by feelings towards the change. The way people feel about a change determines how they will respond to it. The rapid technological innovations, industrialization change in value system, consumerism etc have left the individual ill-equipped to maintain the requisite equilibrium between the self, society and environment. So, when the question arises of self-worth, of basic human dignity, of neglect and suppression, the self-identity is challenged, shaken and with no proper redress, the self is splintered, fractured. This leads to alienation—from the self and from society. How this comes about and how the individual deals with it forms the essence of this paper which aims to address the perspective for a deeper understanding of the dilemmas as also trace the positive growth in the character with deeper insights in to the process of reclamation, the self-realization.

Namita Gokhale is a daring and talented writer whose works successfully portray the recurrent theme of woman's struggle for self-realization and self-definition. Her novels touch upon the psychological aspects with a focus on women characters while underplaying the male characters and have a frank exposition of the hush sexual lives of her women. *The Book of Shadows* is about the past and the present and future and falls in the genre of New Age Fiction where imagination transcends the mundane and is stretched to include other realms, different states of being, space / time continuums, spirit entities, supra-consciousness and such phenomena—with a desire to explore the higher reaches of human potential.

Action in the outer world has its effect on the inner world of man and vice versa. Rachita's one wanton act of physical involvement with her best friend's husband is enough to turn her hitherto complacent life topsy-turvy, and has far-reaching repercussions. Anand, Rachita's fiance, feels cheated and the only way he sees fit to resolve this conflict is by ending his life. Though his suicide note is melodramatic in tone, his reaction is that of a man, heart-broken by the treachery of his beloved who doesn't conform to his ideal of womanhood and through his fatal action, he seeks vengeance for her betrayal, "Goodbye, cruel world . . . Tell the faithless one, the Delilah, that her betrayal will cost her dear . . ." (5).

His sister too resolves the conflict by nurturing hostility, giving vent to violence by throwing acid on Rachita's face to mar her beauty and avenge her brother's death. And Rachita is left with no recourse but to flee, to withdraw from the mocking and prying eyes of society, to escape. She retreats to her childhood home nestled in the Kumaon Hills, at the foot of the Himalyas, ". . . to heal, to hide, to forget. To forgive, to be forgiven" (6) and it is not just the physical scars she seeks to hide but the psychological ones also for she "needed solitude and soliloquy to come to terms with what had happened" (7). Severing all links with society family, she seeks to define, analyze and comprehend her identity in terms of what she has faced because she is now disfigured and nursing a bruised self. That she is aware of her trek downhill even though she makes claims to the contrary is clear when she says:

> I have not looked into a mirror for months now, and my face; that familiar index of my being, has dissolved into

> absurdity and abstraction.... The avengers of my vanity have broken me, humbled me . . . leaving me less than I was. (7)

Veiled, to hide her disfigurement as also to draw a curtain on the inner turmoil she is facing, she seeks solace from the house which carries memories of her happy child hood and the company of the old caretaker Lohaniju who regales her with folklore and ghost stories for:

> . . . it sends delicious shivers of anticipation down my spine, it suspends my disbelief and so, conversely, ups the ante with my belief—in myself, my childhood, my life; in who I am. At this stage I need more than anything to believe, and if I can believe Lohaniju, I can believe anything. (16)

This renewal of belief in what is around her is essential to the purpose of her being, her *raison-etre*. She follows a routine of filling up notebooks with his stories and painting her nails red every two days so as not "to fall into physical and emotional disrepair," adding that "Sanity is like nail polish, it chips easily, it has to be restored and renewed"(19), and through these activities seeks to maintain a hold on life and herself. Her holding on to the stinging nettle to avoid falling down is a lesson that:

> A firm hold on anything, even reality, hurts less than a timid half-way encounter. Pain is a precondition to life, a prelude to joy. It is a teacher, not a tormenter. Lack of stimulation leads only to a lack of sensation. Better, then, the pain. (71)

That the house is going to have a deeper significance is hinted at with "There was an overlay of perception and memory, a mass of recollection that struggled to be set free" (10). The solitude and silence of the house plays upon her and sets a chain of reveries, reminiscences and more eerily, the panorama of the lives of the previous owners unfolds through the voice of a ghost, the raconteur of their deeds. All this forces her to question herself:

> Am I the perpetrator or the victim of this dream madness—do I inhabit these phantoms or do they inhabit me? Although I can still view things from the outside, yet I am irresistibly drawn into this internal and external disorder, this doubling of consciousness. (67)

Soon she finds herself undergoing some inexplicable experiences—an iridescence suffusing the room, of her floating, her fiancé Anand's voice booming out instead of the song she expects to blare out. Lohaniju has found an old journal, written by the man who built the house, an English missionary William James Cockerel and from a sordid world of reality to another dimension, a supernatural and mysterious atmosphere is woven:

> Some impress of memory was set loose from my mind. Images fluttered out of nowhere and sprung to life in full form. A procession of people came out from all directions to meet me. They stood there, in the flesh, no phantoms or fantasies but people like you and me. (10)

"The mooring of personality had abandoned me." (26) and this shows her awareness that another dimension, the sub-conscious has taken over and all she is right now is a detached observer, a vehicle, a medium of exploration of all that has transpired in the house, in the lives of the owners, and is a correlative of her pain and dilemma.

Withdrawal, however, is achieved at a price and fighting through the subconscious where her mind leads her tortuously and inexorably through fevered, shifting nightmare landscapes towards recognition of her own true identity and the responsibility, which she must take for her actions. As she runs from the conflicts of the physical battleground, she is drawn into the depths of her insanity, an experience which may lead her towards recognition of the truth of her situation, but is fraught with its own dangers—madness and the risk of never being able to return.

This separation between the self and world belongs to the Romantic tradition which descried a conflict between the world and man. To redeem this self, the Romantics rebelled against the tyranny of the materialistic world and sought escape—through rebellion or violence, withdrawal, spatial dislocation or wandering; using imagination and supernaturalism as tools. Imagination revelled in magic and mystery of universe and is connected with intuition, perception and insight while the supernatural incidents are linked with the working of human psychology.

While the journal of the missionary carried his and his wife's impressions about India, its mystical charm, the abounding superstitions or otherwise, their experiences and losses, his recounting of the death of the hill-girl Lali and his witnessing the procession of spirits escorting their native God Airee, heartbreak at the death of his wife Fanny, it also gave her food for thought; ". . . memory is capable of delusion, and the mind of man falls prey to many fancies" (56). And reason to surmise his progressive breakdown, so that she is forced to say, "I have to let go, before I can return to myself." (63). This is indicative of her inner turmoil—she knows where she is headed even though she vehemently denies it. And this is where she questions the presence of others in the house, jostling for space and talks of synesthesia, a literal crossing over of the senses, a demolition of the internal boundaries and constraints that demarcate the territories of experience, wondering if she is suffering from the same. Is she? We can only guess!

By force of habit, being a teacher of English literature, quotes by eminent poets spring forth (even though she claims she hates poetry) but she finds she best identifies with the Hindi poetess and writer Mahadevi Verma: a case of identification or self-awareness?

Here the narrative is taken up by the resident ghost of the house, and we get a taste of the macabre and grotesque in true Gothic style.

There are the homosexual sadistic lovers Marcus and Munro, followers of the infamous magician Aleister Crowley and dabblers in black magic who indulge in wild sexual orgies, satanic rituals and terror by massacring panthers in moonless nights. The human sacrifice of a young boy proves to be their undoing and they meet with violent deaths. Colonel Osborne moves in only to kill himself after raping a hill woman. Father Benedictus who befriends the ghost also dies mysteriously while exorcising other ghosts and his death ushers in Captain Wolcott and his sensuous mistress Dona Rosa in whose sexual exploits the ghost is also a participant. Sexual orgies lead to the death of a traveller. Wolcott too is burnt alive. We also have a wise old crow, black panthers, three dead Sherpas, spirit of a young girl killed before the house was built.

The bizarre happenings expose the unpalatable truths and exorcise a sordid, tragic pattern of life. They showcase the struggle between illusion and reality. It is through the perspective of grotesque distortion that a basically philosophical consciousness probes into diverse problems: such as making sense out of an absurd reality, a seemingly senseless history and, above all, out of an ambiguous and constantly jeopardised identity. Of course the reader is never told who the ghost might be for it describes itself thus, ". . . suspended in time and space, without a body, without a context, ignorant of the reasons and circumstances that have led to this strange exile, this cruel isolation" (124).

Juxtaposing present against past, Gokhale images the state of mind of Rachita and that of the ghost, and through his impressions of the previous owners, the present and the past, making us aware of the different aspects of the characters, embodying two perspectives. Rachita wakes up to a bright morning feeling she "had the right to exist" and accepts:

> My centre, my identity, my selfhood had for a while abandoned the confines of skin and bone, abandoned my cage and run away to cower in dusty corners of other abandoned memories and perceptions. (213)

A look at the mirror erased further doubts for, ". . . Some trick of the light, led me to see not just my reflection but myself, the self I truly am" (218). In piecing together her fractured self, she is also able to dissect her reaction, "My body, I had convinced myself was the culprit.... My mind has stood by me... but it has abandoned my body, leaving it vulnerable to anger, abuse and invasion..." (219). She further observes, "It is not my body, which has betrayed me—it is I who have betrayed this body. My abandonment of courage..." (219), and announces, "There was no one else in the room." (231).

Her least favourite student Zenobia Desai's arrival completes her reclamation for she symbolizes Rachita's past that has inevitably telescoped into the present and signals her willingness to joint back society. Reclamation is painful and agonizing, yet leads to harmony and concordance in spite of apparent contradictions and paradoxes of life for it is a concomitant of proper understanding of the complexities of situations and accepting them as they really are.

Gokhale has attempted to fuse fantasy with perceptual experience in this novel of renewal of life. The re-living of the memories of the past, however unearthly and horrifying, is a process in her protagonist's psychic quest for reclaiming her fractured self. Are the weird scenes actual occurrences or mere products of her distorted imagination? Gokhale leaves it vague, as it probably should be though in her Author's Note she affirms having lived in the house and the novel having a core of truth in it, as also serving as a vehicle to resolve her personal pain.

The detached look at the tragedy, unfolding gradually through the protagonist's memory works. It releases the pent-up tensions and feelings, relieving Rachita of her darker, tragic mood and she turns to embrace her disillusioned self. Her awareness of life as a struggle and a manful management of the trials of life enable her to possess the will-power to face life, change it and renew it. Her hour of reckoning comes from inner strength and her transformation is effected through aesthetic experience—after fierce inner struggles and self-questioning so that she forges a meaningful relation between the self and the world around. Life goes on and she has to have the courage to flow on with the current of life. Man can emerge from the breakdown and the disruption, can contend with the disruptive forces and conquer them. The discord in life is a stage, not a terminus. Life is a pattern of despair and delight and one has to make and re-make oneself for the joie-de-vivre. Life is a search for one's own pattern—for identity through things found to be a 'mirroring' of the 'self'-semi-recognizable patterns, visual or otherwise. So we find the protagonist transformed from escapist to realist, ready to face reality and life, in all its hues when she says:

> To be ourselves we must remain in control of our scripts. We must make and remake ourselves, possess and repossess our world, cast and recast our lot in every precious moment. Above all, we must know what to hold on to, what to discard. (229)

And as Louis Cazamian and Raymond Las Vergnas put it in *History of English Literature*, that to descend to the depth of our consciousness is to discover the immanent being; in this way we are able to penetrate beyond the plane of appearance and sense; it is only in questioning ourselves that we can unravel the universe; the only events are those of the soul. Rachita's reclamation is complete and so she proclaims:

> I had acquired achieved, possessed myself again. (229)

Work Cited

Gokhale, Namita. *The Book of Shadows*. New Delhi: Penguin Books, 1999.

14

Buchi Emecheta's *The Joys of Motherhood*: A Forceful Lesson in the Pains of Motherhood

— Protibha Mukherjee Sahukar

An African proverb states that a woman is a flower in a garden and her husband is the fence around it. Undoubtedly this is a beautiful picture of women in an African society. Yet in *The Joys of Motherhood* Buchi Emecheta's (a Nigerian, non-Western and unhyphenated), *magnum opus* we come across a culture where the worth of a woman is determined by her womb; where labels, roles, terms, spaces are used to categorize human being. The novel illustrates one of the most damaging of traditions that motherhood signifies a rite of passage for a woman.

It is a well-documented fact that a patriarchal society needs to nourish various myths and traditions in order to maintain and propagate its system. Women, who are at the periphery of such a society, suddenly get catapulted to a central position by virtue of motherhood, find this male child bearing tradition irresistible and succumb to the system. In many African cultures the importance of motherhood overshadows every waking moment of an African woman's life. Failure to conceive and to produce male children can result in divorce, ostracism from the tribe or worse. Adrienne Rich aptly delineates the African traditional social milieu when she interprets patriarchy as the power of the fathers: a familial, social, ideological, and political system in which, by direct pressure or through tradition, law and language, customs, etiquette, education, and division of labour, men determine what parts women shall or shall not play, while the female is subsumed by the male everywhere.

The present paper evaluates womanhood and motherhood and explores the victimization relating to African woman's struggle for her identity as a woman and a mother. It focuses on the fact that there is no joy of motherhood when fertility simply becomes a subject matter of statistics and sexuality. The paper studies the victimization of Nnu Ego, a young Ibo woman, also the central character by way of societal, traditional, patriarchal, and cultural means. It dispenses with the romantic portrayal of motherhood and denounces the unscrupulous and misplaced values of life.

Nnu Ego is a classic victim of motherhood. She is a woman who makes devastating choices and sacrifices her health and selfhood in the pursuit of failed traditions, capsulated in the idea of motherhood.

The novel points to the utterly dependent and consequently helpless position of the protagonist as a woman in her society and throws light on the reproductive practices (of the Ibo people) that harm woman by letting her institutionalizing the very idea that a traditional wife should seek only to beget and care for her off springs. The Ibo society obliterates female sexual desire and also effaces quintessential rights by subconsciously brainwashing its woman to carry a 'moral albatross' around her neck.

We witness how fertility becomes essential to a woman who links her feminity to maternity and how the joys of motherhood turn into the agony of otherhood. Emecheta who is herself a Nigerian analyzes a woman's place in the Nigerian patriarchal society and focuses on the dangers of adhering to the harsh masculine ideologies and the ensuing damning societal outcomes.

Since the Ibos are a patriarchal people, marriage is deemed an indispensable factor for the continuation of the family line of descent. Children occupy the central point in Ibo marriage. The first and foremost consideration is the fertility of a woman. Parents long for this and the father of the family requests this every morning in his kolanut prayer. The mother begs for it while giving cult to her *chi* during annual festival. In other words, if you ask the ordinary Ibo man or woman why he desires to marry, the spontaneous answer will be, "I want to marry in order to beget my own children, to get a family like my parents". A childless marriage is a source of serious disappointment and sooner or later, leads to serious trouble. The position of a wife in her husband's family remains shaky and unpredictable until she begets a child. She becomes truly secure only after the birth of a male child. Trying to follow these community norms of the Ibos, Nnu Ego goes through a very hard life. This is the story of Nnu Ego during the first half of the 20th century. She is the daughter of a Great Chief in Nigeria.

By repositioning motherhood from being merely a symbol to social realism, Emecheta critiques the ways in which the myths of motherhood are imposed on Nigerian women and deals with the false consciousness of the Mother Africa trope through the life of Nnu. Emecheta makes an effort to free women from the mystique of motherhood by present-ing not only its joys but also its pains. She tries to drive home the fact that motherhood is slapped on as a 'responsibility', where as it is actually a chain that binds a woman to maternal slavery.

Although Buchi Emecheta is unquestionably Western feminism's preferred African writer yet she can not be considered a typical feminist in the Western mould. Emecheta weaves a mélange of traditional beliefs and cultural standards throughout her story. However, the message contained in is neither plain nor traditionally feminist. We have to understand that Emecheta's conception of tradition is complex, neither accepting nor rejecting entirely. Yet as a Nigerian, and as well as belonging to the Ibo community she is the spokeswoman in literature for the rights of women to function as human beings.

She clearly leads us to understand that beyond these biological and cultural roles, the African woman is also an individual in her own rights. It is the portrayal of a traditional society which successfully negates the importance of women as individuals through its constant valorization of motherhood as a role and function that comes to the fore. Obviously there is truth in the African proverb which says that until the lion begins to write his (or her) own story, the hunter will always be the hero.

The story opens with a hysterical Nnu Ego who is on the verge of committing suicide because her first-born son is dead. She wails at her terrible loss, "But I am not a woman any more I am not a mother any more . . . ." (62). The child's death sends Nnu Ego on an immediate mission for self-destruction because the child is a practical vindication of her womanhood. Her entire worth depends on her motherhood and without her son, she is nonexistent, a zero. It is understandable that a mother suffers extreme emotional distress after a loss of such a magnitude; nevertheless, we are hit in the face by the fact that Nnu Ego is devastated because "she had just lost the child that told the world that she was not *barren*" (62). One can easily see this opening scene as a point against the traditional African culture and how unfair these standards are towards the female gender. Tradition acts as victimizer to Nnu, in her childlessness. Nnu Ego finds herself in the terrible clutches of a soul-killing tradition, which places motherhood above everything. Nnu realizes that this failure brings shame to her family and so suicide seems to be the only way by which she can preserve her dignity and her family's social status. It is important to understand the pervasiveness of the enormity of motherhood in an African society.

Eventually, Nnu Ego has more children than she and her husband can in fact support. She has accomplished her goal as mother, nurturer and life giver. She becomes everything desired in a woman: submissive, nurturing, and devoted to the care and concern of her household. She believes that "if you spent all of your time making money and getting rich, the gods wouldn't give you any children; if you wanted children, you had to forget money and be content to be poor. Money and children don't go together" (81). She plunges herself in her family—her husband and her children. She never stops to make the connection that all these children were actually contributing to her daily agony. Her daily existence seems very agonizing and stressful. She so strongly identifies with being a mother that her vision becomes blurred and she fails to see the significant changes going on around her.

Nnu's victimization by men began long before she was born. She grew up without her biological mother who was a strong aggressive woman. Ona was a very independent woman who if she had lived would have guided her child from infancy to womanhood. Nnu Ego might have had a very different life. She was considered "troublesome and impetuous" because she "had the audacity to fight with her man before letting him have her" (21). Ona was a woman who did not bow to anyone, not even the great and famous chief, Agbadi, so highly regarded in Ibuza. On her death-bed (she dies when her and Agbadi's second baby is still-born) she, poignantly, asks the heart-broken Agbadi to "allow [their daughter, Nnu Ego] to have a life of her own, a husband if she wants one. Allow her to be a woman" (28).

However, despite her mother's plea, Nnu Ego fails to obtain a life of her own. Nnu was raised by Agbadi's other wives. She was taught that children made a woman whole and that male children were favorable. She was guided to think that in old age her children would take care of her.

Nnu Ego's first marriage was childless. By the conventional values and beliefs, she had failed in her first marriage to Amatokwu. It was assumed that it was she was infertile and not the other way round. There was no means of checking for sure. It was generally accepted that the male was not at fault in such situations, so naturally it had to be Nnu Ego. She stands alone in her dilemma despite her status as the daughter of the chief of the tribe, since her father as chief refuses to do anything to restore her dignity. Nnu Ego is full of self scorn, "How can I face my father and tell him that I have failed?" (31). She brought shame to her people for not conceiving and her husband's community looked down on her. She was in fact sent back to her father in shame. As she was not able to produce any heir, her husband married another woman who was able to conceive. Amatokwu's ability to impregnate another woman is a declaration of public humiliation because all of the tribe members now know that Nnu Ego is infertile. Amatokwu can find no compassion in his heart to console his wife; rather, she is considered to be dead in the eyes of her husband. Amatokwu derisively states "I have no time to waste my precious male seed on a woman that is infertile . . . If you really want to know, you don't appeal to me anymore" (32). For Amatokwu's his semen is too precious, and cannot be wasted on a woman that cannot make use of it to breed.

In a society, women are treated inferior to men even when they can bear a child, one can imagine the status of a woman who cannot bear a child results in a complete loss of value within the tribe. No doubt Nnu Ego was deprived of her role as a senior wife and had to work on the farms. She was allowed to help with the newborn baby. Nnu Ego, who had yearned to be a mother, began secretly nursing the newborn baby. She had thoughts of taking the baby and running away. She would often whisper to the baby, "Why did you not come to me? I cried in the night and longed for a child like you—why did you not come to me?" (34). One day, she was caught nursing the baby and was beaten badly by her husband. She was taken back home and with the help of her people was nursed back to health. She felt so ashamed for letting her people down.

Having no other choice, Nnu Ego moves to Lagos. In order to uphold her status in society and in an effort to please her father she settles for the unattractive second husband Nnaife. Nnaife didn't fit the typically traditional physique. He was not tall, lean and muscular as the men she was used to seeing back home in Ibuza. She was appalled at the sight of him because "she was used to tall, wiry farmers with rough, blackened hands from farming; long, lean legs and very dark skin . . .. What was more, he did not smell healthy either, unlike men in Ibuzu who had the healthy smell of burning wood and tobacco" (43-44). She is shocked to discover that Nnaife works as a domestic servant and washes women's underwear.

These negative images of her new husband soon faded when she became pregnant with their first child. She sees Nnaife through different eyes. He becomes the centre of her world. She was actually grateful to him for making her a complete woman. By proving her ability to bear a child, she hopes to bring new life to herself within her tribe. Nnu Ego's relies on her body as a means of survival. Though Nnu Ego does not market her body, she does attempt to use her body to insure her and her family's future.

Nnu gives up everything so that her sons Oshia andAdim can have the benefit of an education. There is never any thought given to educating her daughters. Nnu Ego encouraged her daughters to help her with domestic chores, to chop and sell wood. She tells them "the most important thing is for them (her daughters) to get good husbands" (189). Buchi Emecheta provides us with powerful images to reinforce this theory, "He who roars like a lion. My sons, you will all grow to be kings among men. He who roars like a lion. My daughters, you will all grow to rock your children's children" (29). This poem relates the designated social positions for men and women.

Nnu Ego assumes that her sons will come home to live and will care for her as she grows old. Tragically, the endless sacrifices she makes bring her little reward. She dies a broken spirit whose fertility did not enhance her life as she was taught to believe. She is truly an unfortunate product of her heritage. Nnu Ego's joys as mother remain unrealised because her children fail to reciprocate her love as is expected of them, by taking care of their parents, brothers and sisters. One by one her joys turn sour as each child strives to escape from poverty and depravity of his parent's environ-ment.

No other character in the novel seems to experience unhappiness of this magnitude. The question arises why does Nnu Ego have disappointment? That is because she is enslaved by her inherent devotion to tradition. Nnu Ego's traditional views of marriage and family responsibility are completely outdated. She is entrapped between two cultures. She is a product of her homeland but her life is spent raising her children in a foreign land. She tries to play her expected gender role but she can neither put down her traditional African gender role nor accept the western mould of a woman. The irony of Nnu Ego's predicament is seen when she reflects, "because she was the mother of three sons, she was supposed to be happy in her poverty, in her nail-biting agony, in her churning stomach, in her rags, in her cramped room . . .. Oh, it was a confusing world" (167). Nnu Ego has retains her pride as an African woman and chooses to live in dire poverty. She cannot understand the injustice of it. In her ignorance, Nnu Ego sees this contradiction as 'confusing'. She is a typical woman for her time. She is trapped in her own world of expectations, embedded in her mind from the patriarchy dominance. Towards the end of her life, she realizes that having children does not necessarily guarantee happiness. At the novel's end "Nnu Ego realizes that while nurturing children brought her status in Igbo society, it does not bring her personal fulfillment. Her life was marked with loneliness, poverty, and strife" (190).

The Joys of Motherhood is not only an indictment of African patriarchy, but also an illustration of the failure of inadaptability on Nnu's part in the face of enormous change. *The novel* reveals Nnu Ego's internal and external battle with traditional tribal ways and the new ways of the newly urban, colonized Nigerian city. Nnu Ego is a 'protagonist', but she is not a 'heroine', a woman to be admired or emulated, for in the end she fails. Abandoned by her husband and the male children for whom she worked in order to fund their education, Nnu Ego meets a miserable, lonely end. No 'happily ever after' ends this novel.

It will not be wrong to conclude that *The Joys of Motherhood* composes the most exhaustive and moving portrayal extant of the African woman, an unparalleled portrayal in African fiction and with few equals in other literatures as well.

Work Cited

Emecheta, Buchi. *The Joys of Motherhood.* New York: George Braziller, Inc., 1979.

15

Phoolkunwar—Resistence from the Margin

— Gulshan Das and Shabnam Das Manna

The culture of every nation is reflected in its native society, and to understand this native society, the study of native literature becomes mandatory. India has a rich and varied cultural heritage. It has been a home to several castes and sub-castes, each having its own peculiar literary traditions. Just as the river Ganga can never be imagined without her tributaries, in the same way the wonder that is India can never be comprehended without an insight into the traditions, culture and literature of her native people.

In the West, native literature is a well-established literary genre. We in India are still in the evolutionary process. The newborn state of Chhattisgarh is fortunate to posses not only mines of coal and diamond, it is also the proud owner of something far more priceless—mines of literature. It is the meeting ground of the Aryan and Non-Aryan cultures. The shadow of this melee is also visible in the native literature. It is the misfortune of this fertile state that its equally fertile literature has not been popularized and scientifically studied. The native literature of this state has been abundant, rich and multifaceted for several centuries. Much of it though, exists in 'Chhattisgarhi' the local dialect and in Hindi, therefore is unavailable to the most of India and the rest of the world. Still there are some writers, whose recent trickle of works, both translated and untranslated, have helped this state, still in its 'infancy', to carve a niche for itself in the literary map of India.

Ajit Jogi and Dr. Renu Jogi are names, which need little introduction. The first Chief Minister of Chhattisgarh, Ajit Jogi is not only an astute politician but a sensitive writer as well, with an interest and insight into the lives of the downtrodden adivasis of Chhattisgarh, who form and constitute a major chunk of the native population of the state. *Phoolkunwar* is a collection of short stories, co authored by Ajit Jogi and his wife Dr. Renu Jogi. Encompassing the woes of the native adivasis of Chhattisgarh, these short stories offer us a glimpse into their life, lifestyles, customs and traditions.

Phoolkunwar is the title story of this anthology and had been quite popular when published in the 'Saptahik Hindustan' in 1989. The story is set in a small village called 'Chukti Jhiriya' situated in the Tarai region of the Maikal ranges, bordering Madhya Pradesh and Chhattisgarh. As the name suggests, this story is about Phoolkunwar—a typical native adivaasi damsel of Chhattisgarh—and traces the journey of her life from childhood to womanhood till widowhood. In the process the author sheds light on life and lifestyle of the native Chhattisgaris and offers us a rare insight into stuff that the native women are made of.

Chhattisgarh is primarily an agro-based state, surrounded by rivers, mountain ranges and dense forests. These natural geographical barriers have a two pronged advantage—they have not only helped in enhancing the fertility of the soil and preserving of natural resources of the region, but have also prevented external encroachments of the so called cultured urbanity. This is the chief reason why the native culture of Chhattisgarh is still unspoilt, untamed and untouched by the 'fret and fury of the busy marketplace'. This is precisely the reason why the native soil still smells of generosity, simplicity, tolerance and hard work.

The story opens with Sukhiya working in the 'urad fields', where unaided she gives birth to her third issue, a girl child. Usually the birth of a girl is not a very happy occasion for the parents in India, where even the educated elite yearn for a boy. But when a girl is born to Sukhiya and her husband Manku, their joy knows no bounds. They had always wanted a little sister for their two boys and had even prayed to 'Bara Dev' to bless them with a daughter. Now that their wish had been granted, they lovingly named their daughter Phoolkunwar because her innocence and beauty reminded them of a flower. Soon the little girl catapulted into a ravishing beauty. She was the child of the wild; therefore there was a certain wilderness in her behavior and attitude too. Her beauty attracted young men from all the fourteen villages situated in the Tarai region of Maikal ranges. Clad in a bright red saree, adorned from top to toe, she was the cynosure of all eyes. Belinda like Phoolkunwar threw glances at all, but gave her heart to none. Who this ravishing tribal beauty would choose as her life partner, was a question whose answer every young man sought.

It was not that Phoolkunwar was unaware of her attributes. She was a wise woman who knew how to use her beauty as a weapon. When 'Chukti Jhiriya' was in the grip of a famine the Mukhiya of the village made a wise move of exhibiting Phoolkunwar before the Block Development Officer. As expected, the 'B.D.O. Sahib', immediately mobilized relief measures. He often came on surprise inspections to study the progress of these measures. On such surprise inspections, Phoolkunwar in a 'pre-doctored accident' was made to bump into the B.D.O. Sahib. Phoolkunwar also did not object to using her charms if they could contribute to the upliftment of her village. Wise that she was, she knew where to draw the line. Come rains, the relief operations were no longer needed. The B.D.O. Sahib lost his importance and so Phoolkunwar started giving him the same cold treatment that was meted out to other aspiring suitors.

From her childhood Phoolkunwar was different from other girls her age, that's why it did not come as a surprise when she decided to marry 'Baratiya', a middle-aged widower with four children, whose wife died during childbirth. Ever since she was a young girl she had secretly admired Baratiya, who was the farm manager of Mukhiya. He was dark, robust, well built and rustically handsome. In the fields Baratiya had the last word. It was Baratiya's authoritativeness that set him apart from other men and attracted Phoolkunwar. When his wife died Phoolkunwar decided that this was her opportunity to entice Baratiya into matrimony. In the tribes of Chhattisgarh marriages are solemnized very easily by a custom called 'Churi-Pehnana'. As per this custom the groom slips bangles into the hands of the bride and thereafter they become man and wife. Phoolkunwar also accepted the bangles of Baratiya and became his lawfully wedded wife. This marriage between a teenaged girl and a middle-aged man created a stir and sensation in the village, but because the issue involved the dashing and dynamic Phoolkunwar, none dared to speak eloquently and publicly against her.

It is said that poverty and misfortune are synonymous, but in the case of Phoolkunwar, misfortune had tightened its tentacles the day she had married Baratiya. Epidemic struck Chukti Jhiriya that year and Baratiya lost his four children to it. Phoolkunwar, despite being a stepmother, tried her best to save them. She took them to the local 'Baiga' and even went to the 'Bara Dev's' temple to pray for them, but to no avail. Because of the dearth of medical facilities Baratiya's children could not be saved. As if this was not enough, Baratiya who by this time had become frail and weak also fell a victim to the deadly epidemic and died. The blame for this misfortune fell upon the innocent Phoolkunwar. She was proclaimed an 'evil enticer', a 'Tonhi' in local Chhattisgarhi, who kills and eats human beings. The schoolteacher of the village, the Mukhiya and the priest, who always had amorous eyes on Phoolkunwar but had their proposals rejected by her, decided that this was the best time to avenge their humiliation. They called a village meeting and reached a unanimous decision where Phoolkunwar was accused of being an evil witch in the guise of a beautiful woman. As per the orders of the Mukhiya, Phoolkunwar was dragged to the assembly and the village 'Baiga', the local exorcist started inflicting tortures on her in an attempt to scare away the evil spirit that has possessed her. Phoolkunwar lost consciousness. When she woke up the next morning she was shocked to see her own reflection in the mirror. She was brutally beaten, burnt and bruised, but her spirits were still unbent. She decided to fight back and started walking toward the fields, resuming her normal routine as if nothing unusual had happened. The sight and plight of Phoolkunwar generated mixed reactions in the village. The menfolk, whose ego had been wounded by Phoolkunwar, derived sadistic pleasure in seeing her in such misery.

There were a few who were genuinely moved and sad for her. One of them was a simple village lad named Sudhin. Sudhin had always been a silent admirer of Phoolkunwar, but could never muster enough courage to bare his emotions. So moved was Sudhin to see Phoolkunwar in such misery that gathering all courage, he proposed to her to run away with him to some distant town—far away from the clutches of the Mukhiya. What the simple Sudhin did not realize was that it was only Phoolkunwar's body that had been mutilated; her ego and pride were still unbroken and intact. The once beautiful Phoolkunwar could never accept a non-entity like Sudhin as her mate, even if it meant staying in the proximity of Mukhiya's wrath. She rebuked Sudhin, insulted him and asked him never to indulge in such audacity again.

The same night Phoolkunwar received a message from the old school master stating that if she was willing to surrender herself to him, the 'master sahib' in turn was willing to put an end to her miseries. But Phoolkunwar was only broken. She was not bent. Like a wounded tigress she growled back and refused Master Sahib's proposal, not realizing that this action could have detrimental counter reactions. The intensity and severity of torture to scare away the evil spirit that had supposedly gripped her were increased. When Phoolkunwar did not surrender, the assembly came to the conclusion that it was her beauty and voluptuousness that had attracted the evil spirit. To get rid of the spirit, her body had to be destroyed and her beauty sacrificed. Her cottage was set on fire in an attempt to burn her alive.

The wounded, weak and semiconscious Phoolkunwar decided that this was the time to act before it was too late. She accumulated her remaining strength, gathered the few remains of her burning property in a brass container and jumped over the flames like a doe. Standing in front of her blazing home, the enraged she started shouting and crying till her reservoir of strength depleted. She fell unconscious but her wisdom and power of reasoning were still active. In her semiconscious state, she started evaluating the options that she had before her: should she accept Sudhin's proposal and elope with him? Should she succumb and surrender before the Master Sahib? Should she resume work in the Mukhiya's fields and go on enduring the tortures till they meet their natural death? Just then she saw the rat poison that she had unknowingly brought along with her while trying to escape from her burning hut. Will it not be proper that she should get decked up like a bride and consume the poison so that she can once again unite with her beloved Baratiya, never to part again, thought Phoolkunwar. Her entire life flashed by, before she fell into a sweet slumber—perhaps lulled to eternal sleep by the endless tortures and agonizing pain.

This tribal, uneducated and illiterate damsel is a New Woman in the truest sense of the term. When we talk of the phenomenon called New Woman, the picture that comes to our mind is that of a prime and proper, immaculately dressed, English speaking, educated, urbane, elite and liberated woman. The New Woman is dissatisfied with the inhibiting cultural roles assigned to her by the society. She is fiercely independent, self respecting, confident, conscious of her individuality and sure of her discretion and decisions. Though born and brought up in the untamed region of Chhattisgarh, the knave and nubile Phoolkunwar has all the attributes of the New Woman. Phoolkunwar's mother gave birth to her unaided. There is only a passing reference of her two brothers and father. Phoolkunwar's husband Baratiya also remained in her life for a few months—all this symbolizes the quintessential independence of her character. She lives life without any male help and support. The male characters that do appear in the story have a negative tinge. Instead of being instrumental, they are detrimental to her independence. Phoolkunwar is an egoist. She is proud, beautiful and proud to be beautiful.

Phoolkunwar is an iconoclast. By deciding to marry Baratiya, a middle-aged widower and father of four children, she dared to make a decision that raised many eyebrows. She respects and prizes her individuality. She represents the socially unacceptable and non-permissible aspect of the awakened feminine consciousness. She represents the predicament of a tribal woman placed between two poles—superstition and self-respect. Her struggle can be read as a heroic attempt that brings glory to the individual and adds dignity to the spirit of freedom. Phoolkunwar, the tribal New Woman, had always been a fighter. She went down fighting, as if proclaiming with Robert Browning:

I was ever a fighter, so—one fight more,
The best and the last.

Work Cited

Jogi, Ajit and Dr. Renu Jogi. *Phoolkunwar*. New Delhi: Rajkamal Publications Pvt. Ltd., 2003.

16

Self-Realization and Self-Fulfilment in the Novels of Patrick White

— Shrabani Chakravorty

Man's gregarious nature makes him comfortable being in a group. The sense of belongingness allows him to survive through the ups and downs of life. Alienation is one of the biggest fear of man. In fact, no man deliberately chooses to be alienated but at times circumstances are such that he is removed from his comfortable haven and is exposed to the harsh world to face its stark realities.

Marginalised psyche unfolds the existential anguish of a man who has been separated from his homeland. This anguish is perhaps the outcome of the feeling of alienation of a man who is alone and emotionally devastated in a foreign land. Modern man in the contemporary scenario is a split-self-representing the echoes of the marginalised pschye.

Through this paper I have tried to focus on centering the margin through the writings of Australian writer—Patrick White. In *The National Times*, this title appeared in limelight 'The Puzzling Case of Patrick White', the peculiar mixture of fascination and respect, of hostility and dislike which his work evokes amongst his countryman; his own peculiar love-hate relationship with his native Australia, the undoubted quality of genius in his work, and its marked religious character which appears to go so much against the grain of the contemporary outlook. All this seems highly meaningful, when considered within the context of Jung's Theories of the great artist and his role in society.

Patrick White was awarded Nobel Prize in 1973 for his vital contribution to the art of fiction and also for his achievements in bringing Australian literature to meaningful self-reference. Australian literature has a much more religious character than is generally recognised. The work of Patrick White is seen as making a new departure in its concentration on the inner spiritual crisis and the individual religious experience. White is profoundly concerned with the problem of human isolation, its social and psychological causes and with the individual's quest for self-realisation and self-fulfilment.

In an interview with Craig MacGregor, having admitted his own faith in God and deep concern for religion, White observes that now as the world grows more pagan, one has to lead people in the same direction in a different way. His most clear and unmistakeable statement in this regard has been his words to Clement Semmler. To Semmler he told of what has been increasingly trying to do in his books to give professed unbelievers glimpses of their own unprofessed factor. He thinks that most people have a religious factor, but are afraid that by admitting it they will forfeit their right to be considered intellectuals.

White's own temperament and outlook was of such nature that set him strongly at odds with the currents of philistinism and materialism as he discovered these manifested everywhere in contemporary life. His spiritual affinity was with Blake, Yeats and Eliot, who see the malaise of the modern world as deriving from its gross materialism, its extreme rationalism and mechanization leaving no room for mystery, reverence and worship. Australian scene provided White with a microcosm through which he dramatized a vision universal in its implications.

Through his fiction writing, White shows the intriguing conflict between the ambitious world of man and the devouring forces of society, which culminated in the submission, surrender, and sacrifice of the individual man. Thus we see man is obsessed with life's achievements. His frustration towards society is due to the non-fulfilment of his ambitions.

A survey of White's fiction—*Happy Valley*, *The Living and the Dead*, *The Aunt's Story*, *The Tree of Man*, *Voss*, *Riders in the Chariot*, *Vivisector* etc.—reveals that his pivotal theme is the individual's quest for fulfilment through illumination and its social, psychological and spiritual implications. White directs the modalities of fiction to discover analyze and clarify the complex variety of human psyche and the shifts and shocks experienced by the individual with his self-centred in an abstract way in the marble of man.

The polarization of attitude between intense commitment and sardonic detachment is what makes White different from others. While showing a deep concern towards the spiritual quest and the transformation of an individual White occupies himself in an objective and often ironic study of the social life. He wonderfully correlates between these two attitudes through his typical, original style.

In his novels, White vividly portrays the private world of individual experience, tracing the patterns of inner-growth and self-transformation achieved by the really gifted but extremely enclosed individuals that is the 'margins' who in trying to discover themselves not only define the bigger crisis of humanity but also show the redemptive options open to modern man for spiritual refinement and integrity.

Work Cited

Wilkes, G. A. Ed. *Ten Essays on Patrick White:Selected from "Southerly"*. Sydney: TBS The Book Service Ltd., 1970.

17

Rebellion through Surrender in the Poetry of Kamala Das

— S. K. Tripathi

Kamala Das or Madhavikutty or Kamala Surayya is primarily a poet who has raised her forceful voice against the male dictates and tyrannies prevalent in the patriarchal set-up of society. Though she has always enjoyed voicing her pet hates and desires, the fictional images, however, have been derived from social reality. She believes that the poet's raw material is a blend of personal experience, social reality and fictional images. Writing about 'woman' she makes her stand clear and says, "Whether something happened to me or to another woman is immaterial. What really matters is the experience, the incident. It may have happened to me or to another woman who is probably too timid to write about it." (Kaur 168). She seeks, therefore, through her poetry, to lend voice to the aspirations, desires and plight of the millions of women who have not been able to raise their voices or whose voices have been silenced or have remained unheard. The voice that she lends is not of open revolt but of rebellion drenched in sobs.

The primary concern of Kamala Das in her poetry is man-woman relationship. Risking the perils of society's outrage, she straddles between constraints of tradition and candour of modernity, longing for liberty and compulsion of servility, raging for rebellion and susceptibility to surrender and explores the longings and aspirations of woman, delineates her frustration and anguish, and raises her voice without inhibition against oppression and subjection. Her poetry contains, as Vrinda Nabar puts it, "compulsive candour, a disregard for nice feminine concealments, and an aggressively independent assessment of man-woman relationship" (Nabar 19).

Woman, as depicted in the poetry of Kamala Das, surrenders herself completely to the man she is related with just to feel the warmth of relationship. But her dreams are shattered soon. Failing in what she longs for, she feels strong urge to get liberated from the clutches of dissatisfying relationship in a hostile socio-cultural environment and to pass a happy, healthy life of peace and rest. In one of her poems "I Shall Some Day" Kamala Das writes:

> I shall some day leave, leave the cocoon
> You built around me with morning tea,
> Love-words flung from doorways and of course
> Your tired lust. I shall some day take
> Wings, fly around, as often petals
> Do when free in air....
>
> (*Summer in Calcutta* 52)

Not now but some day and that some day never comes, and so, she has to accept her lot. She bears the subjugation and wears the mask of surrendered self but her emotions explicitly exhibit rebellious roaring- her voice and tone are subdued but her heart is filled with fiery feelings of strong protest. The poems in the three volumes of poetry by Kamala Das—*Summer in Calcutta*, *The Descendants* and *The Old Playhouse and Other Poems*—are replete with the feelings of frustration, anguish and growling. In this paper some most representative poems from all the three volumes have been taken up for exploring the frustration, rebellion and resignation of woman as portrayed by Kamala Das.

She articulates the dejection in her woman persona in 'The Freaks' through the images of repulsion and brings out the emotional emptiness and sterility of her married life. The poem opens with wife's explicit feelings of rejection of her man:

He talks, turning a sun-stained
Cheek to me, his mouth, a dark
Cavern, where stalactites of
Uneven teeth gleam....

(*Summer in Calcutta* 10)

Disgruntled woman does not hide her frustration and groans:

...Can this man with
Nimble finger-tips unleash
Nothing more alive than the
Skin's lazy hungers? Who can
Help us who have lived so long
And have failed in love?

(*Summer in Calcutta* 10)

Kamala Das asserts that the patriarchal conditioning is arbitrarily enforced on woman. The pattern of oppression is not natural but a design to curb her 'urge to fly'. In 'The Old Playhouse', the wife makes a strong protest against the instinct of suppression and possessiveness of her husband who wants her to play a subservient role. She utters her grudging:

You planned to tame a swallow, to hold her
In the long summer of your love, so that she would forget
Not the raw seasons alone, and the home left behind but
Also her nature, the urge to fly and the endless
Pathways of the sky.

(*The Old Playhouse and Other Poems* 1)

Though the voice of her resentment subdues, she complains: "Cowering/ Beneath your monstrous ego I ate the magic loaf and/ Became a dwarf. I lost my will and reason...." (*The Old Playhouse and Other Poems* 1). The woman feels frustrated at the palling summer of her relationship due to 'monstrous ego' of her man and the suffocating atmosphere in the room of their marital bond, lit by artificial lights, closed windows and 'all pervasive male scent' of his breath. She wails over her lot: "There is/ No more singing, no more a dance, my mind is an old/ Playhouse with all its light put out" (*The Old Playhouse and Other Poems* 1).

"The Stone Age" is another poem that depicts an unhappy, rebellious wife uttering her repulsion and warning aloud:

> Fond husband, ancient settler in the mind
> Old fat spider, weaving webs of bewilderment,
> Be kind. You turn me into a bird of stone, a granite
> Dove, you build round me a shabby drawing room,
> (*The Old Playhouse and Other Poems* 51)

When her husband leaves, she drives her 'battered car' to 'the other man' assaulting the dull cocoon of domesticity and asserting her freedom as an act of defiance.

Kamala Das makes her protagonist hammer hard at her husband/partner. She views the bond of marriage as a prison in the patriarchal domestic set-up and expresses her intense desire to break the clutches of captivity. The woman/wife in the 'Substitute' feels betrayed and brawls on the assertion of her husband that their love is only physical:

> Yet I was thinking, lying beside him
> That I loved, and was much loved
> It is physical thing, he sad suddenly,
> End it, I cried, end it, and let us be free.
> (*The Descendants* 7)

Beneath the rebellious façade, however, lurks the true poet who is actually timid and withdrawn. She rebels, growls and wanders but does not break the iron chain of marriage bond and accepts her fate of surrendered self. In *The Descendants* she speaks of the common lot of women:

> We were the yielders,
> Yielding ourselves to everything.
> We shall give ourselves to the fire or to
> The hungry earth to be slowly eaten
> Devoured....
> And she feels "we are not going to be /Ever redeemed, or made new"
> (*The Descendants* 8).

Desperate wife or woman in the poetry of Kamala Das, in spite of being rebellious, accepts her role but devoid of emotional attachment moves in the void periphery of relationship and showing complete detachment surrenders to her man like a corpse. Living a life of subjection within the limitations of marital bond, however, she does not hide her despondency. "The Maggots" reveals this state of her mind:

> That night in her husband's arms, Radha felt
> So dead that he asked, What is wrong,
> Do you mind my kisses, love? And she said,
> No, not at all, but thought, What is
> It to the corpse if the maggots nip?
>
> (*The Descendants* 13)

Her silence speaks of her frustration, her meek surrender, and also her rejection of the relationship. This rejection is nothing else but her way of rebellion.

Kamala Das has depicted her woman protagonist as a rebellion even when she surrenders meekly. Using her art as an act of resistance, she shows us the ways in which small acts of protest and resistance may help change perceptions of people. She attempts to bring into being the symbolic weight of women's consciousness to make the invisible visible and the silent speak. Her rebellion is filled not with fire but with sobs and tears. She does not stamp her foot or shake and clench her fist. With her remarkable sense of honesty and conviction Kamala Das has established an entirely new poetic way to bring out the psyche of exploited, victimized and marginalized woman whose fire of rebellion does not flare but seethes.

Works Cited

Kaur, Iqbal. ed. "I Needed to Disturb Society" *Perspectives on Kamala Das's Poetry*. New Delhi: Intellectual Publishing House, 1995.

Nabar, Vrinda. *The Endless Female Hungers: A Study of Kamala Das*. New Delhi: Sterling Publishers, 1994.

Das, Kamala. "I Shall Some Day", *Summer in Calcutta*. ed. Rajinder Paul. ?: Everest Press, 1965.

———. "The Old Playhouse" *The Old Playhouse and Other Poems*. Madras: Orient Longman, 1973.

———. "Substitute" *The Descendants*. Calcutta: Writers Workshop, 1967.

18

Pieter Dirk Uys' *Just Like Home*: A Search for Home Away from Home

— Shubhra Paikra

Marginalized psyche uncovers the existential angst of the unhoused beings that are dangerously poised between two worlds, and remain without roots or a sense of belonging in either. The forced confirmation to the implied value-system alienates them gradually and the subsequent fragmentation divides the self into two-halves. This split self represents the echoes of the marginalized psyche that keeps pulsating in the interstitial space sharing the heterogeneous features which is nothing but an intersection of the socio-cultured traits between the ruler and the ruled. An unhoused sensibility connotes the psychic dilemma of the 'Marginals' who are conditionally bracketed and thus victimized.

The study of 'Dislocation' on physical social and individual level, has been and important component of colonial and post-colonial critique and enquiry. It attempts to trace out the degree of subjectivity and its consequent impact on the individuality of the colonized. The alienating forces of colonization and the dislocating ones of diasporic and exile aims to keep the 'other' always subjugated. The most consuming malady of the 'subject' is a psychological one: one of depression. The subjectivity thus mars the integrity and autonomy of the human individual.

The dislocated self forms a central subject in Peter Dirk Uys's *Just Like Home*. The play at one instance denotes 'Marginality' as a concept that alienates the subject. At other instance it connotes a 'positionality' that is best defined in terms of the limitations of a subject's access to power. Bill Aschroft, Griffith and Tiffin in *Key Concept in Post Colonial Studies* aptly quoted that 'Marginality' unintentionally reifies centrality because it is the centre that creates the condition of marginality. Imperialism marginalizes and the colonized people are marginalized.

The Marginal thus becomes a victim of a debilitating persecution complex: a psychic state where the subject feels that he/she is trapped. The void within, keeps echoing the words repeatedly that 'I am not whole'. Alienated from the self, the subject descends into the void and is finally bracketed as an exile.

Just Like Home is a powerful play by Peter Dirk Uys, a renowned Afrikaner dramatist. The play skillfully portrays the pain and agony of the African exiles whose identities were brutally crushed by the policy of an 'Apartheid' and the 'Group Areas Act; as a sensible dramatist he knows the landscape of exile where identities are propped up by reliving the past to the extent of play-acting. The dilemma posed by cultural duality and the loss of identity is experienced by the main characters Cathy and Mr. Gupta who share their marginality in the 'other land' as an exile. Their desperate need for selfhood and a spiritual anchor sounds almost pathetic *Just Like Home* artistically echoes the saga of an exile who is forced to construct a distant place or the 'other land' as 'Home', poised between the two worlds with different socio-cultural norms. Andrew Gurr discussed at length on the marginality of such exiles. The existential angst of such unhoused beings forced him to locate their identity. Where is the place of 'home' to be located for such groups? In the place of birth (nateo), in the displaced cultural community into which the person is born or in the nation state in which this diasporic community is located.

The present play attempts to display the functional mode of the settler colonies like South Africa and India whereby the 'native-born' colonial wished to preserve a 'racial' discrimination from the 'natives' that depended on retaining a linkage with the absent homeland.

Out of four the three main characters are African exiles and their past life serves as a main background to the plot construction. The recollections of the past life in Africa unfold its socio-political conditions whereby the racial hierarchy comes on the fore and reveals the brutality of the colonizers. There are four main racial groups in South Africa; the Black Africans made up of some hundred of different tribes officially called as 'Bantu'; the second biggest group is that of the Europeans or Whites split into two parts—the Afrikaners are people of Dutch descent who dominate the political life of South Africa through their Nationalist partly and referred to as 'Boers', then there are the English speaking section which includes 100,000 Jews strong in mining, industry and journalism; the 'Coloureds' form the third dominant group, which are people of mixed descents living mostly in Cape-Province; and the final group is the so-called Indians, who could more correctly be described as Asians since not all of them have Indian origins.

Thus the pluralistic social set-up of South Africa stands as a dominant factor leading to a complex life through the social hierarchy. The Afrikaner accept persons of British origin as equals, but have so organized the country politically as to allow them little say in the conduct of affairs. They look upon Africans (The Blacks) as inferiors who may remain in the Republic provided they work in menial occupations and are content to exercise no political rights outside the reserves set for them. For the Coloreds most Afrikaners feel sympathy, but this cannot, they explain, be translated into action since to do so, would be the 'thin edge of the wedge' that might split the colour bar. In this very context the reaction of the Africans is well quoted by Tom Hopkinson in *South Africa.*

> Some extremist political leaders among the Black Africans increasingly take the view—through the law does not allow them to express it—that the only people with a right to live in south Africa are the Africans themselves and the colored whom they are willing to 'adopt' as being politically homeless. (Hopkinson)

All in all, the population in South Africa is so compounded racially as to form a highly explosive mixture. The policies of the present lay Nationalist government and the forces of change sweeping over the rest of Africa are combining to heat this mixture to a point where the world waits apprehensively for the explosion. The policy of 'Apartheid' was the main explosive that brought a social turmoil in the entire South Africa turning the life of all the Blacks and Coloureds.

The psychic pangs of the exile are very well delineated in the present play. The four main characters are forcibly living an unnatural life in the other land. Cathleen serves as a cook in the famous restaurant 'Taj Mahal' run by Mr. Gupta at London. She is a coloured African who was initially a cook in a Brit family 'The Sharps'. The Sharps were the white Africans who shifted to London during the racial war of South Africa. Cathleen was a bonded labourer and was forced to serve them. So conditionally she was forced to leave her own land and London becomes her second home.

Mr. Gupta too is an exile who shifted to London failing to face the social turmoil in India. Hector was a white African solider who refused to follow the dictates of his Boer surgeant. They ordered him to shoot the Black African kids during the racial war but Hector was compassionate and retorted sharply against that order. Since the Boers are politically superior, he was forced to obey their enforced laws. Hector turned a rebel and shot his boss. He thus flew off to save his life, becoming a political exile in London. Trevor is the nephew of Cathy who has been an active rebel against the Nationalists in South Africa. The Nationalists enforced the policy of Apartheid usurping the natural rights of the Black and Coloured Africans.

Cathleen and Trevor serve as a mouthpiece of the nonwhite majority in South Africa whose lives have been so severely curtailed under the white man's rule. Millions of Africans became exiles in other lands due to their failure to live under the shadow of 'Apartheid'. Cathleen is surprised to meet thousands of such rebellious people living as 'Marginals' in London. She thus exclaims with surprise while talking with Hector:

> But now suddenly every body's here as a refugee who nearly brought down the government back home . . . nearly

> but not quite you know? I never thought I'd meet so many people here who fought apartheid there . . . pity they didn't stay at home and do it properly. So, anyway here they come, all these exiles looking as if they had just come from the hairdresser in sea point and eating my Afrikaan babootie like it was manna from the Promised Land. (*Just Like Home* 189)

The policy of Apartheid was enforced by the Nationalists for an increased degree of separation between the races. Dr. Daniel F. Malan who was Prince Minister from 1948 to 1954 and under whom apartheid, was established wrote quite explicitly about the policy revealing its intention. According to him, theoretically the object of the policy of apartheid could be achieved by dividing the country into two parts with all the whites in one and all the Blacks in the other. For the foreseeable future however this is simply not practical politics.

Consequently the gulf between the two races widened day by day whereby the whites bracketed the Blacks as the Inferiors who would be their subjects forever. Following words of Cathleen very well points out the superiority complex of the whites:

> . . . me standing in the door to the kitchen with my apron on in London England and the master and madam and their fancy expect pals watching our old hometown and bitching about the good times they had making. Money there and then making such horrible comments about those they left behind, superior like they were never part of it once Hector I'm telling you, I hared the cockcrows three times. (*Just Like Home* 189)

The Nationalist produced a spate of legislation designed not only to achieve increased separation of the races but also to render the African legally and economically powerless. The Group Areas Act as its name applies was designed to established segregated areas in which all Africans and others Non whites were obliged to live. Implementation of the 'Act' has inevitably involved the uprooting of thousands of nonwhite families who were living in areas now designated as 'White'. Three quarter of million of people work re-housed but it made life a burden for the Africans. The suffocation of a native African in the ordinary built house is well expressed in Cathy's words:

> Back went the boxes and there trekked the September Family and its cardboard treasures over the sand dunes of the Cape Flats. Then luckily someone died in Athlone out with the cardboard boxes, in with the card board bores, up with the cardboard dividers, making one room four. Yes, that is where the family still is. In a half cardboard house with an outside brick lavatory. (*Just Like Home* 194)

The privileged 'whites' (rulers) on the other hand live in a spacy Bungalow with six or seven attendants, enjoying all sort of luxuries. Cathy ironically points out:

> Polite young Christian cops from good homes, brought up to love God and their neighbour, but not in the same church. Fat white Boere boys. By that I'm ice-cold all over . . . (*Just Like Home* 195)

Every exile tries his/her level best in resisting the homesickness but fails finally. Their roots are very strong and therefore the longingness for the original home is very obvious. The same saga of the unhoused Hector and Cathy is well portrayed when they coincidently met for the first time at Taj Mahal restaurant. Cathy very naturally poured forth her thoughts before Mr. Gupta:

> That very first time he wandered into the Taj Mahal and ordered my curry, and then specially came 'backstage' as he called it, to complement the work and there I stood all hot and sweaty and he said right out : which part of Cape Town are you from ? as if you couldn't tell from just looking at me and all I heard myself say was " Ag Master, I want to go home . . .' We both cried Shame. (*Just Like Home* 200)

The image of the original house keeps resonating within the pulse of every exile living in a foreign land. Although the other land offers its best to these refugees but it is unnatural. Cathy is now an independent woman living a free life as a cook in the 'Taj Mahal'. Mr. Gupta as an owner of the Taj Mahal enjoys his privilege and Hector is a renowned actor who gets a leading role in many T.V. serials but no amount of prosperity can compensate their elemental urge for the original home. They are always painted as 'the other'.

They are dislocated either on individual physical or social level. Thus the locii of the split self is the interstial space. It oscillates between the two worlds belonging to the none. The dialogue between Hector and Cathy reflects this dilemma:

> HECTOR : Yes ; there they kill you with guns !
>
> CATHY : And here I will be killed with kindness. It is a long time since I have heard the dogs barking at me. I miss that too.
>
> (*Just Like Home* 197)

The broken heart just cries painfully finding no solution that could serve as a healing balm. Thus we find Cathy confessing honestly that she has never been happier in her life. Although Cathy, Trevor or Hector are always consciously frightened by the internal conflict of South Africa, still their homesickness sounds very natural. The sense of loss grows day by day. This in turn gradually increases their impulsiveness:

> HECTOR : Yes, imagine hundreds of thousand of exiles marching through Africa, with Miriam Makeba singing and Huge Masekela playing his trumpet.
>
> CATHY : All going house like me.
>
> HECTOR : To build a future for everyone.
>
> (*Just Like Home* 207)

The impulsiveness sounds very natural because the exiles have to compensate everything at the other land, desiring to live a healthy life but at the expense of their personal sentiments. The repressed feeling turns them into a violent reactor. Trevor aptly commented, in Act-II, in this context, 'Anything can happen when there's equality in hatred and violence.'

> But Cathy hopes for a final resolution and question positively;
>
> Ja? And once the comrades have killed all the collaborators and the vigilantes have killed all the radicals, who will remain in to throw a party?
>
> (*Just Like Home* 220)

However Trevor is an active rebel who as an 'anti apartheid' was convicted of aggravated assault and thus he crossed the border of his homeland. So he too is a political exile in London like Hector Prince. But he wishes to be so since the African police takes him now as a dead rebel and his parents life is safe there. This is the irony. The inner turmoil of every rebel is reflected when Trevor says Hector, "Go Home, Hector and if you can, after just one week look at yourself in the mirror and say, 'I once had a conscience." (*Just Like Home* 218).

The Blacks and the Colored suffered all sorts of brutality which goes in the name of the major legislation acts enforced by the Nationalists. So the life of the black man in South Africa is beset by appalling difficulties. He is so hemmed in by laws that he cannot quit his job, or choose a new one or form a union, or go on strike. The coloureds are totally helpless. But still, the motherland has its own bewitching instinct. It is so powerful that any exile in the other land fails to forget it. The fragrance of the other land can tempt them only for a short phase of time, but in the long run they wish to be back; becoming one with their native land.

Thus London to Cathy, Hector, Trevor or Mr. Gupta is 'just like home' but not the actual home. It is a second home; a substituted that lacks the aura of the original home—South Africa or India. So in spite of the internal disturbance Cathy makes her mind to return back to her own land however painful it may be. She is ready to face every odd in her way. Nothing can deter her sprit.

When Hector tested her spirit she confidently proved her excellence:

> HECTOR : After boycotting outspan oranges and Grannie Smith apples for twelve years, you now go back in the belly of the beast ?

CATHY : I'm going back to where the beast live so who cares how . . . ?

(*Just Like Home* 207)

The call of the motherland is so powerful that she boycotted anything that was earned in London, and as a true African she wished to be a part of everything that smelt African. Thus we see that the present play artistically delineates the saga of Cathy, Hector, Mr. Gupta and Trevor sharing the existential pangs in the other land.

Works Cited

Hopkinson, Tom. *South Africa*. 1st Ed. New York: Time-Life Books, 1969.

Uys, Peter Dirk. "Just Like Home." *South Africa Plays*. ed. Gray Stephen. London: NickHern Book, 1993.

19

Lajja: A Voice from the Margin

— Somali Gupta

Nobody told me to protest, but from an early age I developed strong feelings about the importance of fighting against oppression. Nobody asked me to shed a tear, but I did. Today, as I speak, I know that many are being killed. Today, as I speak, many women are being beaten, raped, and murdered. Today, I know, many children are being abused because of hatred and intolerance. The challenge is to educate the world's peoples about tolerance and non-violence. The challenge is to make the Earth livable. Tolerance is a concept that recognizes everyone's human right and everyone's fundamental freedom. People are naturally diverse, and it is only through tolerance that diversity will survive.

"I have cried loudly for equality and justice, justice for all people whatever their religion and gender. I have spoken loudly for the separation of religion and state, for secular law, for secular education.

"During my struggle for a secular and ethical humanism, I tried to defend the poor and also the ethnic and religious minority communities that were being oppressed. It was impossible for me to accept the idea that people living miserable lives did so because they had a different faith, or spoke a different language, or had a different culture. I believe that the diversity of our world's many religions, languages, cultures and ethnicities is not a pretext for conflict, but is a treasure that enriches us all. Diversity is a treasure to be appreciated. There is no superior, no inferior culture in this world, only various cultural patterns that makes up our beautiful multicolored mosaic.

"But, humans should not allow oppression in the name of religion. Humans should not allow torture such as female genital mutilation in the name of custom or tradition. Humans should not allow barbarism, humiliation, inequality, or injustice in the name of culture. Culture should not be and must not be used against humanity." (Nasrin)

They say God created earth and then created some living creatures. They also say that amongst all the living beings he created, Human Beings are his most loved ones. But then human beings started searching for God. They found him in different things. These different things gave birth to different beliefs. And these beliefs in turn gave birth to religions. Now human beings didn't stop at this. They started debating about whose beliefs are true and whose are false. These debates started growing denser and at a point broke into violent physical fights. Hatred had already taken birth. And to add to it, the newborn baby was taught religious differences. So now the hatred grew hereditary. Every father gave his son his land, his money and hatred he had for other religions. Now we have a scenario where humans fight each other for their respective religions. But hey, where is God in the picture? We seem to be on a battlefield of religions where no God stays. Maybe they have turned the God's earth in a 'No God's Land. Let's go to two such lands on this very earth—India and Bangladesh.

Taslima Nasrin's *Lajja* tells a tale of a family caught up as a victim member of a minor community at the hands of the majority in Bangladesh at the times of riots. The controversial novel is an example of religious extremism and man's inhumanity to man. The novel exposes the mindless bloodthirstiness of fundamentalism and also captures brilliantly the insanity of violence of modern times.

Lajja, written by Taslima Nasrin is one book, which changed the author's life forever. The book was banned in Bangladesh for 'creating misunderstanding between communities', soon after it was published. It was then rewritten in Bengali for sale in India and then translated in English for the same. A fatwa was announced to kill Taslima Nasrin and an award was announced for the one who would carry out the activity. Her work was called as an assault on Islam and she earned the wrath of Islamic fundamentalists and clergy. Prior to *Lajja*, Taslima was known for her poems, which were primarily against the sexual abuses and violent assaults on females in the society.

The religious riots that happened in Bangladesh, had a strong effect on the author's mind due to which she chose to write the truth Conversion to Islam at that point of time was probably the most respectable thing to do in Bangladesh, and that is precisely what many did to save their skin and honour. Taslima's was probably the lone dissenting voice, and was indeed a pretty loud one; loud enough to cause sufficient distress to the local religious leaders, who took adequate care to ensure her permanent exit from her homeland. In her own words she became a 'stranger in her own country'. Regarding her current status she writes:

> I am, in other words, a stranger in my own country and a stranger here in the west where I am living now. Where can I go? Nowhere. Exile, for me, is a bus stop where I am waiting for a bus to go home. I have been living in exile for more than 10 years. I still do not feel that any home is my home, any country my country. Mine is a hopeless, helpless feeling. Sometimes I ask myself, is this true, do I really have no home? Actualty it's not true. I do have a home. My home is love, the love I receive from women all over the world. That is my home, the love I receive from rationalists, free thinkers, secularists, and humanists is my home. The love I receive from you is my home. (Nasrin)

Lajja, is set in the backdrop of the Babri Masjid demolition saga, back in the year 1992, which caused a strong religious, political and social impact, and resulted in riots in sensitive areas throughout the subcontinent. The stage is set in Bangladesh and the tale revolves around an extremely patriotic Hindu family. Suranjan, a prodigal middle-aged man with little or no accomplishment in his life to boast about, is a son of a doctor (Sudhamoy) with strong national values. Sudhamoy supported his clan during the national movement and worked for the cause of the nation and in turn, his own countrymen for whom he stood for, rewarded him by mutilating his genitals! Despite all this, he strongly believed that Bangladesh was his home and refused to move to Kolkata (India). An atheist, he believed with optimism that his motherland won't let him down. From the Partition of 1947, to the relatively recent Independence of Bangladesh in the 70s, he had lived and participated through every kind of struggle that his country had to endure. His fundamental ideology in life was, "Why should I leave my homeland and go somewhere else? If I live it will be on this soil and if I die it will be in the very same place" (*Lajja*).

Sudhamoy Dutta's ideas were courageous and blatantly patriotic. His belief was that a he was Bengali first and a Hindu later. Unfortunately, the system in which he lived did not allow such ideals to flourish and repeatedly he was reminded of his minority status in society, whether in the matters of career or personal life. His fight for survival, literally, put him on stake many times. His decisions and choices are what lead his family into an unfair trial, which forms the crux of the plot.

Suranjan despite being deprived of opportunities due to his religious background, very much like his father, loved his motherland. The young blood of the nation, he had ideals similar to his father's but only stronger ten-fold. For him, his country, the way he'd always seen it, was what it was. Religion was the last thing he considered during his daily endeavors and he believed himself to be no different from any of his Muslim friends and acquaintances. He refused to even acknowledge the fact that he had less of access to his fundamental rights just because his religion was not in majority in the country. How his ideas come crashing down like pack of cards and put his family into danger is the high point of the narrative.

Sudhamoy's wife Kiranmoyee is depicted as a very kind and a loveable character that stands by her husband and her family during the testing times. Their daughter Maya, a vivacious lady is distraught with compatriots' attitude towards them and her family's idealism to remain in their country even during the hour of peril. As the sole breadwinner of the house, she is concerned about her family's safety and disappointed with her brother for being unable to protect her family in a time when her family's religion had become their biggest enemy. With hopes and dreams for a better life ahead, she prefers to follow the path of safety, than a fight for righteousness. The story speaks about the atrocities and cruelties inflicted on Hindus in general and Sudhamoy's family in particular during the riots. The story is gripping and the climax is extremely poignant.

At one level it talks about the indignities heaped on a Hindu family of four, right from the time of Bangladesh's liberation. The book brilliantly essays the lives of the minority community in the repressed and restricted environment of the Bangladeshi life. It talks about a Bengali Hindu family who kept hanging on their Sonar Bangla pride despite of things turning worse with each passing day as communal tension gripped the entire country. The book is set during the post Babri Masjid demolition which hurt the religious egos of human beings following Islam. Riots broke out in different parts of this subcontinent. Minorities in their respective homelands were being hounded out and massacred in the name of Religion. In that backdrop, Taslima has brought out chronologically the events that led to the situation that prevailed at that time in Bangladesh.

Let us understand that there was no special emphasis on Hindu hatred in Bangladesh because the same was dynamics operated in certain parts of India too. In Bangladesh, which is a totally different country, Muslims burnt down the Hindu fields, drove away people from their homes, raped the women leaving them with no other option but either to embrace Islam or embrace death. Taslima depicts brilliantly the agony and pain of being a woman when hatred spreads or the virus of communalism rears its ugly visage. It's the women who suffer the most and who more often then not are victims to gruesome acts of cruelty in the name of religion and God. They are assaulted not only physically but also emotionally and their very motherhood becomes a target for the mob. They would molest a woman and in the name of being the self-proclaimed votaries of religion they would force themselves upon her so that the next generation is born to their religion. The story of the Hindu girl in this novel talks about this same hatred, lajja or shame.

One can draw a parallel between the girl of Taslima's novel to that of the main protagonist, again a girl in Sadat Hasan Manto's 'Kali Sarwar', the latter being set during partition times when communal frenzy was at its peak. The gruesome depiction of communal hatred in both Manto and Taslima's book through the medium of the exploitation of the women is indeed telling and painful. Every time the girl is molested she is per force converted to the religion that the perpetrators of the crime belong to, who feel they have fulfilled their moral responsibility by doing so. In the end the poor girl is just reduced to a bundle of flesh. The story is numbing and makes one abhorrent of what had happened then and now in the name of the pious religions we all swear allegiance to.

The cover page of *Lajja* shows a grayscale photograph of a woman with a veil over her head covering the lower half of her face. 'LAJJA' glows in blood red fonts below with a red subscript 'SHAME'. The cover page says 'SHAME'; Shame on us human beings for making our earth an ugly place to stay in. Lajja is a Hindi word for Shame. Here Shame is for being a human being lost deep in the illusions of religious identities.

Nasrin not only presents the dreadful realities hidden under the false claims of equalitarian societies, but also depicts the inevitable psychological devastation that individuals endure in the circumstances of widespread terror. Her account of a family in trouble sheers the heart with a painful guilt of understanding and recognising the relatively insignificant ways in which discrimination takes place on a daily basis. Using factual figures of instances of death and destruction in Bangladesh, she is able to highlight the unknown events that often go unnoticed among the politically and socially more 'important' happenings.

The question, which comes up then, is why are the so-called votaries of religion so disturbed by the bitter truth brought forth by a litterateur. *Lajja* talks about the impact any religion has on minds of people irrespective of their countries or geographical boundaries. A Hindu in a country relates with a Hindu in any other country. A Muslim in a country relates with a Muslim in any other country. But the same cannot be said about a Hindu and a Muslim in the same country. Why? What makes them hate each other? Is the base of something known as a religion enough for someone to hate or even think of hatred about a fellow being? This is a topic which won't ever end till our human race doesn't end killing each other in the name of religions. *Lajja* literally means Shame and true to its title, I believe, that every right thinking human being, after reading this book would be ashamed of the religious fanatism that exists today in different parts of the world.

Lajja is Nasrin's exposition of true and real life hatred that runs in the veins and arteries of religious fanatics and fundamentalists of our subcontinent. Though the novel is rooted in Bangladesh, the story wouldn't be different in any other country, be it our own India or our esteemed neighbours Pakistan. Taslima in her tale buttresses her fiction with facts. Her attempt in this book is not to malign any religion, it is an earnest entreat to the human race to embrace humanity and shun fanatism.

Works Cited

Nasrin, Taslima. Interview. Kolkata, 12 April 2005.

_______. *Lajja*. New Delhi: Penguin Books India, 2000.

20

Destructive Impact of Human Tensions in *Cry, the Peacock*, *Voices in the City*, and *Fire on the Mountain*

— Sucheta Mukherjee

We know that tension takes form only in the human mind, so it cannot be segregated from man; only the degree varies from individual to individual. In Desai's novels also, many internal frustrations arise out of psychological barriers in the form of reality and ethical controls. When this reality and ethical restrains breakdown, her characters get involved in self-recrimination and a feeling of guilt follows.

Desai in the process has justifiably concentrated on unusual characters that inhabit the world of *Cry, the Peacock*, *Voices in the City* and *Fire on the Mountain*. In these three novels, the setting is similar mainly because the protagonists revolt in some way or the other. In doing so, they bring about destruction on themselves and others. Only the degree of their agitation and indignation varies. Her characters, in these circumstances react emotionally and vehemently. They also suffer from loneliness which gives rise to the feeling of insecurity. Their psychological problems leave a restraining effect on their mutual relationships.

In this connection Coleman has rightly observed, "Feelings of insecurity may have widely differing effects on behaviour, but typically they lead to a restriction in activities to fearfulness an apprehension and a failure to participate fully in one's world" (Coleman). Because of this insecure feeling, Desai's characters do suffer and cause suffering for others.

Cry, The Peacock (CP 1960) by Anita Desai presents the story of a young, hypersensitive and neurotic woman named Maya. The novel unfolds with a gloomy atmosphere with a description of her pet, Toto's death. This incident upsets her so much that she finds it impossible to endure the psychological strain. Because of her un-reigned imagination, she feels that death was stealing around her which she could not avoid. The sad demise of Toto produces a terrifying sense of doomsday in her. She suffers from prescience.

Desai has brought about this special aspect of Maya's character to suggest that how sensitive she is. It is the first inkling that the reader gets about Maya's emotional over-sensitivity, which ultimately brings about the catastrophe. In a way she suffers from the tragic flaw that brings about her tragic end.

A cosseted and mollycoddled daughter of a wealthy brahmin, Maya suffers from acute father fixation. As a result, even after her marriage, she looks for the father image in her husband, Gautam, who is also twice her age. She misses the much-needed support from Gautama which gave rise to the feelings of negligence. This suffering gives rise to tension. Of course this tension is self-created. Her deep interest in art, literature and music, probably makes her more sensitive and introspective. In Gautam's family, they debate not only on social problems but political matters also showing their vast knowledge and awareness in variegated fields. But Maya knowing her incompetence cannot join them.

As a result she becomes an easy victim of inferiority complex. So, if this kind of feeling is maintained for long, it not only promotes the cause of tension but self-hate also as the same happens to Maya. According to Abraham Maslow's Theory, every man has the 'Desire to Belong'. Maya in her state of frustration either cries or vents her anger through pillow beating:

> Yes, I whimspered, it is that I am alone, and then gave myself upt a fit of furious pillow beating, kicking, everything but crying. From childhood experience, I knew this to be sweetly exhausting. (CP 9)

To keep her identity intact, we always find Maya in search of some pretext to let out her tensions because it acts as a safety valve. Till she is able to ventilate her tensions, she takes the help of these outbursts. Her condition is well defined by Robert E. Egner:

> Every isolated passion is in isolation, insane; sanity may be defined as a synthesis of insanities. Every dominant passion generates a dominant fear, the fear of its non-fulfillment. Every dominant fear generates a nightmare, some time in the form of an explicit and conscious fanaticism, some times in a paralyzing timidity, some times in an unconscious or subconscious terror which finds expression only in dreams. (Egner 21)

Desai has repeatedly stressed on her loneliness. She has insisted in different novels that loneliness is one of the darkest problems of human existence. But inevitably man tries to overcome his loneliness.

Following the dramatic technique of novel writing, Desai has juxtaposed the characters of Leila and Pomwith Maya. We find that Leila, who is actually suffering in the hands of fate, tries to be reasonably, happy. Pom also had made adjustments and molded herself to the desires of her in-laws. She has no grudge against them but Maya that has no reason to be sad is always in a sick mood. Occasionally, she is aware of her weaknesses and is knowledgeable enough to analyze her reactions.

Her traumatic experience is handled carefully by Gautama, which for the time being calms the storm. But it is not the end. It ends with murder-death and in between there are frequent references to death.

Gautama's dislike for physical communion at the time of emergency gives her the feeling of being spurned by him. Since her neurotic pride is hurt, she feels that she had been let own. Discovering to have no savior whom she can cling to, she experiences a damaging blow. On the other hand Gautama is least concerned with her world of senses. Although normal in every way, he is averse to any physical nearness. A glimpse of his bygone life reveals the reason of this reticence. His life was full of responsibilities, which later developed in him the quality of reserve and restrain. Desai has suggested that childhood experiences leave an impact on the future of man. Gautama apparently is afraid of showing his emotions and so avoids intimacy as it leads to the disclosure of the self.

Maya is unable to wipe out the picture of the priest from her conscience because she is weak and as psychologists say, omen, Prophesy etc., have a greater impact on impressionable minds. This leads to the feeling of insecurity. Gautama in this regard tries to eliminate her fear by alluding to Gita quite often, but all in vain. Thus to hide her deficiencies, she makes herself believe that she is superior to most of the weak mortals. Her exaggerated idea about herself in fact had no connection with reality. All hopes broke down one by one as she was no spirit of nature but an ordinary woman fated to confront all the troubles of existence or else fade away from the picture of life forever. Desai presents Maya's stream of consciousness. From these, she wishes to escape but knows that there is no escape. Only delusions about the world, gives her a sense of security. She dreads the real, the substantial. She demands extra attention from others when denied, be it by her in-laws or friends, failure and defeat causes more depression and frustration. Psychologist Coleman has said, "Anger and hostility are aroused by obstacles blocking need gratification; they lead to a direct attack on such obstacles and efforts to remove them" (Coleman 75). This dread helps to generate many unknown fear besides the constant fear of death lying deep down in the heart of Maya.

Since she believes on self preservation, she convinces herself that, as Gautama does not love life and gives no value to her demands. So he should no have right to exist. She kills him in a rage by flinging him down from the terrace. Destiny yet had many more miseries in store for her. She gets haunted with the feeling of guilt and this psychological imbalance drags her to the world of complete darkness and destruction.

Maya's life mainly erupts from the husband-wife relationship. Though there were other causes also. Maya's relation with her mother-in-law is not very smooth. They have love-hate relationship between them. Her greedy temperament and materialistic attitude creates tension for Maya.

Tensions faced by Gautama and other minor characters have also been highlighted. But their positive attitude helps them to curb out everyday tension and create a harmonious state of existence. Desai seems to suggest that in the busy contemporary world where there is no one to lend a willing ear, an emotional person has eligible chances of leading a normal life. Her technical triumph is undisputed in this novel. It has three equal segments. Unlike the first and he third, the middle segment is very long and descriptive giving a detailed analysis of the protagonist. The first segment deals with the apprehensions and clashes between the two important artists that is Gautama and Maya. Last segment has the sardonic view of the universe where he protagonist has no place to exist and the character of Nila is given the role of the observer narrator because Maya with her mental abnormality was no longer in a state to describe he facts logically.

She uses images as an influential technique to produce the sensibilities and the tragic vision of life, with which she remains preoccupied. The lunar image occupies a significant place as it conveys the ultimate end of her husband in a tragic way. Images of Kathakali dance denote the growing violence in Maya. Maya's longing for freedom is revealed through the dust storm image. The mirror image denotes Maya's dual state of mind. Through albino priest, Desai has presented the concept of fate used by Greek dramatists. It would be wrong to suggest that she is a fatalist. Her intention was only to suggest that under he circumstances and the negative prompting from the priest, one would act as Maya acts. Maya is the story of many Indian women. Through this novel Anita Desai has painted the myriad tensions of Human Life and the ultimate result.

Voices in the City (VC 1965), concentrates more on the psychological problems of the characters than the physical ones. Calcutta city is not a vague reference but a living metropolis, affecting the life of the inhabitants. Her narration joins the four parts into a whole structure. Once Desai had asserted that her aim was to explore and then to convey the significance of things and reality, to her readers. While doing so, she wanted to bead together her effective language, appealing symbols, striking images to produce a startling effect. Ramesh K. Srivastava has presented an interesting viewpoint, "In her novel *Voices in the City*, Ania Desai writes about the predicaments of various artists groping for a vision, and aim, a path conducive to the development of healthy art in a city, which destroys as it creates" (Srivastava 88). The story of the novel is all about-facing, single-handed the ferocious assaults of existence in this world. Monisha one of the central characters along with Nirode faces this problem of existence. Her life as a married woman in the joint family becomes so unbearable that she feels stifled, suffocated in it. Her sister Amla confronts failure after failure in her life, yet she does not opt for the same fate of Monisha. The feeling of loneliness and a sense of tremendous isolation is brought into focus by presenting the jungle city of Calcutta, which is over populated. In spite of this crowd, all three characters- Nirode, Monisha and Amla are lonely. All of them aim for something, motivated by the same force. But they fail in the end. The mutual relationships of these three major characters, their mother's extra-marital relationship clouds their psychological reactions. Nirode's position is something like that of Hamlet, who loves his mother excessively yet cannot forgive her. This is a cross that he has to bear being hypersensitive. It is only Monisha's death that ultimately cements their personal relationship.

This novel is like a puzzle where achievement is inversely related to action. Monisha achieves nothing dies frustrated; Amla achieves something through her action but is not satisfied fully; Nirode also fails to achieve except reconciliation with his family. Desai seems to be projecting that mere honest action may not always lead to happiness and the evils of disintegration can reach the good of integration as it happens with Nirode. The picture is completed with the introduction of two other minor characters, Dharma and David. They are brought into focus as contrast to the people in the city who apparently have solved the problems of living. Artificiality of the city life is projected through the ambitious wife of a businessman who poses to be devoted to the Indian culture.

This novel also depicts the absence of love, whether it is in the life of a man in a society or an artist who is generally true to his emotions. The misfortune hampers the development and as in Monisha's case leads to catastrophe. The lack of love demolishes the expected performance of man. In this gloomy and dreary earth, love and the ability to develop original ideas in a creative way, along may give some true hope to mankind. Nirode's example proves the point. He, after his depression, recuperates through Amla's care and finds consolation in the pleasant company of his friends. Even their mother feels rescued from the life of loneliness as she comes back to the main stream of family life. Tragedy happens only with Monisha who misguided by her emotions, fails to appreciate the values of human relationship.

Desai here stresses the loss of man's basic values and individuality that leads to tension of which Nirode is an apt example. Bande rightly commented:

> As Nirode's basic needs have been frustrated, he alienates himself from his essential nature; his value system is damaged. He accepts neurotic values. Thereby developing Neurotic wants which are destructive, both for self and for others. (Bande 73)

Voices in the City has been divided in to four chapters and they respectively deal with four major characters Nirode, Monisha, Amla and mother. Nirode is like a transient vagabond fleeting in the non-conformist world of Calcutta. Being an idealist, he fails at the materialistic front and experiences vacuum which leads to more tension and depression. Imprisoned in a cell of miseries, which has no door to freedom, get nothing but failure. His search for the meaning in life ends in disappointment, except a few realizations of truth. The root of his tensions begins at home. His early realization of the existing contempt between his mother and father hampers normal growth. Nirode's father's partiality towards his younger brother corrodes him with hate. As a result he is deprived of self-confidence and also faith on others. To avoid pain, he moves away from human beings. He rejects life, glories in his failures but since his failures have made him vindictive by nature, he humiliates others.

A representative youth of twenty for years, Nirode, plays an influential role in the novel. He is unstable, fidgety, talkative and a lawless person. As the novel beings, he is seen to have come to see off his younger brother Arun at the Howrah Railway Station, leaving for higher education. He compares his own blazing failures with his brother's achievements. Nirode suffers from mother obsession. He cannot just tolerate his mother's misdemeanor because it desecrated the ethical and social precepts. So deprived of strengthening touch, he undergoes intense feelings of loneliness. Posing to be a stoic, he deceives himself.

Part two of the novel describes the breached life of Monisha, the married sister of Nirode. Her terms with her husband, Jiban, are marked by isolation and lack of communication. In a distraught manner she tries to find out the actual meaning of her life. Through her diary, we come to know that the absence of 'The Element of Love' has made Nirode and herself 'such abject rebels, such craven tragedians'. Having distressingly failed to gain her mother-in-laws affection and her husband's love she turns towards Nirode for his understanding company. Inwardly seeks for her mother's love but finds the homely surrounding stifling. In vain she searches for her private cloister, where she can cherish her personal pleasures. She is 'whole' only when she is alone. Neither the city nor her family provides the opportunity of being alone. This is one of the dominant causes of her tension

Monisha is a great admirer of Kafka's novels. It reflects her world. Her longing for a little privacy makes it impossible to adjust herself in the alien world of a joint family. Her perceptive disposition and academic background does not make it easy for her to compromise in an orthodox joint family whose associates continuously violate and infringe on her personal likes and dislikes. Jiban's restrained agreement in their united claim hurts her most. This humiliating situation becomes the turning point of Monisha's life. Being disillusioned and frustrated she takes the self-destructive step. Tension escalates when the feeling of inadequacy as a wife and daughter-in-law engulfs her. Emotional incompatibility with her husband acts as fuel in fire.

Desai's portrayal of a sensitive character shows that emotional characters are misfits in the material world. Either they are forced to compromise or are destroyed. After the complex character of Monisha, we come to Amla, a bit more open than her sister, in the third section of the novel. Having completed her training as a commercial artist in Bombay, Amla comes to Calcutta in search of better opportunities in some private company. She visits all glamorous places with a view to enjoy life. Amidst the unfamiliar brother and emotionally disturbed sister, Amla feels lonely. A sense of emptiness strikes and shatters her badly. The description of Jit Nair, that they are a family of 'self-destructive' characters and Aunt Leila's admonitions that she belongs to a generation of 'Diseased' young men and women, becomes the cause of her tension. Her realization that she cannot help her sister Monisha creates mental disturbances in her. She realizes that initially she had ignored the 'real and rough lives in the city', of her brother and sister. Gaining a deep understanding of the complex situation matures her considerably.

To avoid such unpleasant experiences, Amla had flown out of the nest and decided to follow the life of a career woman. The relationship between Amla's parents had gone sour and each of the children had experienced its onslaught. Since Amla too had missed the emotional satisfaction coming from her family, she developed a feeling of affection for Dharma, a painter by profession. But his callous attitude towards his own daughter shocked her; as a result, all admiration melts away. Dharma, a strong character benefits from these various hardships of life and later turns into a sensible and matured painter of portraits. But for Amala it was a sad experience. Her tension filled mind is communicated to us through her dream in which she repeatedly sees a crawling insect emerging from her blue-stoned ring.

The fourth section of the novel is titled 'Mother'. It deals with the mother's problems and her view point. To her, life has been a total waste. The reason is that she was forced to spend the best part of her life with a callous drunkard husband. She had grown an impregnable shell around her to protect her sensitive nature from her husband's animal like behaviour. One can well imagine her tortures in the hands of her inebriate husband.

In India, womanhood is enshrined, specifically in motherhood. A mother is allocated with the most significant activity of bearing and bringing up children mother had also the occasion to prove that she had a great power and control over herself. She was the embodiment of the concept of self-denial. But Arun's marriage to a British nurse in England, Monisha's suicide, Nirode's merciless efforts to exterminate individuality forces her to realize the height of alienation in them, caused by her. She decides never to become sentimental about human relationships. Their family tensions have a redeeming effect on her.

Desai has used human tensions as a destroying and creative factor. The voices of the city go against the individuals. Her success lies in portraying the over populated Calcutta city in all its distorting hideous shabbiness. To portray the truth concealed behind the City, Desai has used symbols and images. The appearance of fog vapours and air not only depict the external realities but also the internal chaos, the thwarting and stifling condition of life. Light and dark images are the hallmark of frightening and upsetting dreams of Nirode and Monisha's spirit indicating their psychological storms, genuine disorder and useless longing for solitude. The image of Goddess Kali is very aptly placed in the novel. Monisha remembers the earth mother when she watches the performing street singer. This mingling of the image is symbolic of the mixing of reality with myth. Monisha's frustration unconsciously compels her to identify herself with the weak, tortured woman. In such circumstances her release can only come through self-destruction. The novel being an extraction from Monisha's thought process is put into first person narration. The other three segments are depicted by the novelist herself. In conclusion, one is tempted to say that though in this novel Desai has presented the concepts of destroyer and preserver yet the final note is not pessimistic.

Fire on the Mountain (FM 1977) is a story of a woman, Nanda Kaul, with a built in streak of feminism. In her younger days, much against her desire, the world was too much with her. She had been the target of all her near and dear ones, who had milked her dry. Her tension ridden mind had craved for release and at last after the death of her husband she had found it in Kasauli, a small Himalayan town. The novel reveals the tensions of human life but the pattern is slightly different. If Maya and Monisha, to a great extent are responsible for creating tension for them, Nanda Kaul the protagonist, experiences tension because it is thrust on her by others. She seeks solitude and wishes to lead a life of detachment. But tension begins all over again with the arrival of her great grandchild.

This novel is divided into three segments and they respectively concentrate on particular incidents, which are equally important. In the beginning we come to know about Nanda Kaul's much cherished" Peace" to be disturbed by a letter containing the information of the arrival of an unwanted guest whom she considers to be "A mosquito flown up from the plains to tease and worry" (FM 40). That guest is none other than her own great grand child Raka. Nanda Kaul had been suddenly compelled to jump into the well of tension. Otherwise before the arrival of the letter, she was apparently enjoying serenity and peace. After a hectic life of harsh responsibilities and duties, her recognition as a hardworking, considerate mother, wife, etc. was always neglected. Theunhappy memories of the past create tension in her. Balram Guptahas rightly commented, "Her past keep surging up in the memory and these reminiscences uncontrollable ripples in her consciousness" (Gupta).

That is why the emptiness of the small town attracts her and she enjoys being left alone. But the question that begs our attention is, that 'was she really happy before Raka's arrival?'

The fact is, man can never wipe out the past memories of the bygone days that stop her from enjoying a smooth life. We drift away to the pages of memory of Nanda Kaul when she was called the Vice-Chancellor's wife. Her husband was actually a great cause of tension for her. His affair with Miss David, the mathematics teacher could not give her any peace though she played the role of a deaf and dumb.

At last Raka arrives. Though they live under the same roof, yet, Nanda Kaul and Raka, try to keep distances between each other. "Both Guard their respective freedoms?" (FM 9). But being matured enough they are bound to collide, no matter where and how. The 'unwelcome' and 'reproachful' look naturally creates tensions for both. It is a problem of human relationships. There are instances when we find that Nanda wants to love Raka, but it is Raka who shuns all her tenderness viciously. To our surprise we find the old lady now more apprehensive as she can very well read Raka's rejection. Raka avoids her when she stresses to give her company for a walk. Nanda Kaul changes gradually with Raka's arrival. We see her taking interest in life, going to places with Raka. If in the beginning Raka is an alien who disturbs her peace of mind, now, she creates tension by not accepting Nanda's positive moods. So Nanda Kaul is in a peculiar dual state of mind.

Desai projects Nanda Kaul as an introvert. The reason may be her unhappy relationship with her children. Usha Pathania comments, "The relationship between Nanda Kaul and her children is also intriguing and ungratifying" (Pathania 112).

Nanda Kaul deceives herself by insisting that she wants a life of a recluse. To carry on the act, her meeting with Ila Dasin the novel is not a happy one. Both of them had been together since their childhood. Ila Das was ever smiling and chattering incessantly. She has no grudge against her destiny. She is presented as a contrast. A sincere social worker, sheis raped and killed by Preet Singh. Desai seems to throw light on the fact hat suffering in human life is inevitable. One cannot just check the chain of events that can take place in one's life. None can live in a state of complete isolation. That is why Ila's death moves Nanda and she is unable to disown Raka at her arrival.

She embraces her as if waiting for her. But she fears the repetition of the past as she lacks the strength and stamina of the past. The issues of fulfilment and dissatisfaction which has great and deep impact on the parent-child relationships cannot be just done away with so easily. Raka as a child has different tensions and moments of anxiety. She is deprived of parental affection because her mother is physically incapable of doing so and the father is an alcoholic. These unpleasant happening and chaos in life, have a disintegrating effect on Raka's personality. She learns to shrink and becomes a "Freak by virtue of never making demand. She appeared to have no needs" (FM 47).

Nanda Kaul correctly compares Raka with herself and finds "her great grand daughter was a recluse by nature, by instinct. Her experiences in life had made her personality perverted. The novel is an interesting study of the protagonist's psychology. It is a dismal but truthful picture of life. Nanda's long life as a wife, mother, a great grand mother had given her nothing but frustration, dissatisfaction, worry, tension and anxiety. Her dream world is shattered firstly by her great grand-daughter's appearance in her well-guarded recluse like life and secondly by Raka's failure to respond to her bottled up affections. This is the story of human life and relations. All the characters constantly encounter with a variety of sufferings and conflicts that in return gives rise to myriad tension. Nanda in the end condemns herself for Ila's death. The death-wish works on her psyche. This psychic-death is followed by Physical death. Like Monisha and Maya, in a way, she brings about her own death. Raka because of the inherent rage and tension sets the mountain on fire and destroys life. That is her reaction to the tension-ridden existence. Again, Desai bares the truth that tensions have an annihilating effect on all.

Works Cited

Bande, Usha. *The Novels of Anita Desai*. New Delhi: Prestige Books, 1988.

Coleman, J. C. *Abnormal Psychology and Modern Life*. Bombay: D.B. Taraporevala Sons & Co., 1969.

Desai, Anita. *Cry, the Peacock*. New Delhi: Orient Paperbacks, 1965.

_______. *Fire on the Mountain*. New Delhi: Allied, 1977.

______. *Voices in the City*. New Delhi: Orient Paperbacks, 1965.

Egner, Robert E. *Bertrand Russels's Besat*. New York: New American Library, 1975.

Gupta, Balram "Anita Desai's Fire on theMountain: A Fictional Metaphor of Existentialist Philosophy" *Perspective on Anita Desai*. ed. Ramesh K. Srivastava. Ghaziabad:Vimal Prakashan, 1984.

Pathania, Usha. "The Filialties—A Bane: Fire on the Mountain" *The Fiction of Anita Desai*. ed. R.K. Dhawan. New Delhi: Bahri Publications, 1989.

Srivastava, Ramesh K. "Artists in Voices in the City" *The Fiction of Anita Desai*. ed. R.K. Dhawan. New Delhi: Bahri Publications, 1989.

21

Rediscovering and Centring Igbo Society: A Study of *Things Fall Apart*

— Swetanjali Pradhan

> O born in days when wits were fresh and clear,
> And life ran gaily as the sparkling Thames;
> Before this strange disease of modern life,
> With its sick hurry, it divided aims.
>
> —Mathew Arnold

Africa, a 'dark' continent of dense forest cannibals, and wild life is no longer a gloomy continent. The silence of thick forest, the beautiful landscapes, the throbbing Congo drums and the primitive customs of Africa have prompted the world. African fiction emerges as a kind of reaction to the Eurocentric version of the Africa portrayed in terms of 'a savage' inhabiting 'a dark continent'. African fiction, the so-called Black Literature, is very much ceased with the traumatic experiences, the scars of which are left behind by colonialism. African novel has been able to establish a tradition and an aesthetic of its own in a short span of time. The phenomenal role played by the African fiction is to involve the people in a nation building activity. Chinua Achebe, Ngugi Wa Thiong'o's novels are committed to this task.

Chinua Achebe, the doyen of modern African writing in English has emerged as a novelist and spokesperson of Africa with the publication of his first major novel *Things Fall Apart* which was awarded the Margaret Wong Memorial Prize. Achebe dispassionately mirrors the strength and weaknesses of the Igbo traditional society in his work. His novels are refreshing, entertainment, didactic and informative. His novels attempt a spiritual search for roots and a rediscovery of African's past.

Chinua Achebe has established himself as a writer of the Post Colonial era. He has established African literature as per the emerging genre in the world literature. Achebe, a major exponent of African literature, has been successful in placing Africa, its culture and literature in the world map.

Things Fall Apart (1958) Achebe's first novel is an excellent piece of work in which Achebe delineates the true picture of Africa in the form of Fiction. He makes an effort to enable the world understand 'Igbo' society's ethics in true sense. In this novel he indicates the facts that Igbo community has its own way of life, philosophy, set of values rules and beliefs. The superstition and rigidity of the Igbo people may not appeal to the world, but they are not meaningless and have a peculiar relevance which can not be refuted. This has enabled him to recreate the past glory of Africa and establish its worth among the Africans and the people of the Western world.

Achebe assumes for himself the roles of 'a cultural nationalist, explaining the traditions of his people to largely hostile world, and a teacher, instilling dignity into his own people' (Achebe "The Role of the Writer in a New Nation" 1557).

Achebe's commitment to show to the Western world and his own world that Africa carries with it a glorious past history, tradition and culture is reflected in *Things Fall Apart.* He has presented the cultural legacy of Igbo society with all its minute details. This maiden novel is like his return to his past—past rituals and roots. He himself observes: "Although I did not set about it consciously in that solemn way I now know that my first book, *Things Fall Apart*, was an act of atonement with my past, the ritual return and homage of a prodigal son" (Ogungbesan). People with great achievements are revered. Their achievement is associated with their skill at war and at producing barns of yam. *Things Fall Apart* opens with a declaration of Okonkwo, the chief protagonist's, fame and achievement. He had won a wrestling match upon Amalinze, the cat. Not only this he had shown great skill at war, moreover, his hard work at field has also earned him fame as a farmer. On the other hand Okonkwo's father Unoka was a failure and therefore, was laughed at and Okonkwo hated him for his failure:

> Unoka, the grown up was a failure. He was poor and his wife and children had barely enough to eat. People laughed at him children had barely enough to eat. People laughed at him because he was a loafer, and they swore never to lend him any more money because he never paid back. (5)

Like any other so called civilized community of the world, Igbo society also entrusted great importance to achievements. Achebe also suggests to the world that Igbo community is achievement oriented and being that strives to gain more success, name and fame; African success as a whole lies in achieving an identity of its own and glorifying African values.

Igbo society did not believe in any leader. Though there were elders and others who presided over the meeting, but the decision making power rested upon the community. It is a pluralistic system with decentralized power vested in small groups- priests, medicines men, and men of titles and elders who constitute the temporal authority. Ogbuefi Ezeugo spoke in the meeting and some other elders presided over the meeting called upon to decide about the murder of Umuofian woman. However the decision was taken by all, but their decision was the result of the set rules of Igbo society. "Many others spoke, and at the end of it were decided to follow the normal course of action". (11)

Decision was made that Mbaino should be given a choice of compensation of a virgin and a lad or to wage a war as per the rules of the society. This and a later trial scene show that Igbo community had a sensible and organized pattern of rules wherein they can settle disputes. "They have their own village council, judicial system that decide cases and settle disputes and quarrels." (Achebe "Named for Victoria, Queen of England" 70).

Igbo traditional society as delineated by Achebe in *Things Fall Apart* favours no individualism. It gives freedom to an individual to grow, but this freedom is only to that extent that it does not harm the community. Individual is a part of the social pattern and therefore has to contribute to society for its betterment. On the other hand, society is there to stand by his side when he needs. Okonkwo, the protagonist, grows in life because of that freedom of his society that appreciated and encouraged him to do hard work and to have determination to rise in position. This does not mean that Okonkwo had all the freedom. Like any established high social order, Igbo social set up also controls the individual from violating the law of the land and in self growth undermining the community. It favours the freedom that pursuits own good in their own way, so long as an individual do not hinders the community and its laws. Okonkwo on accidentally violating the law of land by killing a boy was punished and was exiled.

Umuofia, in *Things Fall Apart,* is an Igbo community and it seems to be a well civilized, far from primitivism, coherent and organized community like any Western civilization. Achebe refuels the meaninglessness attributed to the African culture and society. Their society is governed by certain rules, code of conduct. Okonkwo had to repent his violation of laws in peace-week and his offering to 'Ani' the Earth Goddess, as repentance reflects the discipline loving attitude of Igbo community.

Achebe, like Wole Soyinka and Ngugi Wa Thiong'o, wants to regenerate his society and restore the pride, dignity and glory of African values. He has glamorized the strength of Igbo society and its cultural heritage like corporate living. His description of the celebration of the engagement of the Obierika's daughter and Feast of New Yam reflect this corporate living of Umuofian people.

Obierika's compound was as busy as an ant hill. Temporary cooking tripods were erected on every available space by bringing together three blocks of sun-dried earth and making a fire in their midst. Cooking pots went up and down the tripods, and *foo-foo* was pounded in a hundred wooden mortars. Some of the women cooked the yams and the cassava and others prepared vegetable soup. Young men pounded the *foo-foo* or split firewood. The children made endless trips to the streams. (102).

Achebe depicts the Igbo society as masculine and hierarchal. The emphasis on male activities such as acquisition of wealth and wives, courage and resourcefulness in sport and war is evident from Okonkwo's rise as a great farmer with his own obi, his three wives and his skill at wars. Okonkwo rules his household with heavy hand and this shows the masculinity of this society. However, this is only on the surface land. The female power also pervades the society of Umuofia. In *Things Fall Apart* we observe that all the work in the village is carried out on the basis of the acceptability to 'Ani', the Earth Goddess. The priestess or the Agbala is the one who manifest the will of the clan. Okonkwo's helplessness before the priestess when his daughter was carried by the priestess shows his masculinity weakening before the female power at the larger level.

Okonkwo seems to be an apt example of Igbo man, he is an embodiment and staunch follower of Igbo culture, but he lacks the comprehensive understanding of its ethics. He ignores such time ethics of his clan that leads to his tragic end inspite of his ability to grow rapidly. His clan seeks and respects the true Igbo ethics and culture, which Okonkwo has not been able to comprehend. Female importance in the clan and life is rejected by Okonkwo, but in his clan they had their dignified place like 'Ani', priestess etc. Nwakibie's wife wears an anklet bearing the title earned by her husband shows her place in the life of her husband. Moreover, the individual seeking comfort and security during their despair from their mother is the evidence of women's importance in the Umuofian world. Okonkwo in his exile for seven years live in Mbanta, at his maternal uncle's village. This shows the women factor pervading in Igbo community. Uchendu, Okonkwo's uncle was true in explaining the reason of mother being supreme. His words are philosophic and worth understanding to know the importance of women in Igbo community. An Igbo man must know that "a man belongs to his father land when things are good and life is sweet. But when there is sorrow and bitterness he finds refuge in his motherland. Your mother is there to protect you" (122). And that is why it is said that mother is supreme. Had Okonkwo understood this and such other true ethics of his clan he might not have encountered his tragic end.

Achebe does not only reflect the true spirit of Igbo community by exploring its glorious past, he is also concerned in abolishing the evils prevalent in it so that it can stand erect with pride. Achebe problematizes Ockonkwo's relationship to the values of the society. The killing of Ikemefuna draws attention of the readers to the novel's central concern about the tie between an individual and the community in the Igbo society. Achebe has made an honest attempt to show the real African culture with its good as well as evil. It is so because he wants to reform the prevalent evils. S.A. Khayyoom observes, "Achebe, with his positive commitment to the contemporary issues in Africa, as an insider and critic of his society, participates in future renovation via past," he further says that Achebe has articulated the realities of Igbo 'tribal' life and at the same time refuted the distorted accounts of life in Africa:

> Glamorized the strength of Igbo society (Kinship and Corporate living) and its rich cultural heritage (communal experience and harmony). But he seems to have denounced the inhuman rituals like the brutal law banishing Okonkwo for accidentally killing a village boy in Things Fall Apart. (Khayyoom 37-38)

Achebe also depicts the colonial impact on Igbo society over the years. The marches of the missionaries and Europeans have encouraged the disintegration of the Igbo community. A community that was coherent organized and well established is now loosing its ground. Oknokwo's return from his exile to Umuofia shattered his imagination. He could not see the missionary influence in this village. Even his own son Nowye has been converted in to a Christian. Okonkwo could not resist the advent of missionaries and the loosing grounds of his own Igbo values in his village. He underwent a trauma because of the encroaching foreign power. Through Okonkwo's character Achebe has projected the fact that colonialism brought chaos and disorder and not civilization and order in Africa. It prepared the ground for the falling apart of a traditional way of life and encouraged its disintegration and complete destruction. It had shattered the Igbo society.

Achebe has taken the title *Things Fall Apart* from W.B. Yeats's 'The Second Coming' that reflects the very idea of disintegrating old civilization and emergence of the new. 'The old order changeth, yielding place to new'. The old 'Igbo' Civilization began to move away from its central code of conduct and values with the emergence of the Europeans in Africa. Okonkwo's son Nowye has become absolutely free from the restraints of Igbo values and religion, and Okonkwo on the other hand is left out alone as he wants to remain in the old pattern of life. There is a complete falling apart of the Igbo community.

> Turning and turning in the widening gyre
> The falcon can not hear the falconer;
> Things Fall Apart; the centre cannot hold;
> Mere anarchy is loosed upon the world,
>
> —W.B.Yeats

Okonkwo's efforts to reunite his people and to regenerate his cultural dignity are metaphorically Achebe's effort to re-juvenile the African and restore the past glory of Africa.

The colonial impact had brought about chaos and disorder in Umuofia. The colonizers have started erecting their church and spreading Christianity. The colonizers looked everything in terms of black and white. Black was evil for them and is used as synonym for the Africans. But Achebe is concerned with projecting the fact that what Africa in general and Igbo society in particular possess is not understood by the Europeans. Okonkwo and Obierika's make a conversation on the matter of a dispute of a land solved by Whiteman. "Does the Whiteman understand our custom about land?" "How can he when does not even speak our tongue? But he says that our customs are bad" (160). It reflects the fact that Europeans have no knowledge of the Igbo Culture; therefore they should not have disturbed their life. Their values, pattern of life, mode of living everything is unknown to the Europeans as they don't understand European life style. Ajofia, one of the elders of Umuofia is also true in saying:

"We can not leave the matter in his hands because he does not understand our customs, just as we do not understand his. We say he is foolish because he does not know our ways and perhaps he says we are foolish because we do not know his" (172).

Through the conversation of Okonkwo and Obierika and the words of Ajofia, Achebe propagates the central theme of *Things Fall Apart*. His *Things Fall Apart* is a social document of Igbo society which has not understood the West and the West hasn't understood them. Therefore, the emergence of Europeans with their own culture, mode of living in the African scenario imposing the same upon the natives and their own prevalent culture brought about complete chaos and disorder, and shattered the traditional Igbo society by creating chaos and disorder. Obierika, Okonkwo's friend says, "He (Whiteman) has put a knife on the things that held us together and we have fallen apart." (160). It would be right to say Whiteman was creating the disturbances in the Igbo Community through his own religion, social set up and rules of his nation. "In *Things Fall Apart*, the thrust of the Whiteman is to cause dissensions among the natives through his religion." (Reddy 44)

Achebe paints the Igbo community so vividly that one can really find himself moving among the Igbo people. *Things Fall Apart* glorifies this community revealing the facts related to it. Being an insider Achebe really has the advantage to present the life as it is he has been successful in recreating Igbo values to be understood in its true ethics without any prejudices. As the Red Indians in America and the dalits in India have been ignored for ages and have not been given their due place in society for long, so was the case with the Igbo community in Africa. *Things Fall Apart* has been able to restore the dignity and the place of Igbo community in the world. It reflects that Africa had its own civilization, culture, values and organized pattern of living even before the advent of European. Though they were not exposed to the outer world, but it doesn't mean that they were barbaric and evil ruled them. Rather Achebe glorifies its culture making Igbo culture popular and significant among the native Africans as well as the outsider. This maiden attempt of Achebe has not only rediscovered and centered the Igbo society but also has brought to the Centre the traditional value system, which we lack in this so called Modern World.

Works Cited

Achebe, Chinua. *Things Fall Apart*. New Delhi: Allied Publishers, 1998. Parenthetical references of the text are to this edition.

_______. "The Role of the Writer in a New Nation" *Nigeria Magazine*. 1964. Ogungbesan, Koloawole "Politics and the African Writer" *Critical Perspective on Chinua Achebe*. London: Heinemann, 1979.

_______. "Named for Victoria, Queen of England" Morning Yet on Creation Day. *New Letters* 40.1 (1973): 15-22.

Khayyoom, S. A. *Chinua Achebe: A Study of His Novels*. New Delhi: Prestige Books, 1999.

Reddy, Indrasena. *The Novels of Achebe Ngugi*. New Delhi: Prestige Books, 1994. s, grass fires,t Panchmi and Dirge.In Vasant Panchmi

22

Marginalized Psyche: Protest Against Sexual Colonialism in Alice Walker's *The Color Purple*

— T. K. Sandhu

Oppression is an essentially masculine activity which springs from the male's aggressive need to dominate. In the male's world men and society expects all the women to conform themselves to their strictures. Women's free and independent existence becomes intolerable to them. They resist women's demands for equality. The fact is that women have always been viewed as incapable of any serious tasks. Moreover an institution like marriage traps them and confines the women's role strictly to wifehood and motherhood. This socialization like a sexist culture treats women as inert and inferior—'afflicted with a natural defectiveness'. Women's marginalization and treatment as 'other' objectify them in the eyes of males and make them believe that 'men ought to be superior' to women. This kind of relationship which is 'a relationship of dominance and subservience' between the sexes can be called Sexual Colonialism.

As Kate Millet asserts, "Through this system a most ingenious form of interior colonization has been achieved." (Millet). Men become the colonizers and women colonized. Simone De Beauvoir perceives that the position women occupy in the society is comparable in many respects to that of racial minorities in spite of the fact that women constitute numerically at least half of the human race. This secondary standing is not imposed of necessity by natural 'feminine' characteristics but rather by strong environmental forces of education and social tradition under the purposeful control of men. This has resulted in the general failure of women to take a place of human dignity as free and independent existents associated with men on a place of intellectual and professional equality, a condition that not only has limited their achievement in many fields but also has given rise to pervasive social evils and has a particularly vitiating effect on the sexual relations between men and women. With the rise of 'feminism' many authors and feminist critiques raised their voices against this imbalance of power between the two sexes. With the insurgency of female authors in the 1970s and 1980s, a number of texts projected marginality, alienation, gender studies as their themes. The novelist protested against colonization of women. Perhaps no other race has suffered oppression and victimization as the black race. The black men and women in the U. S. suffered insults and humiliation to such an extent that they lost their 'identities, and became invisible. The white society treated the black Americans as aliens and denied their existence. It was only after the abolition of slavery that they started demanding equality in a hostile environment the black men instead of supporting black women, their co-sufferers started exploiting sexually and economically. The ebony sisters denied of respect and stability became triply jeopardized—racially, economically and sexually. The Afro-American female writers opposed their sexual and racial exploitation.

Writers like Toni Morrison and Alice Walker have enriched their literary tradition by giving voices to the silent marginalized psyches of black women. Alice Walker acclaimed as one of the leading voices among black American women probes various facets of inter-relationship of racism, sexism and colonialism in her novels. Prevalent in the black society Alice Walker calls herself a 'womanist' and is after the 'whole truth' of African-American life. In an interview she has asserted:

> I'm preoccupied with the spiritual survival, the survival of whole of my people. But beyond that, I am committed to exploring the Oppressions, the insanities, the loyalties, and the triumphs of black women. (Walker 192)

The present paper deals with protest against sexual abuse and colonialism as voiced by Alice Walker in the novel *The Color Purple*. This novel is the tale of violence, incest and redemption that starts out in Georgia in the 1900s and goes on for thirty years. Walker delineates her protagonist Celie's mental and physical state through the letters which Celie writes to none other 'GOD'. The black English (folk dialect) used by Celie to narrate her plight is faulty yet its lyrical cadence appeals in the opening pages of *The Color Purple* evoke Afro-American slavery. Celie is a young girl of fourteen years who consider herself 'ugly'. She narrates about her sexual abuse, her victimization. She survives at the hands of her own 'Pa'. As she is warned not to speak out, her first letter to God is preceded by Pa's manipulation warnings about the benefit of her silence.

> You better not ever tell nobody
> But God, It'd kill your mammy (11)

Celie's mother being ill is unable to satisfy her husband's sexual appetite and Pa continues to make brutal sexual attacks on Celie. As a result she becomes pregnant. She being 'big' is unable to move. For Celie motherhood is not a pleasure rather she after giving birth to two children are sold or given away by Pa. Soon after Celie of being 'no use' is handed over (sold) like a commodity to a widower Mr. A. Pa assures him Celie like a 'cow' will serve him. To add to Celie's misery her husband after marriage is of the same 'sorry ilk' as Celie's Pa (step father). He measures his 'manliness' by beating his wife and children. Ill-treated and abused as a slave and whore Celie's oppression increases. The black society has always suffered racial oppression but violence against women whether sexual or domestic is not a new one. The patriarchal society licenses and permits wife beating which makes her plight worse. Through out the world all cultures permits this type of violence. Celie too, 'good for nothing' 'plus Stubborn' because a 'wife' has no control against sexual colonialism and like a 'beast of burden' she bears a kind of stoicism and tolerates her husband's brutality. Her primary concern is to survive. So for her fighting back does not seem an option in the beginning.

Celie as a human being desires to be loved and cared. Walker registers her silence in the letters which she writes to God and later to Nettie, her younger sister. It is through Nettie's letters that she gains her lost sense of individuality. The agent that leads her to autonomy is none other than Shug Avery; the blues singer and her husband's (Albert's) mistress. It is she who works as a catalyst in Celie's metamorphosis. Shug Avery raises Celie from her desperate condition by teaching her to love her body ad respect it. Celie's 'crippled' sense of 'negation' or 'non-entity' had forced her to act as a stereo typed female, conforming to social, patriarchal strictures Sophia, Harpo's wife, too ties a knot of sisterhood with Celie. Sophia, educated, liberated and independent refutes to succumbs to Harpo's desires and authority. She helps Celie in her transformation Celie admires her daughter-in-law and learns the language of revolt and protest.

Walker as a rebel against women's victimization helps her women to protest and actualize themselves with their powers. Celie too, stands up to protest against sexual colonialism dethroning her feminity. In Shug's love Celie finds a refuge. She blossoms with Shug's nearness, who teaches her to sew and stitch pants. It is Shug who takes Celie to Memphis and enter into creation. At Memphis Celie re-organizes her life by becoming economically independent. Shug Avery makes Celie conscious of her powers and Celie develops her faith in her own strength by rejecting her invisibility. Her powerful 'colonialist' her own husband is shocked when Celie uses her angry words and curses Albert. Her mouth is just packed with 'claws' enjoying her back talk Celie now tells her oppressor to pipe down. Earlier Albert had bestowed indignities upon Celie by calling her 'ugly' and 'skinny'; she being 'black' and 'pore', 'a woman' and 'good for nothing'. Transformed Celie retorts, "Though I' m pore, I'm black, I may be ugly.... But I'm here" (187). Celie thus turns the table by expressing herself with so much gusto that her words come out as torrents. Celie's changing attitude to life records a shift in her attitude towards her God also. God in whom she had faith too appears to her "like all the other men's" she knows. God is "Trifling, forgetful and lowdown" (199), as he has not heard her prayers. Further in the novel Shug Avery enlightens Celie by asserting 'God love them feeling'. For Celie religion becomes purely a personal affair. It is a person's personal faith that heals people and Celie is finally healed when Nettie reveals that Celie's fragmentation by an external force, that is by Pa was not their real Pa. He was their step father. Celie eliminate herself from this guilt and shame.

Sophia, Harpo's wife, is another woman in the novel, who though educated, smart and independent is initially liked by Harpo. But soon after marriage she is victimized sexually for her confident zeal towards life. Harpo wants her to fit in the traditional roles of woman as wifehood and motherhood. Physically and psychologically strong she rejects these roles but is unable to fight away racial cruelty against Mayor and his wife. She is jailed for sassing Mayor's wife and is forced to work as a servant in the Mayor's family. Yet she retains her selfhood and builds a kinship with her step mother-in-law Celie. Sophia's inner strength to fight domestic violence helps Celie to pursue for autonomous selfhood. The art of 'quilting' with a bond of 'togetherness' gradually leads towards sisterhood; one of the most suggestive metaphors used by black women writers. Thus the women who are morally and physically marginalized in the society are able to raise their voice collectively against racial and sexual colonialism in the novel.

Works Cited

Millet, Kate. *Sexual Politics*. London: ABACUS, 1972.

Walker, Alice. Interview by John O'Brion. *Interviews with Black Writers*. New York: Liversight, 1973.

______. *The Colour Purple*. New York: Harcourt Brace Jovanovich Publishers, 1982.

23

The Interplay of Margins and Centre: A Study of *Silence! The Court is in Session* and *Kanyadaan*

— Tanjeen A. Khan

Drama in literature has always remained a specialised field that requires special skill and talent in selecting a theme which is presentable on the stage, and in picking up a technique that is appreciated by the audience. India has a rich cultural heritage and 'Natak' is considered here the component of the 'fith Veda' that is the *Natyaveda*. These cultural impacts made Indian drama flourish in regional languages, which are now getting translated into English. English translations of these plays are gaining popularity the world over. These translated plays of writers like Vijay Tendulkar, Girish Karnad and Badal Sircar are cherishing the age old rich theatrical history, and establishing it to the heights of Shakespeare and Marlowe.

Tendulkar, a journalist by profession, contributed to several daily columns in newspapers. He started his career as a creative writer, writing short stories and later, plays. He in his plays has dealt with a number of female characters like Kamla, Jyoti, Leela Benare, Princes Vijaya, Rama, Manik, etc. To quote the words of Shanta Gokhale:

> As characters Tendulkar's woman are among the most convincing in Indian theatre. They are not romanticized, idealized, or forced to live by their creator's symbolic purposes. They are first and foremost human beings of flesh and blood who draw their features from the widest

> range of observed examples. They are allowed inherit the entire spectrum from the unbelievably gullible to the clever, from the self sacrificing to the grasping. (Gokhale 81)

Among them Leela Benare of *Silence! The Court is in Session* and Jyoti of *Kanyadaan* are the most witty, lovable, hardworking, rebellious girls, very loyal towards their duties. Work in worship is the motto for Leela where as social equality is for Jyoti.

For Leela Benare, to do one's job honestly is sufficient for a smooth social life. She is a young spinster of 34, working as a school teacher, loves life and is full of spirit. She is very proud of her performance as a teacher and feels that her life is her own and no one has the right to interfere in it. Being a human, Benare too is a slave of her emotions. Her feminine wishes and qualities make her heart long for a safe-shelter and she had searched for that safe-shelter since her childhood days. This very search proves to be a flaw in her character which makes her a prey to the machinations of those who stand nowhere in front of her. Those, who accuse her, are themselves failures in their lives. They heap up their frustration upon the one who is no doubt superior to them. She was a Lioness in the beginning of the play but the society in which she is living, is full of those who very well know how to tame a furious Lioness. To quote N. S. Dharan:

> Silence! However, makes a change in Tendulkar's attitude towards his favorite subject i.e. the middle class man, for the first time in his dramatic career, he began to look into the psyche o his subject and focuses his attention on the ugliness he detected there in.
>
> (Dharan 95)

Jyoti, Tendulkar's heroine in *Kanyadaan* is inspired by her father, who is determined to uproot the evil of casteism from the society and has taken up the experimental task in the play by marrying a dalit. She and her father, with a very positive aspiration determine to reform the society. She tries persistently to bring her dalit husband to a higher stature, but because of the deep-rooted difference between a dalit and a high caste, and above all between a male and a female, her husband doesn't want to rise up to those moral heights. Jyoti goes to bring him out of that dirt but she herself submerges in it.

Silence! The Court is in Session focuses and in fact begins with Leela Benare, a member of an amateur group of actors of Bombay who perform plays around the city as the occasion demands. She arrives at a suburban village for a performance. Being the first to come there, she takes the help of a local hand, Samant. Other members of this amateur theatre are the Kashikar's, Balu Rokde, Sukhatme, Ponkshe, Karnik, Professor Damle and Rawte. They all belong to the urban middle class of Bombay. Mr. Kasikar is the Chairman of the association while Mrs. Kashikar is a housewife. Rokde is adopted son of Kashikar's, Sukhatme is a lawyer and Ponkshe is a clerk, Karnik, a struggling actor and Prof. Damle, a Professor in college. Damle, though not physically present, plays a very important role in the play.

Benare's conversation with Samant in the opening scene displays a very strong and different personality of her. When she talks of her career as a teacher, saying her pupils, are 'so much better than adults' she adds, though her pupils are scared of her, still they adore her. They will do anything for her, or she would give 'the last drop' of her blood teaching them though her fellow teachers and even the management are extremely jealous of her. Samant becomes 'embarrassed' when Benare tells him that the management is holding an enquiry against her 'just because of one bit of slander'. Ignoring the fact that she is in the presence of a stranger, who is in no way connected with her speech she says:

> Throw me out? Let them! I haven't hurt any one. Any one at all, if I've hurt anybody its been myself. But is that may any kind of reason for throwing me out? Who are these people to say what I can or can't do? My life is my own. I haven't sold it to anyone for a job! My will is my own. My wishes are my own. No one can kill those—no one! (Tendulkar 58)

Suddenly she realizes that she is going too far and changes her mood with the arrival of the other members of the group. But before their arrival she sarcastically introduces them all to Samant. In this introduction, she spits venom describing Damle:

> And we have an intellectual too means someone who prides himself on his book learning. But when there's real life problem, away he runs! Hides his head. He's not here today. Won't beg coming either. He wouldn't dare! (Tendulkar 60).

The real play starts with Sukhatme's suggestion to stage some sort of mock-trial to pass time as they have got enough time for the actual performance. Here, there is just a short absence of Benare from the scene, which provides a chance to her fellow members to conspire against her. When Benare returns, Ponkashe suddenly blasts upon her with assaulting lines:

> Miss Benare, you have been arrested on suspicion of a crime of an extremely grave nature and brought as a before the bar of this court! (Tendulkar 61).

Benare in the next scene stands bewildered on hearing these charges. Judge of the mock-trial declares her guilty of infanticide. She tries a lot to behave normal. The trial slowly becomes violent and Benare, hearing these charges mounted against her, becomes furious. She understands what started as a mock-trial is a real dreadful trial for her. All of them are setting their scores with her in the name of the mock trial. She knows very well that her relation with Prof. Damle is the matter to which they are trying to indicate. Tensed and stunned Benare, who remains mute till now suddenly cries as she cannot bear this any longer. With watered eyes, she addresses them all, "what can you do to me? Just try!" and exits into the wings. She, with beaten steps goes to the door to open it. She finds the door locked from outside. Like her co-actors her fate too is making a prey of her.

Defeated and dejected Benare admits all her crimes. But she points out that her private life is her own business. She will decide what to do with it. Everyone has a bent, a manner, and an aim in life. What has any one else to do with it? She boldly admits her love affairs with these two men and both of whom had deceived her. They only loved the flesh in her but not the woman. Neither of them had the boldness to marry her. Her long monologue at last with a feeble voice and sometimes with sudden screams leaves us wondering over the matter.

> I offered up my body on the altar of my worship. And my intellectual god took the offering—and went his way..... And now it carries within it the witness of that time—a tender little bud.... I want my body now for him. (Tendulkar 118).

These conspiracies in the play make psychological assaults upon a woman, who is a very strong individual, and pleads, to the readers to stand by her side. Likewise, Jyoti, daughter of Nath and Seva invites our attention. She belongs to a socialist family who worked hard for a long time. Jyoti inherits her father's idealism and loves Arun Athavale, a dalit poet, whom she meets at the socialist study group. Nath reacts positively and appreciates Jyoti's decision of choosing Arun as her husband, dismissing Seva's argument and questions concerning the boy's background and occupation. Without any 'Storm of hidden passions' Jyoti decides to marry Arun. Gradually the artificial and polished behaviour vanishes and Arun in a very straightforward manner starts telling Jyoti the harshness and ugliness of his life in the ugliest manner. The real man in him comes out and feels more shocked than hurt. Knowing all these Nath still is in favour of this marriage and Jyoti follows his ideals.

After the marriage circumstances crushes Jyoti totally within a few months of her married life. She answers the questions hardly in one or two sentences. It is revealed here that Arun often gets drunk and beats his wife mercilessly. Jyoti tried for separation but her ideals and her father's aspirations retained her compels her to remain in that ugly life. Later, Arun publishes his autobiography. Nath praises his work, but is suddenly suspended in his appreciation when he comes to know that Jyoti is in her sixth month, and is suffering an internal wound in her stomach as Arun had beaten and kicked her. This induces so many questions in Nath's and the reader's mind as well.

Here in these pages has been described the humiliations Arun has undergone with extraordinary sensitivity, "... and the same man kicks on her belly? How...? How dare he?" (Tendulkar 47). Jyoti, who was aspired to create a casteless society, is now yielding to the complications. Instead of achieving something, she is losing her ideals. She hates hypocrisy but now she witnesses that her father has yielded to deliver a hypocritical speech at the function. In utter despair she blames her father for her misery. She says, "I was deeply offended by your hypocrisy. I thought, why did this man have to inject and drug us every day with truth and goodness? And if he can get away it at all, what right had he to close all our options?" (Tendulkar 69).

When Jyoti declares that she is not going to stay, Nath asks her who will take care of her during delivery, she replies harshly, "I am not Jyoti Yadunath Devlalikar now, I am Jyoti Arun Athavale, a scavenger ...." (Tendulkar 70). Saying these words she leaves the house, obviously never to return. She tolerated the violence of her husband and tries to cope with the conditions, just to prove that she is above all the walls of caste and class but her dreams are shattered and she got nothing except a chaotic world where there is no space for idealism.

Tendulkar started these two plays with the heroines in the centre just like in Shakespearean romantic comedies. But at the end these heroic heroines are marginalized in the plays. This struggle is far from being over. To quote the words of M. Sarat Babu, "Human beings have to strip their souls of all the enveloping cultural layers and reach the inner core, their true nature, humanness on the one hand and on the other they have to dissolve their cultural world in order to reintegrate with nature" (Babu 16).

Nature is not a word but it is a theory. World didn't come into existence fortuitously, it was willed by God by creating man and his female consort. If he leaves his female alone, which is nature and which includes all created things, it will turn wayward and may destroy everything. Benare and Jyoti, two such conceptions of nature cannot be put in the margins like this. They are counterparts of supreme creation and if drifted to the margin they may explode and cause a deluge to divine creation.

Works Cited

Gokhale, Shanta. *Speech and Essay.* New Delhi: Katha, 2001.

Dharan, N.S. *The Plays of Tendulkar.* New Delhi: Creative Books, 1999.

Tendulkar, Vijay. "Silence! The Court is in Session" *Five Plays.* New Delhi: OUP, 1992.

_______. *Kanyadaan.* New Delhi: OUP, 1996.

Babu, M. Sarat. *Indian Drama Today.* New Delhi; Sangam Books, 1997.

24

History Retold—Bapsi Sidhwa and Attia Hosain on Partition: A Version of the Marginalized

— Uma Ram

Bapsi Sidhwa and Attia Hosain have the distinction of being the first women writers of Pakistan and India respectively, on partition. Both share similar views on the calamities of partition. Sidhwa's third novel *Ice-Candy-Man* and Attia Hosain's *Sunlight on a Broken Column* are examples. Sidhwa's novel set in the politically volatile period of India's partition in 1947 depicts the climactic end of partition, a terrible period of her country's (she is a Parsi living in Pakistan) history. This was renamed *Cracking India* by the American publishers and was made into a successful film '1947—Earth' by Deepa Mehta. Her counterpart Attia Hosain in her novel depicts the ugly scenes of communal violence as a fall out of partition. Both approach the subject of partition with empathy and compassion of a humanitarian feminist.

Partition of the Indian sub-continent has been a green pasture for Indian writers writing in English. Kushwant Singh's *A Train to Pakistan,* Chaman Nahal's *Azadi,* Manohar Malgaonkar's *A Bend in the Ganges,* Amitav Ghosh's *The Shadow Lines,* Salman Rushdie's *Midnight's Children,* are significant male voices. Sidhwa and Hosain represent the female voices. They have provided a feminine, a gyno-centric perspective to the problem of partition. Both of them stress the vulnerability of human lives. Partition results in inhuman, pitiless killings, annihilating whole families, leaving deep, unhealing wounds on both sides. They maintain a commendable impartiality in their understanding of the event but they show their natural bias, Hosain (though a Muslim) writes from an Indian point of view while Sidhwa has a firm Pakistani tilt. *Ice-Candy-Man* with its backdrop of partition makes it a politically motivated novel. In a conversation with David Montenegro, Sidhwa admits:

> The main motivation grew out of my reading of a good deal of literature on the Partition of India and Pakistan...What has been written by the British and the Indians. Naturally they reflect their bias. And they have, I felt after I researched the book, been unfair to the Pakistanis. As a writer, as a human being, one just does not tolerate injustice. I felt that whatever little I could do to correct an injustice, I would like to do. I have just let facts speak for themselves, and through my research I found out what the facts were. (Sidhwa 'Interview' 36)

In the first two novels, *The Crow Eaters* and *The Bride*, partition has been significant but not the shaping force. In *Ice-Candy-Man* partition is the shaping force. Sidhwa's use of a marginalized narrator—an inquisitive, eight-year-old girl, Lenny, a polio victim, a member of a minority community—is well suited to her purpose, as Ralph, J. Crane points out, "through the various marginalized narrators and through the experiences of the many marginalized characters in her first three novels, Sidhwa gives voice to hitherto silenced groups of India and Pakistan and in so doing tells other versions of her country's history" (Crane). Sidhwa herself as a child was a polio victim and could attend school only in brief patches, thus "lacking the friends one makes in school, enormous chunks of my early life were spent either reading or fantasizing. Factors that, like solitary confinement, incline one to story telling and self expression" (Sidhwa "Why do I Write?"). This observation also holds good for Attia Hosain. Cast in the autobiographical form, *Sunlight on a Broken Column* covers a period of about twenty years before and after independence in the life of young Laila, the narrator, during which India passed through a number of crises. An orphan, Laila is brought up by her relatives in Lucknow. She joins a university and belonging as she does, to an influential Muslim family, realizes that the political turmoil and upheavals become an integral part of their existence .The secular- nationalists under the congress banner are challenged by the Muslim League. The politics of the public places by force seem to invade drawing rooms and dining tables.

> No one seemed to talk anymore; every one argued, and not in the graceful tradition of our city where conversation was treated as a fine art, words were loved as mediums of artistic expression, and verbal battles were enjoyed as much as any delicate, scintillating, sparkling display of pyrotechnic skill. It was as if someone had sneaked in live ammunition among the fireworks. (*Sunlight on a Broken Column* 3.12).

This development has even strained family relationships where father and son find themselves in opposite camps. She observes Indian leaders increasingly urging the people to fight the British in India. College students are drawn into the politics of rebellion and slogan shouting. Physical violence was met by non-violence. For a Neeta or an Asad then to encounter lathis was not unexpected. Laila describes the council chamber, where the procession of non-cooperation had been halted, and the police had charged them with heavy wooden lathis. She had vowed, "to fight for our country's freedom as the satyagrahis did, to lie on the spit stained pavements in front of the treacherous shop that sold foreign cloth, to march in peaceful protest, to defy the might of the arrogant whites" (*Sunlight on a Broken Column* 7.2). But this gradually turns into a fight among them selves as India becomes independent. She discerns the British game of divide and rule, in which Hindus and Muslims become easy pawns, allowing the British to have the last laugh. One is reminded of Mark Antony's words after inciting the crowd against Brutus and his men, "... mischief thou art afoot/ Take what course thou wilt." (*Julius Caesar* III.iii. 265). However she feels that the Indian freedom movement suffered a setback the moment religion entered politics. In the twenty years that saw Laila changing from a fifteen year old orphan to a widowed mother India moves from the British India to a free India, but at what cost?— at the cost of an 'un-childing' 'un-fathering' outcome of the partition of the Indian sub-continent.

Bapsi Sidhwa's narrator Lenny, the Polio stricken little Parsi girl has a keen sense of perception of things around her. Her physical debility makes up for her mental agility. All her energy is directed towards a keen observation of happenings around her. Retelling history from a child's point of view appears to be a successful strategy adopted by Sidhwa as Aamer Hussein observes in her critique:

> We believe we are witnessing the events of partition through the eyes of an innocent child, but strategically placed flash forwards signal, in a subtle manner, that the adult Lenny is actually reliving the past in order to make sense of events that baffled her when she was too small to comprehend. Simultaneously she restricts herself to the experiences and sensory perceptions of the child she was. Thus we are given a double- even a dialogic-perspective that layered innocence on experience, introspection on hind sight. (Hussein 3)

As a child exposed to the tumultuous political upheaval she is disturbed when she hears that India is going to be broken. She is bewildered at the very thought, 'can one break the country? What happens if they break it where our house is? Or crack it further up on Warris road. How will I ever get to the godmother then? She becomes aware of not just the religious differences but class differences being artificially created and deliberately fostered' (*Ice-Candy-Man* 92). She foresees differences widening between Hindus, Muslims, Sikhs and Christians. Ayah being carried away by a renewed devotional fervor:

> Expends a small fortune in joss-sticks, flowers and sweets on the gods and goddesses in the temple... Imam Din and Yousaf, turning into religious zealots... crammed into a narrow Religious slot they too are diminished: as are Jinnah and Iqbal, Ice-candy Man and Masseur... Hari and Moti, the sweeper and his wife Muccho, and their untouchable daughter Papoo, become even more

> untouchable as they are entrenched deeper in their low Hindu caste. While the Sharmas and Daulatrams, Brahmins like Nehru, are dehumanized by their lofty caste and caste-marks. (*Ice-Candy-Man 93*-94)

English Christians look down on Anglo-Indians while the Parsees are reduced to irrelevant nomenclatures.

Sidhwa with her 3P identity, 'I'm a Parsi first, then a Pakistani, specifically a Punjabi' (Sidhwa "Ice-Candy Woman") argues that partition favoured India over Pakistan and its leaders. In an interview to Laurel Graeber, she points out that Jinnah was no monster, as it was projected by the Congress, "Gandhi really sowed the seeds of partition and turned the whole independence struggle into a Hindu movement. It is hard for the people in the West where he is deified to regard him as a petty manipulative politician" (Sidhwa "The Seeds of Partition" 11). She, in fact, defends Jinnah. She feels, the British glorified Mountbatten and Indians, Gandhi. And today, forty years later, in films on the lives of Gandhi and Mountbatten, in books by British and Indian scholars, Jinnah, who for a decade was known as 'Ambassador of Hindu-Muslim unity, is caricatured and portrayed as a monster. She quotes Sarojini Naidu eulogizing Jinnah as a perfect human being:

> ... the calm hauteur of his accustomed reserve masks, for those who know him, a naïve and eager humanity, an intuition quick and tender as a woman's, a humour gay and winning as a child's- pre-eminently rational, and practical, discreet and dispassionate in his estimate and acceptance of life, the obvious sanity and serenity of his worldly wisdom effectually disguise a shy and splendid idealism which is of the very essence of the man. (*Ice-Candy-Man* 161)

Sidhwa establishes her Pakistani identity by focusing on the worst Indian (Sikh) atrocities committed on the Muslims in Punjab. The event of partition creates an unbridgeable chasm between Hindus and Muslims, which culminates in utter hatred and enmity. She comes down heavily on Gandhi referring to his visit to Lahore. She seems to deliberately demystify Gandhi's personality. His speech which focused more on enema and clogged alimentary canal, repulses Lenny:

> ... flush your systems with an enema, daughter,' says Gandhijee, directing his sage counsel at my mother, 'use plain lukewarm water. Do it for thirty days... every morning, you will feel like a new woman.' 'Look at these girls' says Gandhijee, indicating the lean women flanking him. 'I give them enemas myself- there is no shame in it- I am like their mother. You can see how moist and smooth their skin is. Look at their shining eyes.' (*Ice-Candy-Man* 87)

Lenny considers him to be something between a clown and a demon, "I am puzzled why he is so famous." For her he is nothing but an eccentric dietician. For Ayah's lover Masseur he is just another politician whose business is to suit his tongue to the moment. She is deliberately trying to be an iconoclast in her attempt to reassess Gandhi's deified personality as a political saint. She feels she has tried to humanize Gandhi. Her Pakistani bias is quite apparent in her remarks on partition:

> The Hindus are being favoured over the Muslims by the remnant of the Raj. Now that the objective to divide India is achieved, the British favour Nehru over Jinnah. Nehru is Kashmiri, they grant him Kashmir. Spurning logic, defying rationale, ignoring the consequence of bequeathing a Muslim state to the Hindus... They grant Nehru Gurdaspur and Pathankot without which Muslim Kashmir cannot be secured. (*Ice-Candy-Man* 159)

Nehru is a shrewd politician:

> 'that Nehru, he is a sly one... He's got Mountbatten eating out of his one hand and the English wife out of his other and what not...' and Jinnah, 'he will stick within his rights, no matter whom Nehru feeds! He is a first rate lawyer and he knows how to attack the British with their own laws!' (*Ice-Candy-Man* 159)

Sidwa's stance seems to lack rationale. Shashi Tharoor, in fact, takes serious objection to this pointing out that Kashmir was not gifted to Nehru, as it was a part of India.

Attia Hosain's protagonist Laila reveals the trauma of partition through her memories and insights of the Talukdar family disintegrating on the eve of partition. Her cousin Zohra who is married in Pakistan returns to her ancestral home in Hasanpur. She quarrels with her cousin about the protection of Muslim culture and language. Like Lenny, Laila also shows the cruelty of parting ways, "in the end, inevitably we quarreled and though we made up before we parted, I realized that the lies which had kept families together for several centuries had been loosened beyond repair." (*Sunlight on A Broken Column* 303). Laila, like Lenny, is both nostalgic and restless. When Laila wanders around her ancestral home after partition, memories come back to her. Though there is no more nostalgia in her to return to the old order, she has come to detest dogmatism, either in the name of religion or radicalism. Her mature perspectives on life developed after an intense personal struggle enables Laila to tackle the loss of her husband Ameer and the trauma of partition without rancor. Both Laila and Lenny realize that there is no easy solution to communal violence except a focused struggle against dogmatic thinking.

Attia Hosain upholds Laila's concerted efforts at breaking from traditional customs, the negation of despair and recognition of struggle, as Mulk Raj Anand in his introduction to the novel says that Attia Hosain exposes the denseness of a society which had become moribund. Sidwa too shows that there are no easy winners in the communal holocausts of partition. But being a Pakistani writer her sympathies are generally with the Muslim victims: "The Sikhs perpetrated the much greater brutality—they wanted Punjab to be divided. A peasant is rooted in his soil. The only way to uproot him was to kill him or scare him out of his wits" (Montenegro 36). In fact the Sikh faith came about to create Hindu-Muslim harmony. But it proved quite contrary.

Ice-Candy-Man, a historically situated and politically informed novel, affirms that partition is as much a Pakistani part of Indian history. It not only questions the British and Indian versions on partition but also writes an alternative version of that 'shared horror'. Through this novel, Sidwa, 'the

Grand Dame of South Asian Anglophone writing' provides a distinct voice to the hitherto silent groups, the Parsi, the Pakistani, and the girl-child. Perhaps Sidwa and Hosain are pioneers in woman-centred writing in the genre of partition novels. They have, by filtering history of the sub-continent through the consciousness of the girl-child, contrived to highlight the points that had remained marginalized in history.

Works Cited

Crane, J. Ralph. "A Passion for History and Truth Telling-The Early Novels of Bapsi Sidhwa" *The Novels of Bapsi Sidhwa.*ed. R. K Dhawan & Novy Kapadia. New Delhi: South Asia Books, 1996. 48-60.

Hosain, Attia. *Sun Light on a Broken Column.* New Delhi: Penguin Books, 1991. All parenthetical references of the text are to this edition.

Hussein, Aamer. "Bapsi Sidhwa, the Storyteller" Introduction. *The Bapsi Sidhwa Omnibus*. New Delhi: OUP, 2001.

Montenegro, David. "Points of Departure" *International Writers on Writing and Politics*. ? 1989.

Sidhwa, Bapsi. "Why Do I Write?" *Novels of Bapsi Sidhwa*. eds. by R.K. Dhawan and Novy Kapadia. New Delhi: Prestige, 1996.

———. *Ice-Candy Man.* New Delhi: Penguin Books, 1988. All parenthetical references of the text are to this edition.

———. Interview by Bachi Karkaria. "Ice-Candy Woman" *TOI*. Sat, Feb19, 2005.

———. Interview by David Montenegro. "Points of Departure-International Writers on Writing and Politics" *Massachusetts Review*. 31 (1990): 513-33.

———. Interview by Laurel Graeber. " The Seeds of Partition" *New York Times*. Oct. 6, 1991.

25

Cultural Conflict in Bharati Mukherjee's *The Tiger's Daughter* and *Jasmine*

— Usha Masram

When a person leaves his own culture and enters another, his old values come into conflict with the new ones he finds. The expatriate writers face a multi-cultural situation, which may be combined with a personal anguish due to discrimination or a sense of rootlessness, if rejected by their host countries.

Bharati Mukherjee is one of the most significant contemporary novelists in English; her writings have received worldwide recognition. Her novels represent the nomadic impulses of Indians who, in their search for a materially better life, migrate to the West and have to face the tensions of adaptation and assimilation. She is at her best in the depiction of cultural clash between the East and the West.

In her novels *Jasmine* and *The Tiger's Daughter*, Bharati Mukherjee has shown a dual cultural shock. Her characters like Tara and Jasmine leave their respective countries in search of their dreams. This cultural transplant leads to a crisis of choice. Bharati Mukherjee pushes them to the edge of their worlds and liberates them for a new world order.

The Tiger's Daughter pursues an opposite direction with the return to India of Tara, 22 year old daughter of a wealthy and prominent Bengali brahmin. Vassar educated Tara has married an American and has been away from home for seven years. Although she has always regarded herself as an Indian, she discovers she is more an outsider than a native, concerned with the complex and confusing web of politics, poverty, privilege and hierarchies of power and class in India. She has dreamt for years of this return, but now finds herself imbued with the ' foreignness of spirit' attributable not only to her American domicile but also to her early education in Calcutta at a private school run by Belgian nuns.

When she returns to Calcutta after her sojourn in the West, we find her greatly changed. The friends she had played with seven years ago, done her homework with Nilima, debated with Reena at the British Council, but now after her return from America, she fears their tone, their omissions, their aristocratic oneness. She finds that she is admired neither by her family nor by her friends. Tara realizes she has become rootless and out of place both in India and America. So David had bought books on India. This innocent information enraged Tara. She thought the latter was really trying to tell her that he had not understood her country through her, that probably he had not understood her either. She became afraid that David no longer wanted to make her over to his ideal image, that he no longer loved her. Mother also no longer loved her for having wilfully abandoned her caste by marrying a foreigner.

Tara in *The Tiger's Daughter* finds it difficult to relate herself to her family city and culture. Sivarama Krishna considers the novel 'voiceless' and 'visionless'. The heroine finds it difficult to relate, since her marriage to an American and her Western education brand her as an alienated woman. Tara's attempts to reconcile the two worlds: the Western one with its secular orientations with the Brahmin one with its traditional non-secular orientation.

On her return from America, Tara finds it not only difficult but impossible to communicate with her family. She finds that her father, though slightly disappointed her, had said nothing, of course, but then had never really talked about important things.

The Tiger's Daughter presents a segment of society that Bharati Mukherjee herself grew up in and is familiar with: the upper middle class convent educated Westernized boxwallah society, a hangover from the British Raj. It is the autobiography of a class rather than an individual, feels Bharati Mukherjee.

As in *The Tiger's Daughter*, *Jasmine* also reflects the confrontation between illusion and reality. In *Jasmine*, the immigrants are wily participants in the dominant culture, understanding that their code is crucial to appreciating the novel. The potential of fluidity, which Mukherjee attributes to American culture, is epitomized in the main characters 'metamorphosis' from Jyoti, a Punjabi village girl, to Jasmine, a loving and devoted Hindu wife, to Kali, incarnation of destroying goddess, to Jazzy, a remade, non-immigrant, to Jase, a nanry in the home of a New York college professor, and to Jane, live-in partner of a bank official in love. Each of these character transformations is marked by changes in behavior and personality, such as her successive 'rebirths' seems analogy to Hindu transmigration of the soul. While examining the codes associated with each of the six permutations, we discover that while some codes disappear, certain qualities do in fact 'transmigrate' from one young woman to the next. Jyoti, born in Punjab, is a survivor. The quality remains constant. She escapes infanticide, and kills a rabid dog in self-defence. Intelligent, beautiful and self-willed, she finds her way to America after widowed. Prakash, her husband, dies in a bomb blast.

Bharati Mukherjee has carved out the assimilation of third world immigrants into the American melting pot, which is itself enriched by those she describes as 'new pioneers' Jasmine is one of those pioneers, a survivor with courage. Using flashbacks and cross cuts, the novel forges ahead weaving the story of the heroine's life, from her early days in Hasanpur to her extraordinary adventure in United States. Jasmine herself is dizzy at the speed of her transformation, the fluidity of American character and the American landscape.

The narrative shifts between the past and present, between India of her earlier life and America of the present. The past is Jyoti's childhood in the small village of Hasanpur, Punjab, her marriage to Prakash, the young ambitious city man, who always thrashed traditions. Pygmalion-like he had given her a new identity and new name Jasmine for she was small, sweet and heady and would quicken the whole world with her perfume.

The present was her life as Jane in Iowa, where she was a live in companion to Bud Ripplemeyer, a small-town banker. Bud was fascinated by her foreignness, but he never asked her about India. It scared him. He courted her because she was alien.

In the process of her transformation, Jane was seized by a longing to belong. She closely identifies herself with Bud's adopted son 'Du', a Vietnamese because he was an immigrant like herself. Both had seen death closely. Both Du and Jasmine were in a hurry to become American. They tried to forget the nightmares of their early lives. Assimilation in America was easy.

America, the land of dreams had many disillusions in store for her. Lillian Gordon, a kind Quaker lady in Florida, offered her a home, and also to several illegal immigrants. In New York, Jasmine was shocked by the sight of beggars, one of whom cursed her as a 'foreign bitch' when she refused him alms. The taxi driver in New York was a migrant doctor from Kabul, who lived like dogs, because they had taken everything from them. On the streets of New York Jasmine saw more greed and more people like herself.

The experience with the Professor's family was even more frustrating. The biggest shock to Jasmine was the truth of the Professorji's means of earning a livelihood. He was not a Professor but an importer and sorter of human hair. America had not robbed him of his self-respect.

The next identity of Jase was thrust on her by the Hayse's family, where she worked as a 'care-giver'. The twist given to the narrative where Jase falls in love with Taylor is a weak link in the chain of events. The transformation of Jyoti had come half-circle. Jyoti was now a sati-goddess. Jasmine lived for the future, for Vijh and wife and Jase lived for today. Bharati Mukherjee supplements Jasmine's immigrant experiences with similar experience of Letita from Trinidad, and Jamaica from Barbados.

The final crisis of the story comes when Jane is confronted with the souring of the American dream, through the suicide of Darrel. Du's departure from home in search for his family destabilizes her. She is caught between her duty towards the cripple Bud and her love for Taylor. She makes the final choice. She doesn't feel guilty, but relieved. She has stopped thinking of herself as Jane. She feels potent enough once again to reposition her stars. Time would draw its own conclusions about her true identity.

There is a strange fusion of Americanness and Indianness in the psyche of Bharati Mukherjee's characters. The attitude of her characters who feel crazy for foreign things, dresses and items but do not approve marriage with foreigners makes a criticism of the conservative attitude of the Indians. Though Bharati Mukherjee describes herself as an American author, after reading her novels the readers feel the Indian impulse throbbing in her.

Works Cited

Mukherjee, Bharati. *Jasmine.* New Delhi: Penguin, 1990.

_______. *The Tiger's Daughter*. London: Chatto and Windus, 1973.

Tondon, Sushma. *Bharati Mukherjee's Fiction a Perspective*. New Delhi: Sarup & Sons, 2004.

26

Intriguing Tale of Loss and Loneliness of (New) Woman in *The Girl*

— G. A. Ghanshyam

> Out of loneliness, all of us seek a source of love that will fill up the lack we feel inside, and that's exactly what happens, no more and no less.
>
> —Deepak Chopra

No matter who we are or where we are, we always crave for companionship. Bacon in his essay on friendship says that a person who loves isolation must have something of the beast in him for no man can live alone. Modern age has brought in its wake many benefits and feats of progress yet lurking in the shadows are despair and loss. In the race for success men are losing out on their humanity and emotions. Growing materialism and consumerism are gnawing at the roots of the spirit; love, relationships, family, are some of the casualties of this age.

The woman of this era is the New Woman; confident, bold and independent; quite a far cry from the submissive, silent and suffering woman of the bygone ages. The new woman is the face of Piya in *The Hungry Tide* (THT 2006), Kashmira in *Shalimar the Clown* (STC 2005) or Sai in *The Inheritance of Loss* (TIL 2006). But behind the veils of such self-sufficient success stories are also the whispers of pain and anguish; the stories of Boonyi in *Shalimar the Clown* or Leela in *Beautiful Thing* (BT 2010). This woman; disillusioned and lost is still a fighter and a dreamer who stakes her soul and spirit till the very last to realize her dreams. She is the 'Other' side of the face of the new woman who is not so new after all. She is all human, like she always was; unacknowledged yet trying to grasp the last wisps of life within her and be her true 'self'.

Sonia Faleiro is a young talented writer who has given a voice to the silent pangs of loss and loneliness within the soul of the (new) woman; free yet bound by her own insecurities and yearnings. In her maiden novel *The Girl* (TG 2006), Faleiro has portrayed the anguish and pain of a young, sensitive woman, shattered and betrayed by her own.

The Girl is every girl for the author has given her no name. She is the story of modern life that has hyped the need for space to such an excessive extent that it has failed to comprehend the subsequent loss of love and relationships; the breakdown of the social structure that are in fact the roots, the anchor of an individual. The family that was the basis of one's life and the foundation of one's identity is gradually losing its hold and shattering to pieces.

In the novel, we are introduced to the Girl who is a victim of the breakdown of filial relationships. It is through her diary that her life is revealed after her death. She lost her mother in a car accident and the loss of this important link to life pushes her into an aggravated state of loneliness. "Mother is dead. I am dead." (TG 62).

The Girl lives in an old house in a small town in Goa. She has in her family, her grandparents and her uncle, aunt and cousin, but none to take the place of affection that was held by her mother. Her grandmother soon dies and her uncle sends her grandfather to a home for the elderly after selling the family home to a builder. The family home, the cradle for new relationships, the harbor that cradled the relationships together crumpled like a stack of cards beneath the weight of greed and monetary considerations. The Girl was left all alone, bereft of a family, relationships and love. "And she wept for herself, because she knew that never again would she weep for another" (TG 87).

The family is the most important social structure that forms and shapes an individual's identity, especially for a woman because, "A woman's experience is primarily defined through interpersonal, usually domestic and filial, relationships. Her identity exists largely as being—for—others rather than being-for-itself" (Waugh 43). The Girl loses all; roots, security and identity. She has no one to call her own or shelter her from the pain and fear of an empty, strange world outside. Leaving her crumbling home she watches the stone and mortar shattering under the weight of bulldozers.

> She stood outside the rickety iron gates watching the avalanche of noise and brick, clutching her knapsack and three plastic bags knotted tightly to protect their contents. Photographs in cracked wooden frames, diaries as old as the lines on her hands, some clothes. She stood alone. (TG 87)

The Girl moves to Azul, or the Village of the Dead. Prone to introspection and loneliness, she is however unable to connect with the people around her. She lives alone and gives in to her fears and apprehensions. She is pushed to the edges of consciousness and gradually becomes a neurotic; scared of the sights and sounds of the dark shadows of the night. Her loneliness engulfs her so fully that she is completely alienated from her surroundings and her own 'self'. She reminiscences about her home and her loss, agonizing in pain and frustration.

> My childhood home on the Rua de Amelia Barreto is no more. Mere wreckage of forgotten lives amidst palm trees and overripe fruit. From where I sit, staring at the emptiness of the sea, there is no one but me. It is unbearable, this utter loneliness. (TG 94)

Hope in a human heart never fails to conjure new visions of happiness. And so for the Girl, Luke is the new hope that she felt would fill her life with love and care. But her dreams are mere illusions for Luke is a traveller, a wanderer who leaves her not once but twice. His betrayal breaks the Girl completely and she is again faced with the prospect of living a life alone and empty. Her life is a tale of loss and loneliness that become her constant companions. In desperation she questions herself, "What does one do when rejected not once but twice by someone who purports love with a pair of kind eyes that you know cannot tell a lie?" (TG 102).

People and religion give her no comfort for she grew up with none. Home schooled and without any friends, the Girl never learnt to build relationships; she was always a loner but the relationships that she did form where the ones that abandoned and betrayed her trust. She lost her mother and the only other person who she felt offered her a life, left her.

"Pain does not stop when you want it to. It stops when it has had enough of hurting you" (TG 105). The pain and torment that the Girl endures throughout her life does not stop with her loss of love. She realizes the beginning of a new life within her but the realization does not herald a new beginning for her; a new hope. Her life and identity were so completely fused with loss and loneliness that her despair is further aggravated with this new development. Life seems to be an ordeal of pain and isolation that she does not wish for her unborn child. For herself and her child the end is the only way out of the emptiness and isolation, the only escape and release. Yet even in her ultimate release she yearns for recognition and care; a desire to be found out, a longing to be missed by someone when no more. "Like most people, I want to be found" (TG 110).

The story of the Girl is the story of every individual who have lost a love, a relationship or faced the breakdown of a family. She is alone and can live her life on her own terms but the yearnings of her heart crush her down in misery. Earlier the family was a close knit structure that sheltered its members from the storms of life but today individual space has taken over and torn the weave of security. A son is burdened by his ailing father and forgets all about him; leaving him to die a stranger's death in loneliness. And so is also the fate of the Girl, who is not alone but her surviving family is not bothered with her existence. Such is the price of our progress that we are losing out on our humanity; our emotions, family, relationships. In this modern, materialistic, liberated age, every individual is free but not like the bird in the sky that still has its flock to guide its way across but like the rudderless ship on the high sea; lost and alone without a sense of direction and destination.

The breakdown of family relationships and the resultant disintegration and degeneration of the individual forms an important theme in the novels of Ruth Prawer Jhabvala, which is referred to by R. P. Singh as ". . . the unnatural death of traditional centres of culture and an entropic decline of generations and their disinheritance" (Singh 75). In his analysis of Jhabvala's *Three Continents*, Singh refers to the wanderings of Harriet through the ruins of a palace as the, ". . . pathetic wandering of a tragic heroine through a succession of broken mirrors with her fragmented image caused by her wily embrace of self-destruction" (Singh 76). Alienated and fragmented, characters like Harriet lose their sense of direction and find a release from their pain only in self-annihilation.

In modern life and fiction we come across characters, real and fictionalized who are strong, confident and free yet in the depths of their consciousness lies the shadows of loss and loneliness. Leela in *Beautiful Thing* by Faleiro is a victim of greed and exploitation, starting from her own family, her father who sells her for money. She realizes her own worth and escapes to live her life on her terms but the path chosen for her gives her no emotional or social security. She is bold and fearless but her insecurity leads her to cling to an illusory dream of love and a family. Likewise Boonyi in Rushdie's *Shalimar the Clown*, flees from love, relationships and family in order to live out her life and her dreams; free and unrestricted. But freedom is not so free; it is illusory and deceptive, often leading to false identifications of its worth at the cost of the true 'self'. Even in stronger and liberated characters like Kashmira in Rushdie's novel suffer from the pangs of loneliness and loss of relationships. Dysfunctional home environment pushes her towards drugs and violence and it is only through her father's care and love that Kashmira is rescued back to a normal and healthy life. Loss of her father and knowledge about her dead mother torments her but she finally finds peace in her true identity as their daughter and in her relationship with Yuvraj.

Sonia Faleiro has very strikingly and with great sensitivity represented the face of the new woman; aware and free but lost and alone. *The Girl* is truly an intriguing tale of loss and loneliness that captures the most genuine essence of one's self; a self that gets shape and form from the cares and concerns of one's heart. The security and warmth of relationships are the roots that one needs to survive no matter how high the flight of life is or how far the horizon of one's destination is.

The new woman is every woman who has struggled and emerged victorious over the restrictive norms of the patriarchal society. She is the individual who has carved out a niche for herself and asserted her true identity. She is all the woman she was, and she is all the woman she is; a harmony of the past and the present, a perfect blend of tradition and modernity; an individual and an anchor of relationships and love. The (new) woman accepts her myriad roles within and outside her family and relationships; her identity is an amalgam of the various 'I's that combine to render her a complete image. She is the Saru of Shahsi Deshpande who asserts her identity in acceptance not in negation of her many roles and she is also the Paro of Namita Gokhale who deludes her 'self' in negation of truth and loses herself forever. No matter what her name is or who she is, the (new) woman is confronted with loss and loneliness; a struggle in which either she triumphs or one in which she is wiped into oblivion.

Works Cited

Chopra, Deepak. http://www.single-women-today.com/lonely-quotes.html

Faleiro, Sonia. *The Girl*. New Delhi: Penguin Viking, 2006.

Singh, Rishi Pal. "Identity and Sexual Politics in the 'American' Novels of Jhabwala." *The Quest*. Vol. 21 No. 1 June (2007): 73-81.

Waugh, Patricia. *Feminine Fictions: Revisiting the Postmodern*. London and New York: Routledge, 1989.